High-Impact Teaching Strategies for the 'XYZ' Era of Education

High-Impact Teaching Strategies for the 'XYZ' Era of Education

Richard Howell Allen

Green Light Education

Allyn & Bacon

Boston   New York   San Francisco
Mexico City   Montreal   Toronto   London   Madrid   Munich   Paris
Hong Kong   Singapore   Tokyo   Cape Town   Sydney

Series Editor: Kelly Villella Canton
Editorial Assistant: Annalea Manalili
Senior Marketing Manager: Darcy Betts Prybella
Production Editor: Gregory Erb
Editorial Production Service: Omegatype Typography, Inc.
Composition Buyer: Linda Cox
Manufacturing Buyer: Megan Cochran
Electronic Composition: Omegatype Typography, Inc.
Cover Designer: Linda Knowles

For Professional Development resources visit www.allynbaconmerrill.com

Between the time website information is gathered and then published, it is not unusual for some sites to have closed. Also, the transcription of URLs can result in unintended typographical errors. The publisher would appreciate notification where these errors occur so that they may be corrected in subsequent editions.

Many of the designations used by manufacturers and sellers to distinguish their products are claimed as trademarks. Where those designations appear in this book, and Allyn and Bacon was aware of a trademark claim, the designations have been printed in initial or all caps.

Printed in the United States of America

10 9 8 7 6 5 4 3 2 1   RRD-VA   13 12 11 10 09

Allyn & Bacon
is an imprint of

PEARSON

www.pearsonhighered.com

ISBN-10: 0-13-714426-1
ISBN-13: 978-0-13-714426-6

About the Author

Richard Howell Allen is a highly regarded educator and master trainer with more than 25 years of experience coaching teachers. Founder and president of Green Light Education, he has taken his Impact Teaching strategies beyond the United States and Canada to such diverse countries as the United Kingdom, Australia, New Zealand, Hong Kong, Singapore, Brunei, Russia, Jordan, and Brazil. Dr. Allen is also a popular keynote speaker at international education conferences and works with schools and school districts to embed effective teaching methods into mainstream curriculum.

Dr. Allen started his educational career as a high school math and drama teacher. In 1985 he became a lead facilitator for SuperCamp—an accelerated learning program for teens—and has since worked with more than 25,000 students worldwide. Dr. Allen completed his doctorate in educational psychology at Arizona State University, where he studied how the human brain receives, processes, and recalls information—knowledge that informs all aspects of his teaching strategies. The author resides in the U.S. Virgin Islands on the sun-kissed paradise of St. Croix, and can be reached at his email address: rich@drrichallen.com.

Contents

Preface   ix

Acknowledgments   xi

Section One   1

Understanding the Dynamics of the 'XYZ' Era
of Education

Section Two   15

High-Impact ABC Strategies

A	=	Acknowledgment	15	N =	Novelty	127
B	=	Being Open	22	O =	Ownership	133
C	=	Crest of the Wave	29	P =	Pause	140
D	=	Directions	42	Q =	Questions	146
E	=	Entertainment	58	R =	Revolutions	153
F	=	Frames	66	S =	Socialization	163
G	=	Getting Responses	76	T =	Tiers	171
H	=	High-Quality Responses	85	U =	Uniquely Memorable	179
				V =	Vocal Italics	190
I	=	Involve, Don't Tell	93	W =	Walk Away	195
J	=	Jump Up	100	X =	X-Ray Vision	199
K	=	Keen Visuals	105	Y =	Yesterday Lives!	205
L	=	Labels	110	Z =	Zones of Instruction	209
M	=	Music	115			

Section Three — 215

Lessons in the Language of Learning

Lesson 1: The Presence of Chlorophyll in Leaves — 216

Lesson 2: Natural Resources — 218

Lesson 3: Using Question Marks Appropriately — 220

Lesson 4: Know Your State — 222

Lesson 5: Sentence Types — 224

Lesson 6: ABCs on the Move — 226

Lesson 7: Photo Journal Review — 228

Lesson 8: Native American Legends — 230

Lesson 9: Animals in the Ocean — 233

Lesson 10: Plotting Points on the Coordinate Grid — 235

Lesson 11: American History Time Lines — 237

Lesson 12: Can You Dig It? — 239

Lesson 13: Review Baseball — 241

Lesson 14: Docent of Your Own Museum— Understanding the Visual Arts in Relation to History and Culture — 243

Lesson 15: Carrying Capacity of a Landscape — 245

A Final Thought — 248

Appendix — 249

Stories

The Strawberry — 250

The Traveler — 252

The Animal School — 254

The White Horse — 255

The Castle Wall — 258

The Two Seeds — 260

The 1958 World Series — 261

The Caterpillars — 262

The Bicycle — 263

References — 265

Index — 269

Preface

In the eight years since publishing *Impact Teaching: Ideas and Strategies for Teachers to Maximize Student Learning*, a whole new raft of technology has entered education. PowerPoint, interactive whiteboards, MP3s, and the Internet have brought stunning changes to all levels of learning in schools throughout the world. As teachers, however, the biggest change we face is not the technology itself, but how that technology has shaped the current generations of students in our classrooms.

Kids who spend their formative years immersed in the intense stimulation of the digital age are hard-wired for different patterns of learning. They have shorter attention spans and greater expectations of learning experientially. As teachers whose brains developed in a slower, gentler age, it may be hard for us to truly appreciate the gap between our own education needs and those of our current students.

We need an intense and immediate focus on closing this generational fissure in our classrooms. The issue is urgent—the span of the divide appears to be increasing almost exponentially. Traditional teaching methods may still help some students, but they are hampering more and more students with each passing year. The sooner we can build a conduit of understanding, the sooner teachers and students can join together again in creating an effective and efficient learning environment.

This book offers some building blocks for that connection—a host of practical strategies, illustrated in real-life lesson examples. These strategies will engage, empower, and excite the digital natives in our classrooms. They will help to transform any academic content into a relevant and compelling learning experience for students of all ages.

If we make a studied, conscious effort to span the generational gap by using High-Impact Teaching Strategies, the learning of today's students can soar. Without it, our lessons will become increasingly distant from our students' reality, losing relevance and impact with every passing day.

It does not matter if our lesson plans have always worked in the past. The first rule of High-Impact Teaching is to "teach people—not content." Thus, as our students change, so must the way we teach them.

For time-poor teachers appalled at the idea of rewriting lessons, let me offer a beacon of hope. As the contributors to this book will attest, High-Impact Teaching Strategies do not merely empower students, they also re-energize teachers. Revisiting the way we teach is daunting. But the results—students engaging with our material, celebrating their achievements, and succeeding beyond their expectations—repay our investment of time and effort many times over. With High-Impact Teaching, academic results, classroom behavior, and student attitudes all improve—as does our own personal satisfaction.

I believe, if we act together to bridge the gulf between traditional teaching and today's learners, we can renew education as a vibrant, relevant, and vital contributor to society. I hope you join the teachers whose ideas and lessons populate this book in driving toward that goal.

—Rich Allen

Acknowledgments

I am grateful to many people for their contributions in helping to make this book possible. First and foremost, however, I must thank Karen Pryor for her pure writing genius. With a few strokes of your pen my hesitant, sketchy, black and white scribbles are transformed into flowing literary images filled with vibrant splashes of color, animation, humor, energy, and life. If this books works for educators as effectively as I hope, much of the credit ultimately belongs to you. You are an absolute *word artist* in the truest sense.

I must also thank Wayne Logue for the brilliant images he created to help communicate the ideas in unique, perceptive, and humorous ways. Your vision and insight into conveying the techniques visually is simply astounding.

Finally, I must acknowledge each of the teachers who so freely contributed their creative, dynamic, and inspiring High-Impact Lessons for Section Three—these practical, applied demonstrations may be the most crucial means of all for bringing the High-Impact Teaching concept fully to life for readers. Deep thanks to:

Tina Bernard	Dana Hand	Cindy Rickert
Kim Cooke	Tamara Hughes	Nigel Scozzi
Jenn Currie	Lisa Johnston	Christy Sheffield
Shelley Deneau	Kris Long	Abbey Stodghill
Laurie Gallant	Tiffany Reindl	Maureen Stolte

Thanks also to the reviewers: Amy Cooper, Wilshire Park Elementary School; Cheryl Dick, Nixa R-II School District; and LeAnn Nickelsen, Maximize Learning, Inc.

Understanding the Dynamics of the 'XYZ' Era of Education

This chapter defines three specific generations of individuals currently in the classroom, introducing the unique dynamics created by the combination of these three vastly different groups. Within this context, it addresses the need for teachers to adjust their teaching strategies to meet the unique needs of their learners while relating these core ideas to other information currently available in the field of teacher education.

The 'XYZ' in the title of this book refers to the three generations populating today's classrooms and the implications this has for teachers trying to create a high-impact learning environment. The term "Generation X" was coined by Canadian Douglas Coupland, whose first book, *Generation X: Tales for an Accelerated Culture*, became an international bestseller and popularized the terms "McJob" and "Generation X." Generations Y and Z took their names in logical progression. Although demographers draw their lines in slightly different places, the following generational delineations are generally accepted:

- Generation X: 1960–1979

- Generation Y: 1980–1995

- Generation Z: 1996–Present

In other words, right now we have primarily Gen X teachers instructing Generations Y and Z. And this particular divide is creating a unique set of circumstances in our classrooms.

Of course, there have always been generational divides between teachers and students—such is the nature of the supreme arrogance of youth. But the differences between the current generations in our schools are unprecedented—because they bridge the *digital* divide. They reflect the extraordinary differences in the way we now communicate, socialize, play, and learn created by the introduction of the Internet. What this means in the classroom is that, for the first and perhaps only time in history, we currently have what Marc Prensky in *On the Horizon* refers to as "digital immigrants" teaching "digital natives" (2001).

This unique situation has profound implications for our classrooms—and not just in terms of technology infrastructure.

For clarity, let me state up front that this book does not address the need for technology in our classrooms or the issue of technical literacy for teachers. Schools are all too aware of these requirements and most are responding admirably. Despite a chronic lack of resources, technology is being embedded in the teaching process: teachers e-mail homework to their students; video conferencing enables cultural exchanges; and educational websites such as Mathletics are being included as core curriculum (www.mathletics.com).

This book addresses a lesser-known consequence of the digital divide—the fact that exposure to digital technology from birth hard-wires the human brain to learn differently. In the online environment, today's kids are exposed to high levels of sensory stimulation and learn experientially. You may notice they don't read the instructions on a computer game—in fact, there usually *aren't* any instructions—they simply immerse themselves in the virtual world and learn by trial and error. And they learn easily and quickly.

For most of these students, their online learning experience isn't replicated in the classroom. In fact, the traditional classroom—so familiar and normal to Gen X teachers—presents Gen Y and Z with an almost *opposite* learning environment from the one they naturally thrive in.

To bridge this divide, as teachers we need to understand not only the world of our students but also our own biases created by our upbringing. No matter how technically literate we might be *now*, we have to remember that our childhoods were technologically barren compared with those of our students. As children who watched Neil Armstrong walk on the moon, we might have felt we were growing up in an age of technical marvels. However, as a mouse click at www.apolloartifacts.com will tell you, Apollo 11 had less computing power than a mobile phone.

Consider the radical differences in standard technologies across the XYZ generations:

Digital Immigrants	>	Digital Natives
GEN X (1960)	**GEN Y (1980)**	**GEN Z (1996)**
TV	High-definition TV	Web TV
Video	Video games	Online gaming
Analog cell phones	Digital cell phones	Bluetooth phones
PCs	World Wide Web	Second Life (virtual world)
Vinyl records	CDs	DVDs
Fax	E-mail	Skype

Consider also the different world of work schools are now preparing students for, compared to previous generations.

The school system for Gen X students was a construct of the industrial age. Schools prepared students to work in a manufacturing-based economy. Factory workers needed to turn up on time, listen to and obey instructions, and perform rote tasks. The traditional school system—ruled by the bell, with students listening in silence and learning by rote—turned out ideal factory fodder.

In stark contrast, Gen Y and Z graduates will primarily be employed as knowledge workers in services-based economies. In these economies, most repetitive functions are automated, and workers are valued for their ability to synthesize information, solve problems, think laterally, and be innovative. At the same time, technology convergence, globalization, and environmental concerns are increasing the number of telecommuters working from home—people who don't have to "clock in" and can choose the hours they work.

As Ken Robinson explains in *Out of Our Minds,* to develop workers who will succeed in this new environment, schools need to foster creativity, self-motivation, and flexibility—without letting the educational model descend into anarchy (2001).

Thus, as teachers today, we are teaching students whose brains are hard-wired differently from ours in a learning environment designed for a different economy. Simply put, we and our conventional classrooms belong to a bygone era of learning.

Which begs the questions: What educational philosophy can we use for today's students? Where do we find new approaches that better fit the generation of students in today's classrooms? Do we need to essentially reinvent the educational wheel?

Hopefully not. But to be effective in today's unique teaching environment, high-impact teachers need to view the entire educational mechanism from a different perspective. We need to base our teaching choices on the generations doing the learning—not on our own experiences of education.

But if experience can't be our guide, where do we look to find the most effective ways to motivate, inspire, and teach? Perhaps the answer is very close at hand. Perhaps the answer can be found in closely observing kids and teens when they are *not* in school. In other words, we need to observe students in their natural world and ask: In this place, what works for them? What are they excited about? What are they interested in? What are they curious about?

If we can isolate and identify what works in their natural learning environment, we can then bring those strategies into the classroom and create lessons that truly work for our new generations of digital natives.

The Alien School

To grasp the significance of the deep divide between the generations, take this idea further and imagine the following situation. A highly evolved race of alien demagogues is cruising the universe studying the ideal learning environments for different species. They arrive at a small blue-green planet, about 4.5 billion years old, three out from a pale yellow sun.

Our alien visitors have never come across human beings before and aren't even aware we have an existing education system. But they have a tried and trusted process for constructing highly effective learning environments. Their starting point is to *learn how humans learn naturally*.

Like zoologists trying to create an artificial environment that captive animals will thrive in, the aliens start by studying how children and teens assimilate new information in their natural habitat. Their mission is to find out what makes these strange creatures interested, intrigued, and curious. Unencumbered by the knowledge of how traditional schools operate, they observe kids in their home environment—at play and with their friends—to discover what physical, emotional, intellectual, and social stimuli promote learning.

What do they observe? Perhaps they notice how movement helps the human body stay awake and engaged.

Perhaps they realize how much kids learn from their peers and the significance of *social interaction* in children understanding, engaging with, and remembering new information. Perhaps they see how small successes build confidence and how much children need the encouragement of celebration.

They're bound to observe the prevalence of *music*—the way kids have a soundtrack to almost every aspect of their lives. Perhaps they recognize the potential of music to encourage positive behavior in the classroom, from using it in the background to set an emotional tone to signaling the beginning and end of activities.

They certainly notice that kids learn best and fastest when they're having fun—or when they can see an immediate benefit from applying their learning. From this they extrapolate the importance of making learning meaningful. As Joe Kincheloe, Patrick Slattery, and Shirley Steinberg explain in *Contextualizing Teaching* (2000), the aliens realize their school would be wise to focus instruction on information that is related to the students' real world.

The aliens also observe the accelerated pace of experiential learning and the impact of visual and audio stimulation on capturing attention and assisting recall.

After more in-depth research, they discover that when kids are scared or stressed they *stop* learning. In fact, when alien scientists study the human brain, they discover that, in situations involving threat or anxiety, brain function changes quite dramatically. Specifically, they find brain activity decreases around the midbrain and neocortex while it increases in the brain stem and cerebellum. This in turn generates behaviors that are instinctive and habitual, while decreasing the higher-order information processing that is an essential function for learning.

Based on this finding, the aliens decide that for effective learning to occur students need to feel emotionally safe. They correctly deduce that, even in a relatively mild threat state, learners will neither perform at their best nor will they process or encode information at a level conducive to long-term retention. They realize that for effective learning to occur, students need to be relaxed, focused, and at ease—generally feeling pretty good about themselves and the learning environment.

Meanwhile, the alien observers notice that kids don't appear to learn well if they're bored and hypothesize that one way to avoid this is to physically engage them in and emotionally connect them to the learning process.

The aliens don't know it, but they have stumbled across an educational theory human teachers have been aware of for over 20 years—the theory of creating an enriched environment for learners, as put forward by Marian Diamond in her book *Enriching Heredity* (1988). Simply stated, Diamond spent years conducting experiments comparing the developing neurology of the brains of rats in enriched environments (these guys had plenty of things to do) with those raised in more mundane environments (these guys were bored most of the time). The results were clear—the more enriched the environment, the better the brain develops.

Finally, after months of research, the aliens move on to the next step: designing their school. Having observed the natural world of human learners and identified the importance of highly stimulating classrooms, what sort of educational environment will our aliens design?

Surely it would be highly interactive and engaging—full of music, movement, surprises, color, and laughter. Students would either enjoy the learning experience or keenly understand the relevance of content—and probably both! Learning would be embedded during play, application, performance, and conversation. Wouldn't it?

How likely is it that our alien designers would suggest the best environment for human beings to learn in is a classroom where kids are expected to sit still and listen to someone else talking for 45 minutes at a time?

In fact, wouldn't this traditional environment seem *alien* to today's students?

Before you dismiss this imaginary situation as simplistic, forget the aliens and think about the difference between the traditional classroom and the world kids inhabit outside school. For example, consider the issue of social interaction. In the world beyond school, students communicate with each other—if not their parents!—*all* the time. They share, discuss, plan, interact, and live life through text, online chat, YouTube, Facebook, blogs, phone calls, and sometimes even real face-to-face conservation.

Yet students stride directly from that reality, where they share every thought with their social network, into a traditional classroom and are told to turn their phones off and be quiet. In this new situation, their only official outlet for verbal interaction is to speak in front of the entire class. For most students, this is not a comfortable mode of communication, but rather an extremely high-stress situation, very *un*like their normal social interactions where they are protected and emboldened by the anonymity of the Web.

This is not to say that students should be permitted to continue with their social lives during class—it merely illustrates that the huge divide between the current adult and youth generations is being replicated in our classrooms.

To bridge this divide, we teachers must begin by setting aside our traditional ideas of how things should be in the classroom and accept that our students really have grown up on a different planet. To create intelligent life in our classrooms, we must study the environment Gen Y and Gen Z thrive in *outside* school and use these stimuli to promote learning.

Essentially, this is how the collection of High-Impact Teaching Strategies in this book developed. They all in some way try to recreate the environment in which today's kids learn easily and quickly—based on our rapidly developing understanding of how the human brain encodes, processes, stores, and recalls information. They are designed to:

■ Reduce or remove any trace of threat from the learning situation

■ Make content meaningful for students

■ Promote physical stimulation to keep brains alert

■ Use social interaction to assist understanding and recall

The strategies are partly based on and use ideas from the constructivist approach to teaching. At the simplest level, constructivists do not believe that knowledge is simply transferred from the mind of the teacher to the mind of the student. Instead, as the teacher speaks, they believe students are processing the information and *constructing* meaning from it based on a wide range of factors.

These factors might include—but are certainly not limited to—any previous experiences the students might have had with the topic, such as their emotional state at the time of the lesson, their feelings toward the teacher, and their feelings toward the topic. Consistent with this philosophical approach to instruction, this book explains how to design instruction so the meaning students construct most closely matches what you intended them to learn.

Incorporating High-Impact Teaching Strategies into your teaching does not mean you have to throw away anything that currently works in your classroom. Whether you are a new or experienced teacher, the techniques are intended to stimulate your thinking on how to maximize the impact you can have on today's students. Naturally, how you choose to incorporate these ideas into your presentation style will depend on the unique combination of your personality, students, subject, and the learning context in which you teach.

Equally, these are by no means *all* the strategies you could use to build, maintain, and facilitate a high-impact learning environment. They were selected by virtue of being practical, realistic, down-to-earth ideas that will help you to create a positive learning environment for digital natives. Specifically, they all meet the criteria of requiring little or no extra budget, offering opportunities for immediate implementation, and reducing wasted effort on the part of the teacher.

This last point is important. Whether you are nurturing young students or guiding teens or even adult learners, most teachers desire a relaxed, pleasant cruise toward learning objectives. The strategies in this book will help you to design lessons that harness the natural energy and enthusiasm of your students. The point is, if we allow students to guide the learning process, we are more likely to move quickly and efficiently toward our teaching objectives, with little if any wasted effort.

Developing teaching techniques that are effective while also being energy efficient is a critical issue for most teachers (Larkins, McKinney, & Oldham-Buss, 1985). Personally, I've encountered very few who, on completing a full day of teaching, are bursting at the seams with energy and exuberance. Not many stand at the door of their classroom, watch their students depart, then race home for a long night of dancing, revelry, and general debauchery. More commonly, they go home exhausted and crawl into bed for a nap before dinner.

For our own sanity, we need to move away from the teaching style in which the teacher is doing the majority of the work and instead involve our students more proactively in the learning process. They are, after all, the people who need to engage with our content. As the following proverb illustrates, simply telling students new information or showing them a slide about it doesn't necessarily achieve that.

Tell me, I hear.

Show me, I see.

Involve me, I understand.

In other words, effective learning requires us to *involve* our students. While this idea appears very simple, and one that many educators would fully endorse, research shows it can be challenging to actually achieve in the classroom (Greenco, Collins, & Resnick, 1996).

Creating high levels of student interaction requires us to pay careful attention to a wide range of details: the emotional mood we set, the language we use, the memory strategies we choose, the methods of connecting students with the content we select, the ways of bringing movement into the classroom we introduce, and the opportunities to create productive social interaction we find, just to name a few.

These and a host of other details are addressed in this book, which focuses directly on how to bring to life the key findings of current educational theories in the classroom.

Doing so in no way detracts from traditional educational psychology or foundations of education textbooks. I fully endorse many of these texts, with three of my favorites being Anita Woolfolk's *Education Psychology* (2000), N. L. Gage and David Berliner's (1998) book by the same name, and Jeanne Ellis Ormrod's *Education Psychology: Developing Learners* (2000).

It also directly supports many of the more nontraditional texts, such as Eric Jensen's *SuperTeaching* (1988) and *Teaching with the Brain in Mind*

(2005), Bobbi Deporter, Mark Reardon, and Sarah Singer-Noire's *Orchestrating Student Success* (1999), or Louis Schmier's *Random Thoughts: The Humanity of Teaching* (1995). All of these books are excellent resources that present important theories any teacher can use to inform and improve their method of instruction.

However, while also being a nontraditional text, *High-Impact Teaching for the 'XYZ' Era of Education* is not about theory. Despite occasionally mentioning both theories and researchers, its central focus is on how you can use these theories at a practical level in the classroom to engage current generations of students.

The strategies it presents are based on a combination of two things: first, 25 years of involvement in the growing field of brain-based research and its applications to the teaching profession; and second, my own extensive experiences in educational systems throughout the world.

However strange a technique may seem to you, please know that *all* the strategies are tried and trusted. I both use them in my own teaching and have observed their successful incorporation into classrooms all over the world.

An Encyclopedia of High-Impact Teaching Strategies

Finally, before you begin to dip into the pages ahead, a word about how to use this text. This is essentially a reference book, packed with ideas to support you in teaching today's students. The sections are not intended to be read consecutively.

As you'll see, the remainder of this book is essentially an encyclopedia of empirically proven High-Impact Teaching Strategies, organized in alphabetical order.

Why the alphabet? Isn't that a bit random? Well, yes it is—and deliberately so. The truth is, there is no obvious order in which to organize High-Impact Teaching Strategies. Depending on your content, your objectives, your students, and perhaps even the time of year, your classroom will need different combinations of strategies at different times.

In other words, these strategies are the building blocks of High-Impact Teaching, in the same way that the letters of the alphabet are the building blocks of language. Put letters together in different ways and they create different words. Put the strategies together in different ways, and they achieve different learning objectives.

Moreover, you'll find some strategies that you end up using almost *all* the time—just as a vowel appears in almost every word, while other strategies—the q and z equivalents if you will—will be used rarely, but to great and interesting effect.

This is merely an analogy. The strategies aligned with the vowel letters in this book will not necessarily be the ones *you* most commonly use. High-Impact Teaching relies on personal choice and interpretation. The teaching "language" you create from these letters is up to you.

But the analogy is useful at a simple level. Just as you don't need every letter in the alphabet to create a sentence, you don't need every strategy in the book to create an effective lesson. Similarly, some strategies will appear several times in the same lesson, just like double letters, while others will naturally and commonly fit together, like the consonant digraphs *th* and *ch*.

Finally, the strategies are presented literally as the ABCs of High-Impact Teaching to stress that we must understand these fundamental building blocks of interactive learning if we are to create meaning and understanding among the 'XYZ' generations in today's classrooms.

These strategies are the key to communicating with today's students because they create the stimuli that prompt natural learning in digital natives. Used correctly in your classroom, they will give you a strong foundation on which to build teaching strategies that bridge the digital divide.

The 26 High-Impact Strategies

A = Acknowledgment

Just as people appreciate being valued in their personal lives, students appreciate having their efforts valued in the classroom. Acknowledgment doesn't just give students an incentive to try hard next time, it's also an important life lesson.

B = Being Open

We must tread carefully when we ask students questions or open up a topic for class discussion. Without careful, conscious attention to the way we phrase these requests, we may accidentally reduce—or even shut down—students' responses.

C = Crest of the Wave

Learning occurs best in short waves of student interest and momentum. If we are sensitive to when learning "crests," we can maximize these moments with clear instruction as critical mass builds up. Then, as the wave begins to break, we can change the pace, simultaneously allowing students to consolidate the information they've just learned at the crest, as well as reset themselves for the new section.

D = Directions

Giving effective directions looks deceptively simple. However, in reality it is far from easy to achieve and relies on technique and practice. To be truly effective when giving directions, we must understand what we are doing, master some basic techniques, and consciously put them into practice.

E = Entertainment

For today's students entertainment is ubiquitous, instantly available, and expected. This is the environment our classrooms must compete with. As teachers, we need to realize that, while entertainment is not education, education may at times need to be more entertaining.

F = Frames

Left to their own devices, students will naturally view content from their own perspectives. In other words, they will *frame* the content, based on their own experiences and points of view. Alternatively, as teachers, we can frame the content for them to shape the learning they extract from the experience.

G = Getting Responses

A primary way to verify student engagement is to ask for frequent responses. However, we need to clearly *specify* how we expect our students to respond. Knowing what they are expected to do will allow students to feel more comfortable with the responses they provide. This will heighten students' sense of security within our classrooms, increasing participation.

H = High-Quality Responses

When we want students to respond with quality responses and engage in a useful classroom dialogue, we need to give them time to organize their thoughts and prepare their answers.

I = Involve, Don't Tell

Within most lessons, there are central, essential pieces of information students most need to know. Instead of simply stating or explaining them, we need to create ways that students can truly be *involved* in learning them.

J = Jump Up

In a High-Impact Classroom, students learn while standing—as well as sitting. While traditional teaching links *learning* to *sitting,* this idea is not based on science. The fact is, students do *not* learn better sitting—sitting reduces blood flow to the brain.

K = Keen Visuals

Teaching usually relies, in one form or another, on *words.* However, the learning process is more likely to be successful if we reinforce these ideas with visuals. One of the primary ways human beings intake, process, and encode new information is through *visual imagery.*

L = Labels

Labels are words that cause a reaction in us because of our prior experiences with them. They can be both positive and negative and are context specific. By using negative labels, we make our teaching lives harder. On the other hand, using positive labels can help our students achieve more than they believed possible.

M = Music

Music should be a natural and consistent part of most classrooms. Properly employed, music can create a heightened social learning context, motivate students to engage more rapidly, and quickly establish a sense of safety.

N = Novelty

Students rarely arrive to the classroom in anticipation of being intrigued, fascinated, enthralled, and mesmerized. So when we introduce novelty, an almost magical rise occurs in their attention and energy levels.

O = Ownership

When students are personally involved in creating, presenting, and evaluating content, a subtle, although important, shift occurs in their perspective of the classroom. It gives them a new orientation toward the class, one of involvement and responsibility.

P = Pause

When we give our students new visual information, we must also give them time to process it. Depending on the complexity of the visual, this may take only a few seconds, or as much as a minute. Regardless, we always need to make time for students to organize a mental image of the material and get used to it.

Q = Questions

How we ask questions is a key aspect of making this part of learning successful. Precisely phrased questions help us achieve the highest possible impact when we align students' thoughts in the proper direction during classroom discussions.

R = Revolutions

The circular nature of expectation and discovery is often the driving energy behind successful teaching. When students become fascinated with solving a puzzle, intrigued by unraveling a mystery, or simply want to know what comes next, they begin to take a high level of ownership for their learning. We can create this effect by introducing an *open loop*, which we then close as the learning comes full circle.

S = Socialization

For teaching to be effective, students need to talk about what they are learning. This is because, when talking about a topic, they must first think about and mentally process the information. As they discuss the content, they verbally process the ideas. As a result, they come to a better, deeper, and more complete understanding of what they are studying.

T = Tiers

An interactive lesson requires carefully regulated, sequential steps that build deliberately and distinctly on each other. Properly employed, this tier structure helps students understand ideas in the fastest manner possible, without unnecessary diversions and distractions.

U = Uniquely Memorable

It's not enough to teach our students content—we also have to teach them how to *remember* that content. One of the most fundamental issues for teaching a truly High-Impact Lesson is to somehow make it uniquely memorable to our students. And that means using explicit memorization strategies as we teach.

V = Vocal Italics

New lessons frequently bring new terms, phrases, and ideas. When students come across these new words, they often need time to fully

understand them before moving forward to related new thoughts and
ideas. In these situations, giving our students a brief well-timed moment of
focus will allow them to understand and remember the new term.

W = Walk Away

When a student speaks as part of a lesson, it is important that everyone can
hear them clearly. If we obey our conversational instincts and move closer
to the student while they are speaking, they will lower their voice. Moving in the opposite direction will have the opposite effect. The student will
speak louder.

X = X-Ray Vision

Our brain constantly creates mental images to orient ourselves to the
world. As teachers, we want to avoid mental images that accidentally
direct students' focus toward *negative* actions or consequences. Instead, we
need to consciously create images of *positive* actions or consequences in our
students' minds.

Y = Yesterday Lives!

Stories help our students gain insight as to how to apply what we are
teaching them and make connections for themselves. No matter how
technologically sophisticated the current generations in our classrooms,
announce you're going to tell a story and even the most cynical student
settles in happily.

Z = Zones of Instruction

Using instructional "zones" builds on the psychological idea that similar
stimuli generate a consistent emotional response. We can use this phenomenon to create a predictable learning environment in our classrooms
by deliberately and consistently giving different types of instruction from
particular locations.

High-Impact ABC Strategies

This section offers 26 distinct High-Impact Teaching Strategies presented for clarity with a common format of seven distinct categories: In General, The Connection, The Big Picture, Focus on Classroom Management, In Practice, Next Steps, and Your Ideas.

A = Acknowledgment

Nine-tenths of education is encouragement.

In General

Just as people appreciate being valued in their personal lives, students appreciate having their efforts valued in the classroom. We all know the benefits of thanking people and being thanked. When people smile at us, we smile back. When we're told we've done a great job, we feel good about ourselves (Emmons, 2007). Acknowledgment doesn't just give students an incentive to try hard next time, it's also an important life lesson.

If we teach our students to value acknowledgment, perhaps they will practice it in the larger world. What better lesson for them to experience in the classroom than the meaningful, purposeful acknowledgment of other people?

The Connection

In the cyber world of today's students, feedback is almost instantaneous. Looking up the length of the Nile in an encyclopedia used to take 20 minutes (excluding the walk to the library); today Google will tell you in 2 seconds. Similarly, video games offer instant trial-and-error correction and constant rewards for learning: Learn how to get over the wall and you get to the next level. Frequent and immediate feedback plays a large role in their personal worlds. Acknowledgment in today's classrooms should mirror this phenomenon students find so common, in ways that are both real and varied.

The Big Picture

The following story provides an interesting viewpoint on the issue of acknowledgment in general:

> Jeremy was in an advanced calculus class offered only to the most elite high school seniors. Near the end of the year, these students sat an important test. After solving a series of challenging problems, he moved on to the final question, which simply asked, "What's the name of the custodian for this classroom?"
>
> Jeremy had absolutely no idea of the person's name. Since the question had nothing at all to do with math, he decided it must be a joke. He left the space for answering that question blank. As he was leaving the classroom, he asked the teacher if that final question would count toward his grade. The teacher replied: "Definitely. Success does not come just from *what* you know, it also depends on *who* you know. In your lifetime you will meet many people. Each of them is significant, and each deserves your attention and care, even if all you do is smile and say hello."

Now, apply this idea of high levels of acknowledgment to the teaching profession. Ask any teacher, "Who are you teaching this morning?" and the answer usually comes in a grade or content format: "I'm teaching ninth-grade math students."

I've been teaching in-services for over 20 years, so I often ask this question at the beginning of my workshops. In more than two decades, not one teacher has ever come back with the answer, "I'm teaching *people*!"

This is not to criticize the teachers attending my seminars. Of course, they respond with the grade and subject they teach. It's like being asked: "What are you driving?" Our instinct is to be highly specific: "A Mazda sports sedan." Rarely do we say, "A car."

But I make the point because learners are first and foremost *people.* Our students have the basic human need for consistent positive acknowledgment to keep them feeling comfortable about moving forward with the learning process. And while each person is unique (Tomlinson & Kalbgleisch, 1998), they almost all require higher levels of praise and encouragement than we currently offer.

It's not that we don't acknowledge students are people—with the exception of those of us having a *very* tough day—it's that this isn't our *first* thought! Our first thought is content and our lesson plan. Which is why we have to work to stay conscious, at all times in the classroom, that we teach *people,* not content.

Undeniably, content is important. After all, in most cases it *is* what the students are there to learn. However, our primary filter should be one of *people first.* Because if the human beings sitting in front of us aren't prepared to learn, it doesn't matter how great our content is.

Focus on Classroom Management

To understand the relationship between acknowledgment and classroom management, consider the image of a sailboat out in the open water of the sea. If a sailing ship encounters heavy winds striking it from all sides, its efforts to move forward will be severely hampered. In a classroom, the same idea applies. If students are acknowledged inconsistently, at times ignored, and occasionally even reprimanded for what might be their best efforts, it is as if their "ship of learning" is being struck by winds from a variety of angles. Not all of them will be propelling the student in the desired direction. In fact, these various winds probably end up canceling each other out, and consequently learning stops dead in the water.

NINE-TENTHS OF EDUCATION IS **ENCOURAGEMENT**

I KNOW YOU WILL DO IT
I'M PROUD OF YOU
GOOD
KEEP GOING
WELL DONE
YOU CAN DO IT
FANTASTIC EFFORT
GREAT WORK
YOU ARE SMART

Not knowing which way to head, students may well wander off in an unwanted direction, even engaging in disturbances in the classroom.

If, however, the same ship encounters a single steady wind blowing directly toward a clearly identified goal, it can move in that direction with a minimum of effort from the captain. In fact, the role of the captain is significantly reduced, becoming more of a gentle guide in the proper direction, requiring only a nudge here or there. In the same way, if students receive a steady amount of encouragement and positive feedback for their efforts, the experience is akin to a steady breeze moving them rapidly toward the primary goals of the instruction. Unwanted behaviors are greatly reduced as their focus stays steadily on the primary objective.

If we use multiple forms of encouragement for our students, and keep it coming steadily toward them, then students are more likely to remain actively involved (Levenson, Ekman, & Friesen, 1990). The encouragement must be genuine, focused on the efforts they are making, and provided frequently enough to keep the learning moving forward at the appropriate pace. These positive emotions might well drive future learning, as students seek to maintain that level of acceptance. If students feel their efforts are truly appreciated and acknowledged, many behavior management issues will subside.

In Practice

How do we typically acknowledge classroom students during the course of a day? We might write a nice comment on their papers, or perhaps when a student answers a question, we might respond "That's correct" or "Good." Maybe we say "Thank you" when students return from a break on time.

A consistent theme runs through all of these situations: In each of them, it is us, the teacher, who provides the acknowledgment, and the student who receives the comment, reward, or verbal kudos. This is the norm in most classrooms. When acknowledgment is to be given, we as teachers do the giving, and the students do the receiving. Although the teacher-to-student flow of praise and reward is useful at times, if we remain stuck in this pattern, we will miss other opportunities for acknowledging students and creating a more dynamic learning environment.

There are other forms of acknowledgment than the teacher–student flow and many more opportunities for thanking students than we think.

Let's start with what triggers acknowledgment in our classrooms. What do students need to do? Do they have to get something right? Or do something the best? Or perhaps they have do something we personally like or value? But these are just the start of what we need to acknowledge. Are there additional possibilities we might have overlooked?

What if we acknowledged every small success, or even honest endeavors that did not work out correctly? Is it possible that acknowledgment could be effectively used even in these moments? Perhaps we could give acknowledgment regardless of results, based on effort expended. When people know their efforts are appreciated, it usually encourages them to try again, perhaps even harder next time. Effective acknowledgment should span across situations and unite students in continuing to put their best effort into everything (Goleman, 1995).

And it should also not just be from the teacher to the students. What about self-acknowledgment, or acknowledgment *between* students? Here are some examples of how these alternative forms of positive feedback and encouragement might work.

■ **Self Acknowledgment:** Students assess their learning by completing a form that asks them which aspects of the learning they fully understand. They can then grade their own paper and be given an opportunity to write three adjectives on the top of their paper that describe their success. With younger groups, we can ask students to stand up and pat themselves on their own back, to thank themselves for successfully handling a particular challenge or task.

■ **Peer Acknowledgment:** In most interactive learning environments, students will be working with each other in a variety of activities (Lazar, 1995). They may be working in pairs, in small groups, or they may be simply chatting briefly with each other. After each interaction, it can be useful to have them thank those other people. The teacher might simply say "Please say 'thank you' to the people you've been talking with" or "Please thank your partners."

The beginning and ending of each class, each day, or each week provides teachers with another opportunity for peer acknowledgment by having students greet and thank each other. At the start of a day, the teacher might say "Please shake hands with at least three people and say 'Glad you could make it today.'" Or at the end of a session the teacher could say "Please thank at least two people for being here today." After lunch, the words might be "Please tell two people you're glad they came back from lunch."

Teachers might develop a "whole class" acknowledgment format where, for example, students turn to the person singled out for praise, put their thumbs up and shout "Well done!" You can have a special phrase that signals the start of this sequence, perhaps: "That's TRULY AMAZING, Sarah. Everyone, let's give Sarah a big well done. 1 . . . 2 . . . 3 . . ."

■ **Physical Acknowledgment:** Physical forms of acknowledgment between students is another option. Athletes use a wide variety of actions to congratulate each other for their successes, some of which might work well in the classroom. The teacher might say "Pat at least two people on the back and say, 'Well done!'" The practice of giving each other "high-fives" (where each person raises their right hand and these hands are slapped together) may also fit very well in some circumstances, especially if students have just been involved in a physical activity. There are endless variations on this form of congratulation: "low-fives" or "high-tens" or even a "behind-the-back-ten."

■ **Compliments:** Compliments, even when done with humor, are another effective form of acknowledgment (Vergneer, 1995). For example, we might distribute materials by having several students hold the workbooks and stand throughout the room. To receive a workbook, the other students must approach one of these people and give a compliment, after which they are handed a workbook. Another strategy is to take two minutes after they have received their workbooks to decorate and "personalize" them with magic markers. When this is complete, everyone stands up and holds their book in front of them. They then proceed to walk around the room, showing their cover design to other students while complimenting each other on their designs. This sequence takes less than three minutes, but helps create a playful, good-natured feeling in the classroom. This approach can set the stage for learning with a relaxed, comfortable tone which will hopefully continue for the duration of the class.

■ **Feedback:** Students and teachers providing feedback for each other is a frequent component of many classes. One form of feedback uses the idea of "gems and opportunities." Gems are those things the person did that worked well. It is important to include the positive aspects in any feedback situation, since these are examples of what this individual is already doing well and can build on in the future. On the other hand, opportunities are those things they might want to consider changing for future efforts.

■ **Young Student "Specials":** Teachers of young students have a unique opportunity for different forms of congratulation, as these students rarely arrive with preconceived notions as to which forms of feedback are appropriate and which are inappropriate. For example, instead of applause, young students may be asked to snap their fingers, wiggle their fingers at the person, or give a "sitting ovation"—making a circle over their heads with their arms while saying "Ooohh." They might want to give a quick three-clap acknowledgment after a person has spoken, where the three quick claps in unison are a way of saying thanks. In these cases, the form of the acknowledgment is less important than the fact that is consistently given and they are a part of it.

Next Steps

The possibilities listed above are merely a sample of potential options for acknowledgment. Given the opportunity, students may well come up with their own.

Some learning environments that are longer in length may use a particular form of acknowledgment that becomes a *standard ritual* for them. For example, students who will be together in the same classroom all year might begin providing acknowledgment for each other by simply saying "Thank you" when acknowledgment is needed. In these cases it is useful to occasionally switch from one form to another when needed to keep things fresh and alive in the classroom. Perhaps in the second month they might be asked to say "You're the best!" or "Thanks for your help" when acknowledgment is required. This will help students avoid falling into patterns where they are acknowledging each other simply because they are "supposed to," rather than meaning what they are saying. Variety is often the key to maintaining a genuine feeling in these interactions.

ASSESS YOUR CURRENT USE OF ACKNOWLEDGMENT

- I use frequent acknowledgment in a variety of formats and explicitly build it into my lesson plans.

- I make sure to acknowledge my students but have not used student-to-student acknowledgment.

- Other than occasionally saying "Good" or "Well done," I have rarely used acknowledgment in any other format in my classroom.

Your Ideas

Take a moment to consider how you might be able to use more acknowledgment in your classroom. Note *at least* three moments during instruction and *at least* three different types of acknowledgment you could use.

Moments during Instruction

1. _____

2. _____

3. _____

4. _____

5. _____

Types of Acknowledgment

1. _____

2. _____

3. _____

4. _____

5. _____

B = Being Open

When the "Open" format is used, students are more Open to engagement.

In General

While any shift from the teacher "telling" is to be applauded, we must tread carefully when we ask students questions or open up a topic for class discussion. Without careful, conscious attention to these particular moments, we may accidentally reduce—or even shut down—students' responses. However, when handled properly, question time can become a fertile ground for discussions and learning.

The questions posed by teachers can be divided into two basic formats:

1. Closed format—e.g., "What is the most important thing to remember here?" This is closed because it indicates there is a single correct response.

2. Open format—e.g., "What do *you* think are *some* of the important things to remember here?" This one is open because it implies students own the answer and makes room for multiple correct responses. The openness frees the student from the fear of being wrong.

The Connection

Today's students are the first generation able to easily find multiple possible answers to almost any question. For example, a past student who asked "Why is the sky blue?" would most likely have been perfectly happy with the answer provided by their teacher. However, when today's student googles the same question, about 6 million possible answers emerge. Some are simple, some contain complex equations, some contradict each other! And some may be better than the one provided by their teacher. In other words, the idea that questions have only one possible answer doesn't sit well with these students. It goes against everything they are learning on the Internet.

One of the greatest things we can teach students of the information age is the value of generating and finding *various* ideas . . . and then analyzing and comparing them before reaching informed decisions.

The Big Picture

Clearly, there are times when a teacher *should* use the closed form of a question. For example, look at the question "What's the speed of light?" There is only one correct response (186,000 miles per second). However, in a surprisingly high number of learning circumstances, opportunities exist for open questions, allowing for greater depth of processing, which may result in higher levels of retention. Using a question stated in an open format allows for a wider range of interaction with reduced risk for the student. One way of stating this would say that closed questions lead to "simple" learning, while open questions trigger deeper learning.

For example, imagine the following situation. A teacher wants to engage her high school students in a discussion, so she opens the class with a question. To her surprise, no one responds to it. Examine what she asked them and see if you can spot the problem.

"What is the most important political issue facing the world today?"

Why might no one have responded to her query? Why was she faced with a room full of blank stares and uncomfortable shuffles? Let's look closely at the form of the question she asked.

The question contains two (in this case) unhelpful assumptions: (1) There is only a *single* correct response to the question, and (2) the *teacher* has this correct answer in mind. These implicit assumptions are the cause of the deadly silence that follows the question. Consider the mental and emotional hoops students have to jump through before they can answer the question:

- Mentally generate several responses

- Evaluate which of these responses they believe best fits the question

- Decide whether their response may or may not match the response the teacher has chosen as the correct one

- Finally, risk participating in a game of right or wrong, where only the teacher knows the criteria for making the final decision

Closed questions like this significantly increase the risk of participating. Indeed, such questions may inhibit students from interacting in the discussion at all. Even those students game enough to risk an answer don't have *time* to go through these mental paces in the split second following the question. No wonder they're not responding.

To decrease the threat factor, thus increasing the likelihood of interaction, the same question might have been phrased a different way:

"What are *some* of the most important political issues *you or your family believe* are facing the world today?"

The form of this question makes it clear that students are merely offering an opinion—it doesn't even have to be their own! It also implies there is more than one possible correct response. Used together, these two changes in the form of the question should significantly reduce the amount of threat students perceive, thus increasing the likelihood they'll participate in the discussion.

Focus on Classroom Management

The issue of an open or closed format extends beyond questions posed by the teacher about content. It's also relevant for the way we give instructions around classroom activities. When we ask students to act, we need to make it as easy as possible for them to have a chance of succeeding in the task. The more they believe they can "get it right," the more likely they are to participate. Consider the following examples:

Closed: "Turn to someone near you and compliment that person."

Open: "Turn to *at least* two people near you and compliment them."

If there were an odd number of students in the room, the original statement would not work out—someone would not be participating.

Closed: "In trios, discuss this question further."

Open: "In groups of three, four, or five, discuss this question further."

Only if the number of students in the room were exactly divisible by three would the closed format actually be possible. Otherwise this might create an awkward moment while the groups get sorted out. One or two people might end up feeling like an "extra" person. It would also require more time for people to make sure everyone was in a trio.

Closed: "Smile if you now know how to do The Twist."

Open: "Smile if at least once you've done The Twist."

The closed statement seems to imply that everyone can now do something called The Twist perfectly, while in fact some of the students may have been successful once or twice, but are not yet feeling that they have the concept down completely.

Closed: "What's the best place you've ever been to for a vacation?"

Open: "What's a vacation place you've really enjoyed?"

This closed format makes the student answering the question perform an evaluation process, knowing that when they make a final choice it must be better than *every* other vacation place they've ever been. The open format allows them to simply pick one of the many places they've enjoyed visiting.

Closed: "When should we use this communication skill?"

Open: "What are *some of* the circumstances where you might use this communication skill to your advantage?"

The choice of *when* may imply to some listeners there is a simple, specific circumstance when the skill under discussion should be used and not at any other time. The use of *some of* relaxes this implied restriction, creating a more open environment in which to respond to the question.

Closed: "What is a Completion Circle?"

Open: "Has anyone heard of a Completion Circle? If so, what have you heard about it?"

The use of specialized terms in learning situations is frequently a dangerous choice. Students may have heard the expression in a different context. Not knowing precisely what the teacher is referencing may make them feel there is a risk of being incorrect. If so, it creates a game where there are winners and losers. Students rarely enjoy interacting under these types of conditions—many will not respond.

In Practice

Here are some examples of closed questions and how they might be rephrased in an open format. Notice there are probably many ways to adjust the words so the meaning stays the same while the format becomes more open. The ones included here show just some ways this could be done.

Closed: "What's the best way to bake a cake?"

Open: "What steps would you use to bake a cake?"

Closed: "What's the best movie you've ever seen?"

Open: "What are *some of* the best movies you've ever seen?"

Closed: "Raise your hand if you're considering going to college."

Open: "Raise your hand if at least once in the past few years you've considered going to college."

Closed: "What are the rules to the game Musical Chairs?"

Open: "Who's played Musical Chairs before? What rules did you use?"

Notice how in the final example the original form of the question implies there is a *single* set of rules, while in fact there may be a number of variations on the basic theme of the game. Think about it. In the whole world, isn't there a fairly good chance that there are at least two different ways of playing Musical Chairs?

Next Steps

The issue of open and closed formats has wide-reaching implications. We need to be aware of the potential effect the *format* of our questions can have on students' willingness to answer or obey them. Without this awareness, it is easy to become frustrated with students for not fully participating, while in fact a simple adjustment in language and sentence structure may dramatically boost their level of interaction.

ASSESS YOUR CURRENT USE OF BEING OPEN

- I make careful, conscious choices in each teaching situation as to whether to use the open or closed format.

- I have occasionally varied my approach between open or closed formats, although so far this has been random rather than planned.

- I have not been aware of the difference between these two formats.

Your Ideas

Take a moment to consider each of the following closed statements. What are some ways you could rephrase each question to allow it to be more open?

Closed: "What was the cause of the American Civil War?"

Open: _____

Closed: "How *should* you solve this equation?"

Open: _____

Closed: "Thumbs up if you know how to play Blob Tag."

Open: _____

Closed: "What is the best way to approach this homework assignment?"

Open: _____

How would you rephrase each instruction to be open, thus reducing potential classroom management issues?

Closed: "Turn to a person near you and discuss . . ."

Open: _____

Closed: "Shake hands with three people near you and say 'Good morning.'"

Open: _____

Closed: "Form a group of four people."

Open: _____

Closed: "Spend one minute at each poster I've put up around the room and . . ."

Open: _____

Finally, write down at least three questions and at least two grouping situations that actually occur in your classroom where you might be able to consciously use the open format:

Questions: _____

_____

_____

_____

_____

Grouping Situations: _____

_____

_____

C = Crest of the Wave

If you're not riding the crest of the wave, you'll find yourself beneath it!

In General

The ocean is relatively calm. In the distance, a swell begins to build. It is slow and steady at first. Gradually, as it approaches the shore, it gains height and momentum. It arches up out of the water, growing ever higher. Soon, critical mass is reached and at the very top, white foam begins to form. Slowly the wave curls in on itself, crashes thunderously forward, and then begins to dissipate. The wave gently washes up on the beach, and all is calm again.

The cresting wave models the fluctuating dynamics of learning. Learning occurs best in short waves—bursts, perhaps—of student interest and momentum. If we are sensitive to when learning "crests," we can maximize these moments with clear instruction as critical mass builds up. Then, as the wave begins to break, we can change the pace, simultaneously allowing students to consolidate the information they've just learned at the crest, as well as reset themselves for the new section.

The Connection

The world of Generations Y and Z is filled with almost constant motion, rapid changes, and sudden reversals. Although previous generations may have experienced the beginnings of this speed-up and proliferation, the pace of this phenomenon accelerated rapidly in the last three decades of the twentieth century. However, it may have been the era of MTV that brought this dynamic to a sudden and remarkable peak. On this TV channel, which was extremely popular among teens throughout the 80s, visual images rarely lasted longer than 7 seconds. The pattern was set: Students developed shorter attention spans but increased their abilities to multitask and rapidly shift topics. Their learning occurred in shorter and shorter bursts.

However, classrooms were slow to adapt to this change of pace. In many cases classroom lessons continued—and to this day continue—to expect students to learn well for periods of time well beyond their actual capacity to stay focused. Instead, many of today's students need lessons full of dramatic action, sudden changes, and shifting points of view to hold their attention and keep them learning. While for Gen X teachers this pace may seem to border on hectic, perhaps even frantic, to today's students this is merely the norm.

The Big Picture

Science tells us every action has an equal and opposite reaction. The words *press and release* could be used to summarize the idea of how to manage the crest of the wave in much the same way. For every *press* situation that students experience, an equal opportunity for *release* should follow. This allows them to return to a more natural, balanced state. When students feel in balance—rather than stressed and overloaded—they can more clearly focus their attention on the subsequent section of instruction.

This is most important when information is being delivered through lecture or direct instruction. Before this discussion continues, however, consider this question:

"How long can you pay attention when someone is presenting?"

Paying attention, in this case, is defined as being able to recall and use the information at a later date. Of course, our ability to focus and give our full attention to a presenter depends on a variety of factors. What are some of these influences?

- Environmental factors (room temperature, comfort of the seat)
- Teacher's presentational skills (vocal changes, facial expressions, hand movements, use of humor)
- Learners' physiology (Did they get enough sleep last night? Have they just had a heavy lunch?)
- Learners' internal motivation (How motivated are they to learn this subject?)

There are many more. However, suppose for a moment that all of the factors listed above are *perfect*—the teacher's fantasy. The room temperature is just cool enough; the chairs are sufficiently comfortable; the students are sharp and focused; the teacher's delivery is both humorous and poignant; each learner has personally chosen to be present at this class and desires to learn more . . . If everything were perfect, once again ask yourself:

"How long can you pay attention when someone is teaching?"

Although answers will always vary from person to person and from situation to situation, academic studies have established some general figures. Given the previous definition of *paying attention,* on the average, adults can focus up to a maximum of fifteen minutes. Yes, that figure is correct. Fifteen minutes—at most. And the younger the audience is, the shorter that figure becomes—naturally! For teens the figure is eight to ten minutes of direct instruction, and for students 12 years and under the figures become even more drastically reduced. (Middle school teachers have occasionally been caught pondering the possibility that some students actually have *negative* attention spans!)

What does this mean for us as teachers? Well, most high school classes last somewhere between 35 minutes and an hour. For the purpose of this example, let's take a 50-minute class. What may happen to the learning in the room if this class is taught in strictly lecture format—in other words, if we present for 50 minutes?

The question takes us back to a 100-year-old educational principle, known today as Ebbinghaus's Curve (Driscoll, 1994). In some of the earliest educational experiments, Ebbinghaus demonstrated that, when studying long lists of content, students tended to be able to recall the greatest amount of information from the beginnings and ends of the lists. True, there may not be a direct

correlation between serial list learning and lecture format. However, we should consider the *tendencies* derived from these early studies.

The dual phenomena of our limited attention spans and Ebbinghaus's Curve mean that, for 50 minutes of classroom instruction, learners will recall material primarily from the start of the class (the first 10 to 15 minutes during which we can actually give our best attention), very little from the middle, and some points from the last few moments of the class. Of course, it's rare for teachers to lecture for the full 50 minutes—many use an activity to provide a single break in the middle of a long class. But this is not nearly enough. We need to allow learners to process information far more frequently to achieve efficient learning.

Simply stated, when we reach a maximum of 15 minutes, we need to provide students with some form of "brain break"—an approach known as the *pause procedure* (Ruhl, Hughes, & Schloss, 1987). When we give students a few moments to process new ideas, they will create *redundant retrieval routes* to the information. This strengthens the primary concepts in their minds and improves understanding and, in itself, may result in greatly increased levels of retention.

This idea of a 15-minute maximum has been academically validated only for a carefully defined situation, where new content is being presented in lecture format. Attention spans for other circumstances vary greatly. For example, most of us can sit through an entire two-hour movie or 45 minutes of stand-up comedy quite easily. Despite these differences, however, the same idea may still apply: Of the 45 minutes of comedy, how many jokes can we actually recall when it's over? How many lines from the movie can we recite from memory?

Similarly, in learning environments, attention spans may be longer in nonlecture situations, for example, when students are discussing ideas in small groups, creating a team skit, or reviewing material in preparation for an examination.

Our job as teachers is to judge when each component of learning crests, so we can shift to another mode of engagement. A useful starting point may be to consider spending much shorter periods of time lecturing or presenting to our students.

To illustrate this point, consider the following example in which a teacher paid strict attention to his beliefs concerning the maximum attention span for his students:

A special high school class was to be taught for three hours after lunch each Wednesday. On that first day, students trudged in and took their places.

The first thing the teacher did was to hold up a small kitchen timer. Carefully, in full view of the class, he set the timer to ring in exactly ten minutes. He said nothing further about the clock, but instructed the students to take out a pen and some paper to take notes. He began to lecture. Ten minutes later the timer rang, and the teacher stopped.

At that point he turned on an overhead projector with a question written on it and asked the students to discuss this question with one or two others near them. After several minutes he asked them to share their ideas with the large group. Then he carefully reset the timer and began to speak again.

This time, when the timer rang, he stopped the lecture, distributed a two-page article related to the subject, for the students to read. Then they formed small groups and discussed what they had read. Afterwards, the teacher reset the timer again, and the class continued in this manner, with an extended break in the middle—for *three hours*.

The class was taught in this style for the entire semester. In the collective experience of the students, interviewed after the class, most agreed that not only had the class time passed rapidly, but they could recall considerably more information from this class than many, if not all, of the classes they had previously attended.

Why was this? The timer meant everyone in the room knew how long the lecture would last, and that there actually was an end in sight. And then each manageable chunk was followed by a pause, with a different mode of instruction.

Remember: We're talking about maximizing a student's ability to pay attention. It is not that learners will get *nothing* from longer sessions, but that beyond 15 minutes (10 in some cases!), learners will have to work harder and harder to stay focused on the information. Eventually, a breaking point will crash in on them, which will be readily apparent on learners' faces. They fall back on that vital teenage skill—stare at the teacher and occasionally nod the head to send a message of interest while spacing out and thinking about anything but what is being taught at that moment. At this point they've reached the information overload level, and the wave has crashed down. When that happens, classroom management problems arise almost instantly.

Focus on Classroom Management

Consider the following situation:

Students have just completed a 10-minute exercise in silence. At the end of the exercise, the teacher intended to spend a few moments discussing what had taken place, developing the ideas of teamwork and communication. However, before beginning to facilitate this discussion in the large-group setting, he gave everyone an opportunity to spend a few moments discussing these ideas in small groups of three or four people.

Why did he choose to spend several precious minutes of classroom time in this manner? In this case, the answer comes from previous experiences this teacher had gone through in similar teaching situations. He had discovered that if he did not allow the students time for *everyone* to talk for a few moments immediately after the silent activity, they didn't pay attention during the large-group discussion. He realized that, if the students were silent for an extended period, they would need at least a few moments to verbalize their own thoughts and feelings before they could fully participate in a general discussion. Without realizing it, he had stumbled across a critical component in creating a successful, dynamic, safe learning environment.

In other words, when students are mentally "balanced," they are in the optimum state for learning.

In the classroom, situations when students have to concentrate on taking in and understanding new information create "press" situations. For the purposes of this discussion, we might think of these pressing situations as the wave building up and rolling along the ocean. Used properly, they create minor levels of stress that are actually quite useful for learning and retaining new information (Sapolsky, 1999).

However, extended periods of pressing will cause students to be moved off balance. This naturally results in a need for "release," some activity or event to bring them back to center.

In the example described above, the *press* aspect of the situation was the need for students to work together in silence for an extended period of time. What the teacher discovered is that immediately afterward everyone started talking in the small groups. The opportunity to talk was the balance they needed at that point, the necessary *release* mechanism in the situation.

Viewed from this perspective, it is understandable how these groups reacted before he added the small-group discussion time. Without it, the need for release was powerful enough to cause them to whisper to each other, fidget, or make silly remarks—anything to release that pent-up feeling in their body. By adding the release component, the teacher allowed his students a chance to retrieve a more useful learning state. Now they could easily turn their full attention to the large-group discussion.

Here are two more quick examples of press and release in a classroom:

■ **Example 1:** In a creative writing class, students experience press as they create a short story or poem. They could release after they write by taking time to share their stories aloud or by exchanging papers and reading in silence—or even by having their papers posted on a wall where they could be read by everyone.

■ **Example 2:** For students whose first language is not English, it is a press for them to concentrate on an English presentation from a teacher or another student. A release could take the form of giving them several opportunities throughout the day to discuss what they have heard and how they might apply it in their native language.

The idea of *press and release* creates a sense of motion in our classrooms. We introduce a feeling of dynamic movement. In traditional classrooms, students may primarily experience a sense of being pressed. If this is their only expectation of the learning environment, it should come as no surprise that they would seek to avoid this unpleasant sensation, whether by spacing out during the lecture or by acting out undesirable behaviors. Or they may simply choose not to attend school. The more they experience appropriate opportunities for releasing within the context of the class, the less threatening the classroom becomes.

The question then becomes clear: How should we respond to the crest of the wave? What release options do we have?

In Practice

Curriculum changes around the world mean teachers are being asked to cover more content in less time. In fact, many of the teachers I meet feel frustrated that they don't have enough time to cover the material effectively. For these teachers, the idea of lecturing for fewer than 15 minutes and then allowing students time to process may seem like a dangerous waste of precious classroom time (Gagne & Glaser, 1978).

In response to this concern, consider the net effect on learning if we continue to speak past the point where students can effectively take in new information. The learning curve drops drastically. Our talking increasingly becomes a waste of time. Who needs that?

Instead, if we allow students the opportunity to process the information through a different modality (talking, reading, editing their notes in silence for a few moments), we create a win–win situation (Litecky, 1992). On one hand, learners have time to reorganize their thoughts, process the material, and thus be better prepared when the next section of lecture is delivered. Meanwhile, we get the opportunity to assess the students' reactions, breathe for a moment, and reorganize *our* thinking for the next section.

Given a few minutes break, when we begin the next section of lecture, we are likely to be more articulate and focused, and thus able to communicate the information more clearly and in a shorter period of time.

Let me leave time-poor, stressed teachers with a final thought on the issue of covering content. A little knowledge, as the saying goes, can be a dangerous thing. However, in some situations, a lot of knowledge can be an even *more* dangerous thing (Glaser, 1984). Certainly as teachers we want students to have a solid base of understanding. However, particularly if we're passionate about our subject, it's easy to forget one of the basics principles of effective instruction: Teach directly to the point! Beware of extraneous information that can cloud students' understanding. Of course, if we had all day, there's a bunch more information we could give our students. But given the constraints of the school day and the curriculum we are expected to cover, we need to say to ourselves: I have 15 minutes; what do they need to learn?

State Changes

When we recognize the crest of the wave and move forward to something else, we change the "state" of our students—their physiology as well as their mental state. Thus, the term for creating a "release" or moving back to "press" is called a *state change*.

A state change occurs when an educator changes the method of instruction for the class from one modality to another modality.

When a state change occurs in a learning environment, it causes the brain to refocus attention on what is happening (Schacter, 1990). For a brief period of time, it will feel like the start of something new, a condition in which the brain tends to be in a heightened level of awareness. Thus, using frequent state changes can help students maintain a high level of attention for most of the 50-minute lesson.

We have countless options for creating state changes. For example, after a brief lecture, switching to small-group discussion is a state change. Moving then to a large-group discussion would be another state change. State changes can be very brief or continue for some time. They can be subtle, such as moving from direct instruction mode into telling a story, which would cause a subtle change in how learners listen to and process the verbal information. They can also be quite dramatic, such as moving from indoors to outdoors for the next section of the class.

Here's an example of how one teacher makes creative use of one simple state change:

The teacher lives in the southeastern United States. He is a calm, soft-spoken individual. In addition to teaching math, each fall he also tours the schools in several states and gives two-hour lectures in an auditorium setting to high school students, usually in groups of over 250. The topic he covers is "Getting involved in today's politics." Attendance is frequently mandatory.

Not surprisingly, the students are seldom very pleased to be present. However, at the appointed time, he quietly begins his lecture. After about ten minutes, he pauses to ask the audience a simple question. When a student answers, he turns around in silence, takes something off of the table behind him, and tosses it to the student while saying thank you.

When this happens, many in the audience sit up and take notice, wondering what just happened. What was thrown out to that person? There is the sound of crinkling paper, and suddenly it becomes clear—it was a piece of candy! With this realization, the game is afoot . . .

Meanwhile, the lecture continues. A few minutes later, the teacher asks another question. What happens? Many hands are raised. Another piece of candy is distributed.

Throwing candy out to audience members is the *only* state change this teacher uses in his entire presentation, and the audiences stay right with him for the entire two hours. To keep it lively, he occasionally announces he feels "random" and heaves out huge handfuls of candy. But that simple state change is enough to keep his audience focused, smiling, and paying attention.

As this example shows, the conscious use of state changes, even quite subtle ones, can have a powerful influence on the audience's ability to stay focused on the material. For example, simply by varying the tone of voice using *vocal inflection* (*see* V—Vocal Italics), a teacher can help learners to focus longer. Most dynamic teachers change their method of presentation quite frequently, even within a single class session. They will alternate between storytelling, focusing on main points, brief student involvement, and using humor. If we incorporate these ideas into direct instruction, we may be able to continue to teach effectively well past the 15-minute limit previously discussed.

Teachers of younger audiences may want to consider this same discussion from the opposite perspective. Given that younger students are quite naturally full of adrenaline, motion, and excitement, perhaps instruction should be geared toward activities that release that boundless energy. The crest of the wave may then come in the form of those brief, quieter, more focused moments where we deliver primary content.

Also, be aware of the possibility that state changes can be overdone. Which kinds of state changes to use and how frequently they can be introduced will depend on the ages of our students, our content, our time frame, and the physical learning environment.

The following two examples may help clarify when and how to use state changes.

■ **Situation 1:** It is early in the year. The teacher's objective for this sequence is to allow students to meet others in the room one-on-one. The students form into dyads, choosing who will go first and who will go second. The teacher provides a question to be addressed and informs them that each person will have two minutes to answer the question. The teacher will tell them when it is time to switch to the second person. The first person begins.

Here is the critical question: Does the teacher always give the first person the full two minutes? The answer depends on understanding the crest-of-the-wave principle. First, it is necessary for the teacher to observe and listen to what is happening in the room once the conversation between students begins. Initially, the sound level in the room will build. However, as some students run out of things to say, they will stop speaking, and the overall sound level will decrease. At this point, the crest has been reached.

The crest of the wave can also be identified visually. As the first person runs out of things to say, she may begin to feel uncomfortable and look away from her partner's eyes. Or she may begin to shift, fidget, or twist and turn to see what else is happening in the room. These are visual cues indicating some of the dyads have reached the crest.

Consider what happens if nothing is changed at this moment. As time continues, students will feel increasingly uncomfortable. When the next activity is introduced, they may be hesitant to engage in it, since they have now had a mildly unpleasant experience. While it may be subconscious at first, with repeated experiences, a teacher may suddenly find the group has become "difficult," unaware that a simple matter of timing has created the particular group dynamic.

Once the crest of the wave has been identified, how could the teacher respond? In this case, perhaps the teacher might say, "Please take 10 seconds for the first person to complete." With this statement, those who are already finished will be relieved that the discussion is almost ready to switch, knowing they can survive for 10 more seconds, while those pairs still talking know it's time to complete their conversation. The most important point is the teacher *must react* in some manner to the fact that the majority of the people in the room are ready to move forward.

■ **Situation 2:** A lecture has been given, and the teacher has opened the floor for student comments. Several questions have already been answered. As another one is asked, the teacher is aware of several people shifting slightly in their seats and looking around the room. This movement informs the teacher that the questions have shifted from those that were of concern to the large group to those that are of concern only to one or two students.

The crest of the wave for this session has just been reached. The teacher responds to the present question, perhaps adding, "This will be the final question for now. We'll be ending class a bit early today so those of you with further questions may speak with me individually afterwards."

As these two examples demonstrate, we need to be responsive to waves of interest and attention within the environment and make appropriate responses and adjustments as quickly as possible.

The bottom line is that we need to become aware of, and respond to, the changing needs of the audience. This is not to imply that students have no responsibility. Quite the opposite. If we are responsive to the needs of the students, students often respond to the needs of the teacher and the situation, choosing to become much more actively involved than they might otherwise have been. With continued exposure to this form of instruction, learners frequently demonstrate a greatly increased level of personal responsibility for their education.

The following list of state changes—some already discussed, and some additional ones—are merely a beginning. As you discover for yourself which state changes seem to work best for you, create your own personal list. Carry it with you at all times. Build on it whenever you can. Then, when you realize that the crest of the wave has been reached and the learners are ready for a state change, you will have some prepared options to fall back on in case your creative genius is unable to spontaneously generate an idea.

- Find a new place to sit.

- Stand and stretch.

- Tell a story.

- Drink a glass of water.

- Play a 30-second game.

- Stand and shake hands with several people nearby.

- Greet at least three people wearing the color blue.

- Have someone stand and read a part of the text.

- Role-play a related scenario.

- Give two minutes for students to edit their notes in silence.

- Let students talk with others near them about their reactions to the new information.

- Take 30 seconds to celebrate learning something new.

- Take a three-minute walk outside, perhaps in pairs or trios.

Next Steps

Much like waves building, peaking, then crashing down, there are swells, crests, and tumbles in the classroom. When students start finding it hard to draw useful learning from a mode of interaction, we've reached the crest of the wave. At this point, we need to shift to some alternate manner of instruction or distinctly change the pace to recapture student focus and interest.

On closer inspection, you'll find multiple "waves" happening simultaneously within most learning environments. There are small ones, such as how many seconds of silence to allow students to observe a newly introduced visual (*see* P—Pause for Visuals), how much time to give a group to read a particular passage in a book, or when to use directed questions instead of a general question technique. Larger ones may consist of how long to give lectures, how much time to allow for small-group discussions, or how much time to devote to a particular lecture. By carefully managing and responding to these various situations, we help students pay attention longer and learn more.

As you consider which ideas to use in your own classroom, know that in general there are basically two primary types of state changes: obvious ones, such as movement or group interactions, and more subtle ones, such as vocal changes. It's up to you to choose which ones to use, and when and how frequently to use them. Remember: Not all state changes work with all students, of all age levels, in all classrooms!

ASSESS YOUR CURRENT USE OF CREST OF THE WAVE

- I am constantly aware of the crest of the wave in my classroom, and make appropriate adjustments.

- I sometimes respond to the crest of the wave by doing a state change, but have not really thought about this consciously.

- In general I tend to stick to the lesson I have planned, regardless of how the students are reacting.

Your Ideas

Write out *at least* seven different kinds of obvious state changes that might be appropriate to use in your classroom with your students.

Obvious State Change Options: _____

_____

_____

_____

_____

_____

_____

_____

_____

Write down *at least* seven more subtle state changes that might be appropriate for you to use at the crest of the wave in your classroom.

More Subtle State Change Options: _____

_____

_____

_____

_____

_____

_____

_____

_____

_____

As mentioned previously, consider using what you've created here as a beginning point to developing your own "master list" of state changes to use in your classroom. The more options you have handy, the more likely you are to find the most appropriate one to use as each new crest-of-the-wave situation arises.

D = Directions

Effective directions make interactive learning efficient.

In General

One of the least appreciated techniques in teacher training is the "art" of giving effective directions. The choice of the word *art* is deliberate. Effective directions are truly an art form unto themselves. Like many pieces of art, effective directions look deceptively simple. However, in reality they are far from easy to achieve and rely on technique and practice. To be truly effective when giving directions, we must follow the same path as the budding artist. We must understand what we are doing, master some basic techniques, and consciously put them into practice.

The Connection

More than ever before, we need to teach today's students in an interactive manner. Interaction is their primary mode of learning. On the Internet, with electronic games, listening to iPods, or texting with cell phones, learning is intuitive and experiential. The new generations don't read manuals—they learn through doing.

One of the many implications of this shift in learning is that, as teachers, we will find ourselves having to give far more directions. If we're going to use more activities, we will have to guide our students through those activities. If we don't give directions effectively—if it takes students a long time to move between activities—we will lose precious teaching time. Thus, the more rapidly we can give precise, coherent directions and get students effectively engaged, the more time students have to learn.

The Big Picture

Giving effective directions requires different techniques from presenting a lecture, relating a story, or facilitating a question-and-answer session. The contrast between directions and these other modes of teaching should be as sharp as the contrast between the English and Russian languages. We need to move consciously into direction-giving mode, signaling this change by using different words and a different tone of voice. Even sentence structure and our pauses between sentences will be different.

It's surprising how many directions we need to give within a single fairly conventional learning session. In interactive classrooms this number is magnified as students shift rapidly from activity to activity. Some of the instructions we need to give will be short, others will be long, but all share a common objective. In every case, we want students to move as efficiently as possible to the next task, with minimum uncertainty on the part of the learner and minimum repetition on the part of the teacher.

If our directions aren't clear, we create a variety of problems. Students who aren't clear about what is required may hesitate to involve themselves for fear of doing something wrong. They may quickly wander off task, or worse yet, they may *believe* they are on task, but end up spending precious classroom time on an inconsequential tangent.

Few teachers enjoy the moment when a student raises a hand and says: "What are we supposed to be doing?"

It's easy in this irritating situation to wish our students listened more carefully. But wait. Instead of blaming our students, perhaps we should first consider the possibility that we could have delivered the instructions more clearly in the first place.

Focus on Classroom Management

If we don't give clear instructions, our classrooms will regularly dissolve into anarchy, making us battle to regain control of the room. Moreover, regularly having to repeat ourselves or clarify what we say can undermine our credibility—creating an environment where students find it easy to be disruptive.

EFFECTIVE DIRECTIONS
MAKE INTERACTIVE LEARNING EFFICIENT

Consider the following situation. It's early in the year of a long course, and the teacher wants to warm up the students with some introductions. He says, "Please turn to the person on your left and introduce yourself!"

Can you see it coming? Imagine what would happen if everyone actually did follow this instruction. If each person turns to his or her left, every student would end up facing the back of someone's head. Additionally, the people at the left end of each row would be facing a wall!

In practice, most students would probably laugh when they realized the absurdity of the instruction, and adjust by finding someone near them to meet. But the damage will be done. The teacher has unintentionally communicated a powerful message. The subconscious implication is: If this simple instruction doesn't make sense, what else in the lesson won't be clear? Does this teacher know his content? Does he know how to teach?

Let's not raise such ideas in the minds of our students. Instead, let's mobilize them and get them quickly engaged with clear, concise, and meaningful directions. In this case, the teacher might have said, "Say hello to two or three people near you."

Now the instruction is easy for everyone to accomplish successfully, and the class moves smoothly forward—without the teacher losing credibility.

In Practice

Before we begin looking at techniques for directions, let us start from a point of awareness. While your directions are clear to you—because you've thought about them, planned them, maybe even written them out—your students are hearing them for the first time. They need help to understand them.

Here are seven key ideas to make your directions more effective:

1. Be clear and concise

2. Give directions one at a time

3. Make sure students can see you

4. Use a "step check" whenever possible

5. Be congruent

6. Directionalize

7. Use the "four-part sequence"

Clear and Concise

Directions are very distinct from a conversation or a lecture—they require different words, different phrases, and sometimes even different sentence structures. But one of the biggest distinctions is that they require *fewer* words.

Which words in this statement don't we need?

"I want you to turn to page 42."

Look at the first four words, "I want you to . . ." What purpose do these words serve? In reality, none at all! Of course the teacher wants students to turn to page 42! He is the person speaking! Saying these words is not only unnecessary, but can eventually interfere with communication, since students tend to tune out repetitious phrases. All the teacher needs to say is "Turn to page 42."

The rule with directions is to only say the *essence* of the communication. If we stick to what is essential, students are more likely to hear, understand, and do what they're asked.

Beware of the following phrases, which can get in the way of clear directions.

- "I want you to . . ."
- "I'm going to . . ."
- "What I'd like you to do is . . ."
- "What we're going to do is . . ."
- "What we have to do is . . ."
- "OK, now, we'll just need to . . ."
- "OK, everybody, here what's coming next . . ."
- "I think now might be a good time to . . ."
- "I think what we'll do is . . ."
- "So, then, why don't we just . . ."

It's easy to develop an unconscious habit of using one or two "pet" phrases. But if students hear a particular phrase too frequently, they begin to stop hearing it at all. This may well start a treacherous trend. If students become accustomed to not listening at certain points in class, then how long will it be before they stop listening during the spaces *between* those moments? Probably all too soon.

So try to avoid unnecessary words and phrases. Say only what is necessary, and avoid getting caught in repeating words or phrases that add nothing to the communication. Your directions will be more effective when you present them clearly and concisely.

One at a Time

How many directions can students remember? The key here is to realize this is not a question about how many *things* students can remember, but how many directions. The trouble with remembering directions is that the second students are told the first direction, they start thinking about doing it. This thinking diverts their attention from listening to the second direction. If they don't hear the second direction, any further listening is irrelevant—they won't get the sequence of directions right.

This is why the most effective directions are given *one at a time.* We give our students one direction, and then wait until it has been completed before moving to the next. To see why this is so important, consider the following real-life example.

At the very start of class, a high school teacher gave the following directions:

> "Good morning everyone. Today we'll be continuing the discussion from the last class. To start off, here's what we're going to do. In a few moments, we'll be getting into groups of about five or six. Each group will appoint a discussion leader. This person will facilitate a conversation about the topic so the group can remind itself of some of the key issues we were looking at last time, specifically concerning challenges in creative writing. After four or five minutes, each group will need to decide which two potential solutions to these issues they believe will generate the most success. Then select someone to write your two ideas on the board so we can see which ones are similar to those that other groups have come up with. Oh, and let's make sure that each group's ideas are written on a separate part of the board, so we may make notes near them. OK, let's begin!"

As soon as the teacher said, "Let's begin," the students, who had grasped the first instruction, organized themselves into groups—but no one knew what to do next. Rather than draw attention to themselves and actually ask, a general murmur of conversation filled the room as each group spent several minutes debating what they were supposed to do.

The teacher had been looking down at some papers. Soon, however, she realized the students were not on task. She reminded them to choose a discussion leader and get the conversation under way. Prompted, they quickly chose leaders and were soon talking animatedly to each other.

However, after five minutes, no one had approached the blackboard to write their answers to the original question. The teacher again reminded them—this time with considerable exasperation in her voice—of their assignment. Then, as various members of each group began to write on the board, she was further annoyed that no one had remembered to spread their responses out so other notes could be added later. At one point, she rolled her eyes as if to say, "Why did I get the class of slow students?"

Finally, the students put their answers on the board correctly and the teacher began the group discussion. But the emotions in the room didn't support enthusiastic conversation. The teacher was cross about having to repeat herself and the time lost while students debated what to do and sorted out the errors on the blackboard. Meanwhile, some of the students were feeling aggrieved—they hadn't *meant* to annoy the teacher—whereas others felt stupid about not knowing what to do. Why, they wondered, was it all so hard?

This is an excellent question. Why is it so hard? Why couldn't the students recall all the directions in the order they were given? Let's consider, in slow motion, what happened when the students heard the teacher's words.

The first direction the students heard was to organize themselves into groups. Instantly, where did their attention go? Naturally, they looked around to decide who they wanted in their group. While they were glancing at other people, their attention was diverted from the teacher, who was continuing with her list of instructions—*important information to which they were not listening.* Once students missed the link in a series of connected directions, it was virtually impossible for them to get back on track and figure out what they were supposed to be doing.

What does this mean to us as teachers?

We need to consider directions in the light of how they will be heard and processed by our students. For example, whenever we give an instruction that directs students' attention away from us, we must allow them to complete the task before giving them further directions.

In the original example, the class would have run more smoothly if the teacher had begun by saying:

> "Good morning, everyone. Today we'll be starting with some group work, so you'll need to organize yourselves into groups of five or six. Please do that now."

. . . and then *waited* until the groups were organized before continuing:

> "Thank you. Next, please select someone to be your discussion leader."

Then, she could pause until every group had a discussion leader before explaining the discussion topic and telling them to begin. Once she felt confident the groups had covered the important issues, she might say:

> "Pause there. Now, see if your group can come up with at least two potential solutions to these challenges."

Again, after sufficient time, she could give the next direction:

> "Now, please select someone to come to the blackboard and write your group's solutions to these challenges."

And as the students approach the blackboard, she could complete this sequence of directions by saying:

> "For those of you writing on the board, please leave plenty of space around your responses, so we can add some notes to them later. Let's get those ideas up on the board now."

By giving directions one at a time like this, the teacher would have avoided the frustration of feeling that her directions were not heard, acknowledged, or acted on. Even more important, the students would have felt confident about what was expected of them and found it easy to quickly achieve each short-term objective.

This point is, hidden in her original directions were actually six separate instructions:

1. "Find a group."

2. "Select a discussion leader."

3. "Have the initial discussion concerning challenges."

4. "Have the second discussion concerning solutions."

5. "Select someone to write on the board."

6. "Write responses, leaving space around them."

And the teacher needed to wait until each was accomplished before giving the next one. That way, she wouldn't have had to repeat them—and they would have been carried out in about half the time.

Of course, not every situation calls for us to give one direction at a time. Some directions are inherently linked: "Please take out your geography book and a pencil." It's up to us to judge about how many directions our students can handle in different situations. However, in general, we will give our students the best possible chance to achieve every step of an instruction sequence when we give that sequence *one direction at a time.*

As a final note, there is a hidden challenge in using this strategy. You'll probably notice the number of times this section talks about "waiting patiently." This is the challenge! We have to *pause* after giving a single direction and wait in silence until it has been successfully completed. At first glance this may appear a simple thing to do, yet in practice it can prove a tremendous challenge. With all this waiting patiently, it may seem as though directions are taking forever. Console yourself during the seemingly interminable waits for students to comply with simple instructions that you are actually *saving* time by giving directions that are clearly understood in the first place.

See Me

Consider the following situation. Suppose a teacher is carefully sequencing his directions—*one at a time*! First he asks the students: "Please get into small groups, with approximately six to eight people in each one."

The teacher waits patiently for the groups to be organized before giving the next direction: "Please put your chairs in a circle."

Again, he is patient as the groups form circles. When all groups are ready, he continues speaking. For his third instruction he begins explaining their discussion topic. But about 20 seconds into his explanation, he notices students fidgeting and not paying attention. What's going on?

If you consider the physical arrangement of the classroom, you can see what's happening. By getting his students to move their chairs into a circle, the teacher has created a problem. *No matter where he chooses to stand in the room, approximately half the students will have their backs to him.* This is a problem because being able to *see* the teacher strongly supports students' ability to understand and recall instructions and directions. Seeing the teacher's facial expression helps students maintain their focus and pay attention while the information is being presented. By contrast, facing other students is incredibly distracting.

Yes, but surely it doesn't matter. At least some of the students in each group *can* see the teacher. While this is true, with half the class distracted, the whole dynamic of attention has changed. Once the students who can't see become disengaged, they immediately distract those that can—and the domino effect disrupts the whole room. Even a small loss of attention by a small number of students can quickly distract an entire class.

How can the teacher adjust to this potentially frustrating situation? Quite simply, by asking the students to turn and face him before giving the next direction: "Please move your chair so you can comfortably see me."

With this statement, the teacher has given clear permission for the students to adjust their chairs so they can see him while he gives the next set of instructions. They will not feel as if they are failing to follow the previous directions asking them to form a circle. Now the students are facing him, they are less likely to be distracted by interactions with their peers. In this position they can maintain their attention on the next set of directions.

Note the use of the word *comfortably*. It may be useful to include this word, or a similar one, in instructions like this to give students a clear visual image of what we are asking them to do. Alternatively, we might say:

- "Please turn so you can see the board."

- "Move your chairs so you can face me."

- "Turn to face this direction."

- "Please look up at me."

- "Make sure you can clearly see my eyes."

The key is to give the students permission to face the teacher.

We talked previously about waiting until the first direction had been completed before providing a second direction. The same concept applies here. If we ask students to turn and face us, we need to *wait until everyone can see us before continuing* with the next instruction. If we begin talking too soon, we run the risk of some students missing the first part of an instruction. For clarity, wait patiently—yes, again!—until every student is ready before giving the next direction.

We can apply the See Me technique whenever students are facing away from us. For example, students might be looking down at their notebooks or texts when we are ready to give another direction or some more information. Or they might be scattered around the room, working in small groups or talking in dyads. In these situations, we can still ask students to look up to receive the next direction. We might say:

"Please pause for a moment and look this way. [Wait for students to pause.] Thank you. Now listen for a moment for something else you can consider in your discussions . . ."

Whatever the physical situation, make sure your students can see clearly and comfortably from the position they are in before giving them directions or additional information. When your students can see you, they can better give you their full attention—at least at the start of the directions. Then it's up to you to keep it!

Step Check

If every student needs to complete a direction before we give the next one, we need to know when this has happened. Sometimes we can tell this easily—are the students all in groups or not?—but, in other situations, it's easy to inadvertently leave students behind. Consider this example:

A teacher is using a workbook with 25 students. The teacher wants the students to consider a specific line from their workbooks. She says, "Please turn to page 12 and follow with me."

She then looks up from her workbook and briefly glances around the room. From a quick glance, it appears everyone is following along. She continues, saying, "Now, look at the second paragraph. Do you see where . . ."

However, as she begins discussing the line in the book, something obviously isn't right. The class has fallen into three categories: One group of students has rapidly located the correct page and is following along. A second group has found their workbooks, but has yet to locate the correct page or line. And students in the final group *are still looking for their workbooks!*

These students are busily looking under their chairs, checking in their desks, or turning to see if they had left their workbook on a side table in the room. Their focus is entirely on finding their workbooks—meaning they aren't listening to a word the teacher is saying.

What this teacher needed, after the first direction, was to give her students a quick *step check*. A step check is a means of visibly verifying that students are keeping pace with the directions or the information being presented. When you give a hard-to-verify direction, a step check allows you to be certain that all your students are at the same spot.

For example, instead of leaving half her students behind, this teacher could have made sure everyone was keeping up with a step check by saying: "If you have found page 12, please hold your workbook up in the air."

Now she knows which students, if any, need an extra moment to locate their workbooks—keeping her little flock together before taking the next step. Taking the necessary 30 seconds at this point to make sure everyone is at the same place may save a much greater amount of time later in the day—when it suddenly becomes necessary to go back to ideas discussed earlier for those students who weren't keeping up.

Here's another example: Imagine a teacher is about to give a mathematics test on which students are only allowed to use a pencil. The teacher might want to verify that each student has a pencil. She says, "Please hold up your pencil. Thank you, you may begin."

When their pencils are all in the air, the teacher can be certain that all students have the necessary tools to begin taking the test. The teacher has avoided the disruption of having a student walk up after the test has begun, announcing that he or she doesn't have a pencil.

A step check is an invaluable tool for keeping all members of a class moving forward at the same pace. It's a quick and easy means of helping students to keep up—which means we don't have to catch up individuals later, and students feel more successful in our classrooms.

Congruence

The world's greatest orators—John F. Kennedy, Martin Luther King, Jr., and Winston Churchill—all shared one critical characteristic: their ability to communicate their message with power, conviction, and passion. This skill was not an accident. How did they make their audiences feel this way?

How did they project their feelings so powerfully when speaking before very large crowds? The key is that *every aspect of their delivery* was communicating the same message. Their choice of words, tone of voice, pacing, use of pauses, eye contact, and physical gestures were all focused on that one key idea. The term used to describe this effect is *congruence*.

This quality of being congruent is equally important in instructional settings—particularly when giving directions. While we don't have to teach everything at the level of intensity these speakers demonstrated, we can occasionally use congruence to reinforce key points of information—like directions. High levels of congruence generate a strong impact on our students. The stronger the impact, the more deeply they will encode the information, and the longer they will remember it.

We need to make three elements congruent when giving instructions.

1. Our tone of voice must support the fact that we are giving directions—don't shout, but be authoritative.

2. Our hand gestures must add clarity—demonstrate the circle you're asking your students to make; hold up fingers to reinforce numbers; point in the direction you want them to move.

3. Our body language must further emphasize the idea—turn your body in the direction they must go to get a handout; lean to one side if they must lean over to talk to another student; walk toward the door if everyone is heading to another room.

Each of these elements adds to the level of impact our directions will have.

Directionalize

Because we often give directions while facing our students, our "left" is their "right," and vice versa. Thus, directions involving the words *left* and *right* have a huge potential to confuse students. Consider what happens if we give this instruction:

> "All the boys please form a group on the left side of the room, and all the girls please form a group on the right side of the room."

On hearing this, our students hesitate. They wonder: Are we referring to our point of view, or their point of view? A few students start moving tentatively toward one side of the room or another, watching out the corner of their eye for our reaction to see if they have guessed correctly.

In choosing these ambiguous words, we are unintentionally undermining the emotional safety in our classroom. Forcing our students to guess what we mean triggers a subtle game of right or wrong. At best it merely slows students down as they tentatively guess at our intention—at worst it causes them to disengage from our lesson. Either way, it is strongly in our interest to give them clear, unambiguous instructions.

In this case, we can avoid the "mirror image" issues by eliminating the words *left* and *right* from our directions. Instead, we can *directionalize* our instructions. This means choosing something everyone can see and using that as the directional object for our instructions.

For example, we might directionalize our earlier instructions by announcing:

> "All boys please form a group near the clock, and all girls please form a group near the health poster."

Now the directions should be clear to everyone, and students can quickly move to the appropriate side of the room.

Here's another example of a potentially confusing situation. Suppose a teacher raises one of his hands and says to a group of students, "Please raise this hand."

As he gives the instruction, the teacher raises his *right* hand. But the students must once again guess what he means. Is he referring to their right hands, since he is raising his right hand? Or is he referring to the hand on that side of the body, mirroring where he is standing, which would mean their left hands? And of course, at least one clown in the class will wonder aloud if the teacher meant *his* hand!

The teacher could avoid confusion by directionalizing the request: "Please raise your hand closest to the window."

Alternatively, suppose he actually does want the students to raise their right hands. In this case he could first *turn his body* so his back is to the class. Now when he raises his right hand it will much clearer what he is asking. He could actually now use his original instruction: "Please raise this hand."

Turning around to face the same way as your students can be useful whenever you want students to copy a physical motion. For example, it could be helpful when modeling a physical skill such as passing a football or hitting a baseball. Or it would even be useful when leading a few morning stretches in class.

The Four-Part Sequence

The following four-part framework for directions helps students to complete an instruction successfully.

First: Establish a time frame for the students to act on the direction

Second: Imbed a trigger to signal the start of that movement

Third: Give the directions clearly and concisely

Fourth: Pull the trigger

Imagine a teacher wants students to move their chairs to the sides of the room. Here are the four distinct parts of the direction:

First: "In ten seconds . . ."

Second: "When I say go . . ."

Third: "Move the chairs to the sides of the room and stack them neatly."

Fourth: "Go."

To understand why this sequence is important, consider some of the possible problems in giving this direction without the framework. Perhaps the teacher states, "OK, we're going to move our chairs and . . ."

Imagine what happens in the room even before the teacher has a chance to complete that sentence. Suddenly, chaos reigns as students begin to pick up and move their chairs. Any other information the teacher has to deliver at this moment is lost as concentration shifts from listening to the teacher to the physical activity of moving the chairs. Why did this happen? Because the original instruction *didn't give the students a time frame to tell them when to begin.* Therefore, most students will simply begin immediately.

We must keep students focused until they have clearly heard and understood our directions. This starts with giving students a clear time frame for mobilizing directions. For example, the first part of the sequence here is:

"In ten seconds we'll be moving the chairs to the sides of the room."

When the teacher uses those first three words, students now know approximately when the movement is going to commence. They know not to move yet, that they have ten seconds to keep their attention on the teacher for further information.

Adding a time frame to the beginning of a mobilizing direction is the first step of the four-part sequence. Subsequent steps follow the same lines of thinking. We don't just need to tell students when movement is going to occur, we also need to give them a clear *signal* or *trigger,* indicating when it is time for the movement to begin.

In this example, the trigger is the word *go.* But you can use anything that works with your students. Other common triggers are "Ready-set-go" or "On the count of three." Or you can use a novel random word or one related to what is happening, such as "When I say 'chair,' please move the chairs . . ." Varying your triggers helps to maintain student focus.

A word of caution: Be sure to "pull" the trigger you originally imbedded in the earlier part of the direction! It is easy to imagine how confusing it can be for students if we use a sequence such as "In five seconds, when I say go, find a partner and stand with them. Ready, *move!*"

Because we established the word *go* as the original trigger, this is what the students are waiting for. Our vocal inflection on the word *move* makes it seem like this is the time to find a partner. But students may not be certain, since we haven't pulled the imbedded trigger. Pulling a different trigger will be disconcerting and cause confusion.

The third component of the sequence is to state the instruction clearly and concisely. This issue has been discussed in depth at the start of this chapter, so let us just repeat the basics: At this part say *only* the words needed for students to know what is expected of them, and nothing else.

In the four-part sequence, each of the components plays an integral role in providing easily understood directions. Giving a time frame allows the students to fully understand when the movement is to occur, so they can take in *all* the information before they move. Including a trigger helps clarify when the movement is to occur. The instructions are then given clearly and concisely. Finally, the trigger is pulled, and the action begins.

Having to repeat instructions is frustrating for both teachers and students. As frustration mounts, it begins to interfere with students hearing further instructions, developing a self-perpetuating cycle of confusion. As confusion around directions grows, students become less willing to involve themselves in the class. Giving clear directions allows students to feel confident about what is expected of them. This encourages them to involve themselves more freely in activities.

Next Steps

Think about how effective your directions are. Do your students ever ask you to repeat directions? Does every student carry out your directions

ASSESS YOUR CURRENT USE OF DIRECTIONS

■ I am extremely conscious of the directions I give to students, and give only one at a time whenever possible.

■ I have become aware how important effective directions are and have been working toward giving better directions.

■ I have never really thought much about specifically how to give effective directions.

successfully? Do you ever see confusion in your classroom? Can you use any of the previous ideas to make your directions even clearer?

Your Ideas

Giving effective directions frequently requires careful preparation. First, select a classroom activity. Then write out the directions you think would work best. Finally, go back over your directions, making sure you are using the key ideas described here:

- Are they clear and concise?

- Where needed, did you provide directions one at a time?

- Whenever you are speaking, can they see you?

- Is a step check needed, and if so, have you included it?

- Did you use the idea of "directionalizing," if needed?

- Did you use the four-part sequence, if needed?

- Are you ready to be congruent with your voice?

Activity 1: _____

Directions: _____

_____

_____

_____

_____

Activity 2: _____

Directions: _____

_____

_____

_____

_____

Activity 3: _____

Directions: _____

_____

_____

_____

_____

E = Entertainment

Memorable teachers don't give speeches, they put on a show.

In General

Good entertainment is highly memorable. We may not remember what we had for dinner on Tuesday night, or the conversation around the table (unless our daughter announced her intention to drop out of high school), but two weeks later we can still recall the plot of the TV show we watched that same evening. Why is this? Partly because stories are inherently easy to recall (*see* Y—Yesterday Lives!). But also because good entertainment engages our emotions. We may have cried, flinched, or laughed many times during the TV episode. And we remember moments that generate strong emotions. Highly emotional events such as weddings, funerals, birthdays, shocks, and celebrations are seared into our minds in intense detail. We can harness this effect in our classrooms by using the principles of good entertainment within our lessons.

The Connection

For Generations Y and Z, entertainment is everywhere: on their phones, on their computers, in their pockets. Every youth-oriented retail outlet plays MTV on a plasma wall. Even car journeys come with built-in entertainment. Ten years ago, kids on the long vacation drive stared out of the window, got travel sick reading, or bickered with their siblings. Today, the family car is often an oasis of silence as kids plugged into headphones play Nintendo or watch the in-car DVD. Thus, for today's students entertainment is ubiquitous, instantly available, and expected. This is the environment our classrooms must compete with. As teachers, we need to realize that, while entertainment is not education, education may need to be more entertaining.

The Big Picture

The good news for teachers is that if we glance backstage, we can easily identify practical strategies to bring the magic of drama into our classrooms—bringing dry material to vibrant life. Deliberately including these strategies in our lesson plans will make our lessons both more engaging and more memorable (Reid, 2000). Guided properly, drama can trigger a wealth of healthy emotions and positive learning for everyone involved in a theatrically designed lesson.

Teachers whose hearts are already sinking at the thought of having to "put on a production" can rest easy. You only need the barest resources to use drama to create magic for your students. You don't have to have costumers or a set—although a basic props box can be useful! And you don't even have to write the script.

When we incorporate drama into instruction, the performance itself can be as simple as a one-minute sketch with minimal props. And we can incorporate learning in every part of dramatic development. Learning can occur anywhere—in rehearsal, behind the scenes, or on stage.

For example, in planning their performance students must understand the material before they can decide how to tell a story. Writing and rehearsing are excellent learning vehicles as students have to carefully review and think about the content. In performances, the actors, the crew, and the audience all learn, the actors and crew because their heightened emotional state strongly embeds the memories, and the audience because the message is encoded in visuals and emotion. Even after the performance, learning continues, as the experience triggers further discussions among the cast, crew, and audience.

Focus on Classroom Management

Incorporating drama in lessons almost always reduces classroom management issues, discipline problems, and disruptive behavior. This is because drama engages even the most normally distracted student. While involved in developing or presenting—or even while watching—a dramatic lesson, students' attention levels tend to soar, leaving precious little energy left for disruptive behavior. In addition, classroom management problems are significantly reduced in any classroom situation where the students—rather than the teacher—are the primary monitors of behavior. And since dramatic works are primarily the result of groups of students working together, peer pressure prevents many kids from acting out (Kagan, Kagan, & Kagan, 1997).

In Practice

We have a wide range of options for building the various elements of drama into many topics—starting with ourselves. Some teachers are natural performers—and if this is your element, then use all your dramatic tendencies to make your content come alive.

Feel free to take full dramatic license and step boldly into any dramatic role you are willing to explore within the classroom. You can act out situations related to your content, become a character connecting to the topic, or simply tell a dramatic story that helps emphasize a key aspect of a lesson.

You don't need to prepare a complex script. What engages the students, what captivates and motivates them, is the energy and dynamics of your dramatic performance. In fact, you might say that teaching is one-quarter preparation and three-quarters presentation.

Of course, not all of us are comfortable in the role of performer. However, regardless of our own level of comfort with acting, we can have the same effect by making even minor variations from our usual selves—perhaps by doing an accent, talking in a funny voice, wearing a hat, or using a prop. Even including these simple dramatic elements can bring a potentially mundane lesson to dramatic life. The courage to do this comes from the knowledge that, by doing so, you are helping your students to learn at a much deeper level than you would by merely *telling* them the information.

If including even simple dramatic elements seems too daunting, don't despair. Let your students become the performers instead. Drama is at its most powerful in the classroom when it involves students.

Here are just some of the strategies you can use to turn content into entertainment.

Student Skits

One of the simplest—and often most effective—ways to bring drama into the classroom is to invite students to perform skits based on the content

(Cruz & Murthy, 2006). Using this approach, your role is to isolate the events students need to focus on and provide support materials for their "productions," such as a box of props or perhaps a few costumes. You can then step back and let the natural learning process take over. When students create their own skits, they must engage with and understand the material—thus they can't help but learn it. Their eagerness to perform, as well as the subtle peer pressure from their group, means they will almost always engage fully with this approach to learning.

Students as Content

This idea offers an unusual twist on the entertainment theme. Instead of *acting out* content, student might actually *become* the content. For example, math has multiple opportunities for students to become numbers, variables, exponents, parentheses, operations, and formulas—and perhaps then move in the way each part of an equation must move for it to be solved. Math can frequently feel like a totally conceptual, abstract topic to students who are kinesthetically oriented (meaning they prefer to learn through physical engagement). However, if taught using dramatic engagement, these students tend to learn the concepts much more rapidly because the teaching process matches their orientation to the world.

Many other subject areas offer opportunities for students to "become" the content. In science class, students might become the different parts of a chemical process. In physics, perhaps they become the parts of a bridge or a catapult as they work on discovering how certain pressure, stress, or acceleration equations are derived. In an English class, students might become verbs, nouns, pronouns, prepositions, and adjectives—and perhaps they could then form a line, based on what kind of word they are, to create a grammatically correct sentence. In music class, perhaps the students could become musical notes and act out a musical sequence. To bring these subjects alive at the dramatic level, the teacher simply needs to find a way for the students to physically become the content.

Acting Out Songs

Here's a variation on the idea of acting out content. Instead of performing a written scene, students could perform movements to the lyrics of a song. Some songs may have deep levels of content-specific information, while others may be simply for enjoyment to complement a topic and make it more memorable. For example, students studying basic math skills might act out "One Thing Leads to Another" by the Fixx, or "ABC" by the Jackson Five. Students at higher levels of math might act out "Opposites Attract" by Paula Abdul—making a connection to negative numbers, or "Turn, Turn, Turn" by the Byrds—making a connection to circles and rotations in geometry. Many more ideas for both of these types of songs can be found in *The Green Book of Songs* (Green, 2005). The key here is that when students act out the words to a song, they frequently understand the writer's intention much more clearly than if they were merely listening to the song itself (Pierce & Terry, 2000). The "deeper meaning" behind the words is often revealed through the movements students create when they act out the song.

Talk Shows

You can use the talk show format in a wide variety of ways to bring entertainment alive in the classroom. Consider, for example, a typical review session—which students often see as a boring revisit to "stuff they already know." In this situation, rather than writing full lines as demanded in the skit approach, students might only need to work together to prep a series of questions for the host of the talk show. Then they might work in groups to prepare how they might answer these questions. In doing both of these tasks, the students have engaged with the material at a much deeper level than during a typical review session, increasing their understanding and encouraging insight. Perhaps more significantly, this verbal processing mode also allows students to enhance their vocabulary (Sutton, 1998).

You can use different variations of a talk show review session. For example, in some situations, maybe the talk show goes as planned for a few minutes, then the audience—other students—could come up with additional questions to ask the characters. Or maybe you could generate a series of basic questions to ask the characters, and your students form groups and plan how they would answer each question if they were that character. Or perhaps *you* could become a character, and the students would ask the questions—then they would have to decide whether your character is being truthful. The only way they'd know the right answers is if they fully understand the material!

Multimedia Productions

Instead of a live performance, perhaps your students could create a video production of content. Video lends itself to deep learning because students will practice many times before the final production is taped. These multiple rehearsals create multiple opportunities for learning. In addition, every time the video is viewed, the lesson is revisited. As students proudly share their video with their friends, parents, and extended family, and view it again and again throughout the year, their learning and recall of the information gets stronger and stronger.

There is another—more subtle—advantage to using a multimedia production. A live play usually occurs only within one physical location. However, using video as the production medium provides opportunities for a variety of stages, and thus *different areas for learning* (Moreno & Mayer, 2000). This means students will experience the content on a much broader scale, and consequently have the opportunity to make wider connections to the information and how it applies to the real world.

One-Act Plays

Most of the time, we simply don't have the energy, time, or resources to create an entire one-act play—even a brief one—around a particular topic. However, if you *can* use this approach occasionally, it is often an amazing learning opportunity. Each separate step provides opportunities for learning, from deciding what order to present the content in, to writing lines, to deciding on costumes. All aspects of developing the play offer unique glimpses at the content that would not happen within more typical classroom approaches.

Of course, once you've created a play, you can use it—or a revised version—in future classes in future years, with substantially less time needed to pull it together. The effort you invest the first time around may seem enormous, but the effectiveness of the strategy will be worth it—particularly as your students will reap the benefits for years to come.

Role-Play as Assessment

Some students simply don't test well in traditional written assessments. Role-playing may allow these students to demonstrate their grasp of the content in an entirely different, yet entirely valid, format. In a history class, a student becomes an important historical figure, explaining why his country must go to war. In a chemistry class, a student becomes a famous inventor and explains how she made her big discovery and what impact it will have on the future. In a PE class, perhaps a student demonstrates his understanding of how to use a weight-training machine by becoming the expert and teaching another student.

Next Steps

At first glance you may feel only a very few topics lend themselves to drama. For example, in history or social studies classes, we can easily see how students might become famous characters and act out well-known historical scenes. And it is certainly true that not all content can be presented in this way.

However, with a little thought, you'll be surprised how much material you *can* teach using at least one or two aspects of entertainment to engage your students. The key is to look at each general topic, each individual lesson, and even each *aspect* of a lesson, and consider if some part of it could be offered to students in a creative, appealing, and ultimately entertaining manner. If you teach even one element of a subject this way, student learning will rise dramatically.

ASSESS YOUR CURRENT USE OF ENTERTAINMENT

- I use aspects of entertainment in my classroom as much as possible, given the information we are learning.

- I occasionally allow some elements of entertainment in my classroom, but not that often.

- I tend to teach more by simply explaining the information and rarely use entertainment as a way to present a lesson.

Your Ideas

Consider your own subject area. Think about a few of your upcoming lessons and the topics you'll be covering. Now review some of the entertainment ideas discussed here to see which you could apply to that particular lesson. In each case, write down the general subject, the specific topic, and then select an entertainment strategy that might be useful to incorporate in your lesson plan. Finally, write a few sentences describing how you will go about integrating the strategy into the lesson.

As a reminder, here's a list of the entertainment strategies presented in this section. Remember: These are only a few of the many unique and varied ways in which you might include aspects of entertainment.

- Student skits
- Students becoming content
- Content-related songs acted out
- Talk shows
- Multimedia productions

- One-act plays
- Role-playing as assessment

Now fill out the sections below to start developing your own ideas on how to harness the power of entertainment and bring it into your classroom.

General Subject: _____

Specific Topic: _____

Entertainment Strategy: _____

How to Incorporate It: _____

_____

_____

_____

_____

General Subject: _____

Specific Topic: _____

Entertainment Strategy: _____

How to Incorporate It: _____

_____

_____

_____

_____

General Subject: _____

Specific Topic: _____

Entertainment Strategy: _____

How to Incorporate It: _____

_____

_____

_____

_____

F = Frames

Frames focus students' feelings.

In General

Painters know it's true. The most exquisite picture can be ruined by the wrong frame. No matter how unjust it might be, the quality of the frame skews the viewer's perception of the picture. A masterpiece in the wrong frame is overlooked by all but the most discerning art expert. An unremarkable picture, beautifully framed, can double in value. The frame, the light, and the way a picture is hung all contribute to how it is viewed, valued, and remembered.

The same phenomenon is true in learning. Left to their own devices, students will view content from their own perspectives. In other words, they will *frame* our content, based on their own experiences and points of view. Alternatively, we can frame the content for them. This frame will shape the learning they will extract from the experience.

The Connection

Framing answers the question: How do we connect today's students with our content? Of course, teachers have always struggled to demonstrate the usefulness of the curriculum. Today's is not the first generation of 13-year-olds who will despair: "But *why* do I need to learn algebra?"

But it's harder to justify to these students why they should learn the date of a battle, when at the touch of a few buttons they can call up not just the date, but the location, number of troops, names of commanders, pictures of uniforms, and actually far more detail than previous generations have ever been made to remember. Today's students are questioning why they have to learn math when their phone comes with a calculator and why should they learn how to write in a foreign language when translation programs are available.

Some subjects will always be easy to justify at a basic level. Understanding math helps you keep score in games, tell the time, or balance your checkbook. But many don't have a straight-line connection between content and life. And, the truth is, given the pace of technological change, we are preparing students for jobs that don't currently exist. Today's content may *not* be useful to today's students in any literal way. We need to find a way to connect disinterested students with content—a way that resonates with their real lives, right now.

The Big Picture

Creating an appropriate frame is important for three reasons.

1. On their own, students rarely create a positive frame for their learning. As teachers, one of our most important roles is to keep students feeling upbeat about learning. If students believe they can't learn, this becomes a self-fulfilling prophecy. The way we frame a lesson is a key factor in creating a positive learning experience—in making students believe they can learn.

2. If we don't create a frame, each student will process the content along an entirely different line of thinking. To ensure a more common outcome for learners, we need to invest time to create a common "frame" that will help guide our students' thinking (Ready, 1978).

3. A lesson's frame helps students connect with the content. Connection creates relevance, helps engagement, and improves retention. What's the point of knowing who runs the government, how to solve a quadratic equation, what colors comprise the light spectrum, or when to watch the midnight sky for a meteor shower? Or as many younger learners frequently express it, who cares? As teachers, we have to give them a reason to care.

Perhaps the effect of frames is best summed up by a variation on the old saying: "We learn from our experiences." While this is certainly true, *what* we learn from those moments is dependent on the frame we choose to hold around that experience. In this case, perhaps the following expression would be more useful:

Experience + Frame = Meaning

Without a frame, an experience is just an experience. Our frame gives it meaning.

Consider this real-life example. Many years ago, during a workshop for 140 teenagers, we ran an informal experiment that showed the power of single word in shaping perceptions.

In the experiment, we showed the students a 60-second movie clip of a car traveling down a dirt road and then hitting a barn. Immediately afterwards, the group was given a written list of questions about the clip. The questions were identical, except the last one, which was phrased differently in half the questionnaires. Half the students were asked, "How fast was the car moving when it *bumped* into the barn?"

The other half were asked, "How fast was the car moving when it *smashed* into the barn?"

We wanted to know whether this single word switch would change the students' perception of the event. It certainly did.

On the average, the group responding to the word *bumped* estimated the car was traveling at 32 miles per hour. Conversely, the group responding to the word *smashed* thought it was traveling at 47 miles per hour! Altering that single word significantly changed the students' perceptions of the film clip. This effect was explored years later in the literature on memory (Loftus, 1992), which went on to influence the way police deal with the accuracy of eyewitness accounts (Loftus, 1993).

As teachers, we need to consider the awesome potential of the power of framing experiences for learners. If a single word exerts this much influence on students' perceptions, what difference can we make by deliberately framing whole activities in a positive and relevant light?

Focus on Classroom Management

When students are first introduced to a new topic, a frequent question is: "So what?" They wonder *why* they have to learn it, *what* could be so important about it, and *how* it could possibly be relevant to them. If the answers to these questions take too long to emerge—or don't emerge at all—students mentally disengage. Regardless of the motivational strategies we may use, many students will still fail to engage with the content for a very simple reason: They don't care (Wells & Arauz, 2006).

However, when we connect learning to things students already understand or care about, we create *relevance*. Relevance makes students interested. They want to know more. They become more willing to engage in the lesson.

In Practice

Here are some practical examples of framing that show its use in creating:

- Relevance through connection
- A positive frame for learning
- A common perspective

Creating Relevance through Connection

We can use frames to offer students a way to see the material as relevant to something they already understand or care about.

Example 1: Teaching the Order of Operations

A math teacher wants his students to understand why it's important to know in what order to do mathematical operations in an equation. He could simply tell them it's important, so they get the correct answer. However, this has little emotional impact on students. While it's true that they need to be able to find the correct answer, he needs to find a way to have them understand *why* it's so important. Instead, he involves them in a brief exercise.

He puts five letters on the board: A, E, S, T, M. He asks them to create as many five-letter words as possible using each of these letters. Eventually, students find there are five words: teams, steam, meats, mates, and tames. Once this has been established, he asks the students a critical question, "Each of these words uses the same five letters, but they do NOT have the same meaning. So what tells us what the meaning is?" The answer, of course, is the order of the letters indicates the meaning. Using this as a springboard into his frame for the lesson, he says:

> "In other words, the order of the letters in the English language tells us the meaning. And here's something you may not know: *Math is actually a language as well!* For mathematicians to communicate, when they work out a problem they need to be able to create the same meaning each time. Therefore, the order in which we do things in a math problem, such as adding or multiplying, is important so we can always have the same meaning. Just as the order of the letters in the English language tells us the correct meaning, the order in which we do math problems tells us the correct meaning, or answer."

By providing his students with this explanation, the teacher "framed" the importance of learning the correct order as being similar to learning to understand the English language.

We can put the students learning this concept, typically around 11 to 12 years old, into two broad categories. Some will like math and science, while the rest will like languages. The students who naturally like math are already intrinsically interested, and need very little to get them excited to learn about this subject. However, for those students who prefer language arts, this frame offers them a connection as to why this content is relevant to things they are naturally interested in. When math is viewed through the frame of language, arts students feel they have a much stronger starting point for understanding the central concept of the lesson.

Example 2: Teaching Fractions

A teacher wants to teach the concept of fractions to her students, ages 6 to 7. Fractions may well be perceived by students of this age as being an absurdly abstract and thus hard to grasp concept.

However, even these young learners can process information at this level of abstraction, if we build a solid connection between the concept they are learning and a concrete reality in their world. Therefore, the teacher chooses to connect the idea of fractions to something they are familiar with—food! Here is how she uses it to teach them about fractions.

First, she gives each student a few slices of bread, a paper plate, a plastic knife, and a small container of peanut butter. She introduces the lesson by showing students her own favorite kind of sandwich— peanut butter, of course! She tells them she is not hungry enough to eat all of it and asks them for ideas on what she could do so it doesn't get wasted. The unanimous answer is to share it. So she puts it on an overhead projector, and proceeds to cut it in half. However, she doesn't cut it into equal parts and the kids all shout, "No fair, the pieces aren't the same size!" "Exactly," she says, "You have just discovered the secret to fractions—*equal parts*, which means having each part be the same size!" So she slides the sandwich together and cuts it again, correctly this time.

Next she starts the guided practice part of the lesson by having them take a piece of bread and cut it into two equal parts. Students practice cutting the equal parts both horizontally and vertically. Then she explains that they cut the bread in *half*, explaining that the word *half* means *two equal parts*. She continues with the lesson in this manner, and the use of food makes the lesson truly meaningful for them.

This frame demonstrates a wonderful connection between the potentially abstract concept of fractions and the very concrete idea of food. Food is something familiar to these students, so the information they are learning is connected to something *real*, something *solid*, something *tangible* (Prensky, 2005).

Creating a Positive Frame for Learning

Frames don't just connect students with content—they can also change students' attitudes toward content.

Example 3: A School Summer Class

It was the first day of class. The teacher picked up a large stack of papers, containing copies of eight articles that all students were required to read. Her hands laden with this frightening collection of reading material, she faced the class again and said:

> "OK, now, I know it's summertime, and reading may be the last thing on your mind. But we have to do this, because it's required by the school that you at least do *some* reading for this class. We'll have to buckle down and do the best we can with it."

Consider the frame the teacher has just created for the students around reading these articles. The first visual image the students have in this moment is a *heavy* stack of papers, definitely not a good start toward making a positive first impression. Next, by telling them they shouldn't like reading because it's summer, an enormous negative image is immediately formed. Then come the words "But we have to" and "it's required by . . ." These phrases build further on the negative base already established. The final blow is delivered as she concludes the frame with a sentence containing the phrase "buckle down," implying seriously dreary times ahead. Given this frame, even the student with the most positive attitude in that classroom might have contracted at least a mild case of depression.

Here's a different approach the teacher could have taken with this same situation. She begins by separating the articles out into eight *small* piles, a key starting point for visual effect. Now the first impression the students have will be that these are thin articles and thus quite short. Next she frames the distribution of the articles by saying:

> "I'm not certain if you knew it, but this class was supposed to have a required text. It's this one here, and costs $90 at the bookstore. [She holds up the text, which is quite thick.] However, in looking through it, I decided there's no way we're going to get through all this material. If each of you were to buy this book it would be a waste of both your time and money."

She sets the text down—to sighs of relief from her students. Then she says:

"Instead, I've spent some time locating a *few* articles that speak directly to the topics we'll be exploring. This way you won't have to spend time sorting through a heap of irrelevant material. You should be able to complete the reading quite easily, so you can continue enjoying your summer. Please come forward and take one article from each group."

What a difference a frame makes! The students are now mentally comparing that massive text to the thin stack of articles and perhaps feeling that they got off easy. This should begin to put them into a more positive frame of mind concerning the required reading for the class. Additionally, they are pleased to discover they didn't have to spend the $90 on a book which, for the most part, would go unused. And finally, she implied that their reading will go quickly, so they can return to "enjoying their summer," a positive picture to leave her students with.

Of course, this frame may not turn nonreaders into avid ones. However, it should at least give them a head start toward forming a healthy perspective concerning the articles. This more positive outlook may go a long way in having the students *choose* to do their homework, which in turn may have a significant impact on their learning.

Example 4: Using a Four-Letter Word

Suppose there are two minutes remaining in a test situation. Learners are hunched over their papers, busily working on their math problems. The teacher wants to let them know their time is almost up, so he announces: "You have just two more minutes!"

In this situation, what effect does the word *just* have on the communication? It can easily be interpreted as putting pressure on the students. The simple use of the word *just* has framed the final two minutes as being stress-filled. But a testing situation is inherently filled with pressure, so teachers should do what they can to avoid unnecessarily increasing this state of anxiety. Most researchers agree that adding significantly more stress decreases student effectiveness (Covington, 1992; Covington & Omelich, 1987; Woolfolk, 2000). In this case, rather than stressing his students with the four-letter word *just,* the teacher could simply leave out that one word, and in a calm tone of voice announce: "You have two more minutes."

Now the communication is more straightforward, lacking any implied urgency. We could even take this situation one step further, and actually try to ease learner stress by saying, "You have plenty of time. Please make sure all your answers are written as clearly as possible during these final two minutes."

The point is, every time we communicate with our students we have a choice about the emotions our words encourage. It's up to us to frame learning situations so our students get the most out of them—and perform at their best.

Example 5: Students Teaching Math

While teaching an advanced math class for high school seniors, I stumbled on another framing idea. The material in this class was a partial review for many of the students, so I made them an offer. If anyone would like to teach one of the chapters from the book, they wouldn't be required to take the test for that chapter! Of course, they needed to prepare lesson plans and personally review them with me well in advance of each class. Additionally, they needed to create the final test, plus generate an answer key with the solutions written out completely.

I was concerned because I knew the level of work required in preparing to teach a single chapter of math. It far exceeded the work normally required of a learner, whose primary responsibility was simply doing their homework and taking the test. Much to my surprise, students leapt at the opportunity to teach a section of the class. It was only later that I understood what now seems very obvious.

Simply put, the frame of *not having to take a test* was too powerful to resist! I had forgotten that their world was filled with tests, and the chance to avoid one seemed too good to be true, despite the work required. They dove into their respective chapters and produced impressive results. It made me realize one of the basic concepts of teaching:

"We learn best what we teach to others."

Without becoming consciously aware of it, many students took quantum leaps forward in their overall understanding of math, given they now clearly understood the information from the one chapter they had taught. The frame of not having to take one chapter test ultimately produced better results for both the "student teachers" as well as for their peers.

Creating a Common Perspective

If we don't frame material for our students, they will use their own frame of reference.

Example 6: The Maze

The teacher was illustrating a concept using a maze activity. She introduced the exercise by saying, "Welcome to The Maze! Here's how the game is played . . ."

What does this "frame" tell her students? Why are they doing this activity? What's the objective? How does it relate to the class they are currently taking and the topics they are focusing on today?

As you can see, there's no frame at all. Without a frame, students are free to think anything they'd like to about the activity. Perhaps they decide this activity doesn't have anything to do with them and stop paying attention to the directions. Perhaps they think it's a competition and lose the point of the entire exercise. Perhaps . . . well, who knows what they'll think.

This teacher later changed her approach to the maze activity. The next time she used it, she said:

> "Welcome to The Maze! The Maze is a puzzle. While solving this puzzle, several issues may emerge that will be useful to our understanding of innovation and creativity. Experiencing them firsthand will show us how different people approach innovation."

This frame tells learners about the activity's purpose. Knowing it is supposed to further their understanding of innovation will change the aspects of the activity they pay attention to—sowing the seeds for a more productive discussion afterwards. Giving them a purpose through which to process the experience will help create a common learning experience.

Next Steps

These are merely a few variations on the vital theme of framing. You'll find this idea demonstrated in many other examples throughout this book. The bottom line is: Application is everything. Without it, nothing else matters. If the learners cannot find a way to rapidly integrate the knowledge into something they know and are familiar with, the information may quickly fade from their memories.

ASSESS YOUR CURRENT USE OF FRAMES

- I frequently frame lessons, explaining how the new information is relevant to the students.

- I occasionally frame new learning if a connection occurs to me, but do not consciously plan one for every lesson.

- I rarely frame new lessons, because I expect students to make their own connections and come to their own understanding.

Your Ideas

How will you make your lesson more relevant to the students in your class? In many cases this takes careful forethought and consideration. Below, write out at least two general topics you teach, as well as at least two specific lessons you expect to be teaching your students in the near future. In each case, write out one to three sentences describing how you would frame the overall topic or the specific lesson. The more *specific* you can be, the more helpful this exercise is in preparing you to frame your content appropriately for your students.

General Topic: _____

The Frame: _____

_____

_____

_____

_____

General Topic: _____

The Frame: _____

_____

_____

_____

_____

General Topic: _____

The Frame: _____

_____

_____

_____

_____

Specific Lesson: _____

The Frame: _____

_____

_____

_____

_____

Specific Lesson: _____

The Frame: _____

_____

_____

_____

_____

Specific Lesson: _____

The Frame: _____

_____

_____

_____

_____

G = Getting Responses

Getting responses drives the interactive classroom.

In General

One of the primary ways we can verify students really *are* engaged is to
ask them for frequent responses. However, many students have learned

the hard way that responding in a classroom can lead to them feeling fool-ish. So we need to clearly *specify* how we expect our students to respond. Knowing what they are expected to do will allow students to feel more comfortable with the responses they provide. Consistent, conscious, careful use of this technique will heighten students' sense of security within the classroom, leading to increased levels of participation by all students, even the potentially less confident ones.

The Connection

While technology allows Gen Y and Z to communicate far more prolifically than previous generations, much of this communication has ceased to be face-to-face. Text and chat with friends is through the impersonal inter-face of a phone or computer. A MySpace page may seem like the ultimate exposure—but each blogger chooses what to reveal. In the anonymity of a chatroom, or as an avatar in a computer game, these kids are amazingly uninhibited. But in real life—in front of a room full of their peers—they are often uncomfortable.

Ironically, the connected generations are even more likely to resist responding in the classroom limelight. In the interactive classroom, how we as teachers set up, handle, and complete student responses becomes a critical factor in the success of the lesson.

The Big Picture

The teacher is about to ask a question of the class. However, he has noticed that when he has posed other questions to the group during the past hour, few students have been responsive. Why can't he get a greater level of response, even to some of his simpler questions? There may well be very good reasons why his students are hesitating.

To understand some potential hazards in this situation, examine in detail a single student's response to a seemingly simple question. Suppose the class is asked: "How many of you have been to Hawaii?"

It appears to be a straightforward question, seeking a simple answer. However, is responding to this question really so simple? Consider the decision-making process the students must go through before making a response. The problem is, if students have been to Hawaii, they are now faced with a decision about how they are supposed to respond. Should they raise their hand? Should they nod their head? Should they speak out loud? But the words the teacher used gave the students no clue as to how they are supposed to respond, so it is left to each student to guess at the response their teacher is seeking. This seemingly small level of uncertainty is enough to dampen the class's response.

What frequently happens in this type of situation is the students who have been to Hawaii will tentatively raise a hand, perhaps only halfway. They choose this option of how to respond since raising a hand in the classroom is the most common form of response. At the same time they are careful to avoid committing too strongly to a course of action, in case it's wrong. If the teacher were looking for people to answer out loud, then the one person who chose to raise a hand may look foolish. The tentative response is the result of the uncertainty of how to respond.

Instead, the teacher might have avoided potential confusion and a dampened response by rephrasing the question: *"Raise your hand if you have been to Hawaii."*

STUDENT RESPONSES ▶ DRIVE INTERACTIVE CLASSROOMS

With this slight change in the language of the question, the teacher has *specified the response* he is seeking. The guessing game has been eliminated. Now everyone is clear what is being asked of them and how they are expected to respond. Those who have been to Hawaii can respond easily and with confidence. They might be even more inclined to respond if the teacher were also to raise a hand, since now students are seeing the desired behavior clearly modeled.

Forcing students to play a guessing game in the classroom is a dangerous choice. As students consider their options, they know one response may be right while another may be wrong. When students sense they are running the risk of doing something wrong, their willingness to engage is immediately reduced. The threat factor has been introduced, as the fear of looking bad in front of others has reared its ugly head.

To avoid this, we often need to *specify the response* when asking a question. This will make students confident about what is expected of them, and they can respond freely and easily, without fear of embarrassment—while staying fully involved in the current lesson.

Specifying the response isn't just important for encouraging classroom interaction—it's also vital if we're "checking in" with students. For example, consider the following situation. The class has just read page 27. The teacher asks, "Is anyone still reading?"

And when no one tells him otherwise . . . "No? Great, let's continue."

The problem is, the teacher hasn't given his students an easy means of communicating that they're still reading. Unless some students were comfortable enough to quickly raise their hand, or to ask the teacher to pause for a moment, the lesson was going to continue regardless of whether everyone was ready or not.

Instead, this teacher might have rephrased his request for response like this: "When you've finished reading page 27, please nod your head."

Presented this way, the teacher can watch the students and wait until all students have nodded their heads. Now he is deciding when to proceed based on solid visual feedback—and all his students should be able to keep up.

Focus on Classroom Management

In any classroom situation, there may be multiple reasons why students fail to respond to questions. Clearly, some of these causes are out of our control as teachers. If left unchecked, however, this issue can quickly build into a significant problem as students become hesitant about responding and mentally withdraw from the learning process. We should pay close attention to factors that *are* within our power, since they play such a critical role in maintaining student focus and attention on lessons.

Disengaged students are far more likely to become discipline problems as their level of disinterest, disconnection, and detachment eventually leads to acting out. As their boredom grows, they begin to spin a "web of distraction." And like a spider, soon enough they snare the attention of other students around them, creating a ripple effect of disruption and disturbance.

However, if we control these moments so that students respond properly, it will help us to keep all students engaged and on task at a high level. Appropriately handled, frequent student responses are an essential building block in the learning process.

In Practice

Asking students to raise their hands is only one method of specifying the response. The following are some comparisons between questions that lack a specific response and some options for how these questions might be rephrased.

No Specific Response	An Option for Rephrasing
"Have you got the right page?"	"Nod if you're on page 16."
"Is everyone ready?"	"Smile if you're ready."
"Did you have a good lunch?"	"Hold your pen up and wiggle it if you had a great lunch!"
"Does this make sense?"	"If this concept makes sense to you, give me a thumbs-up."
"Am I right?"	"If you agree with me on this, raise one pinky."
"Who's finished?"	"If you're finished, turn your paper over."
"Does everyone have the handout?"	"Hold up the handout if you have received one."
"Are there any questions?"	"Those of you who have a question, please come to the board and write it down."

Several of these options may seem childish, but they are actually used frequently and successfully with adult learners. That said, if they don't fit with your teaching environment, develop some that do work with your students and your teaching style.

In developing your own response mechanisms, keep in mind the value of specifying unusual responses. Appropriate yet creative choices can often keep the atmosphere of the room light and relaxed. A positive atmosphere in the learning environment is useful to learning for students of all ages. Even in more serious, technical classes, specifying the response by asking students to look up if they have completed an assignment may be sufficient to achieve the desired outcome.

When consciously choosing a response to specify, we should also be consciously aware of *what* we are specifying. Even when simply asking students to raise their hands, by specifying the response, teachers are asking students to be public. This can create a potentially negative situation. For example, consider the potential problem with asking a group of students the following question: "If you have not yet completed the assignment, please raise your hand."

Presented this way, those who are still working on the assignment must now raise their hands and publicly "confess" that they are slower than other students in the room! This puts them into a situation where they may feel embarrassed. Given this potential for public humiliation, some students who are still working may decide to not raise their hand. Now the teacher is making decisions based on incomplete information.

The key is to *focus on the positive*. The statement used in this example could simply be rephrased as: "If you have completed the assignment, please raise your hand."

From the response to this question, the teacher can still effectively know how much more time to give them to complete the assignment, without running the risk of embarrassing those who are still hard at work.

Of course, you don't always have to specify the response. Often, both students and the teacher inherently understand what is expected, especially several weeks into the school year. If you've already set a pattern of raising hands, students will understand this. Specifying the response is most important early in establishing the dynamics of the relationship between teacher and students. The earlier we introduce and reinforce this pattern of interaction, the more comfortable our students will feel.

Next Steps

Two additional issues are important to address once we decide to specify the response—first, students often need to be *primed* so they are ready to respond, and second, we must *complete the action* we have asked them to do. Let's look at each of these to understand how to set up getting the most effective student responses.

Priming means asking yourself the question, "Are my students ready to do what I'm about to ask them to do?" Here's an example of what happens when a teacher does *not* successfully prime students for the desired response.

The students are vigorously taking notes as a guest lecturer is speaking. At the conclusion of her remarks, the regular teacher says, "Please give our speaker a nice hand for being here today."

However, the response from the students is somewhat quiet. The teacher, disappointed by this minimal reaction, turns to them and says: "Wait a minute. Is that any way to thank someone for coming here today and talking with us? Please, give her a really big round of applause. Let's hear it for all these wonderful ideas she has shared."

This time students applaud with more enthusiasm and increased volume. The guest lecturer departs, and the class continues.

Here's the critical question: Why had the students not responded immediately and with more energy the first time they were asked to acknowledge the speaker? A closer examination of their behavior reveals why. The first time the students were asked to acknowledge the guest speaker, something was physically obstructing them from completing the request. Remember what they had just been doing—jotting down written notes. Taking notes requires holding a pen. Giving applause, however, requires both hands being free. When they went to applaud they were still holding their pens, so it was nearly impossible for them to do what was asked of them. They were forced to do the best they could, so they clapped while still clutching their pens.

However, the second time, they could see what was coming, so as the teacher was repeating the request they were placing their pens on the desk so they could fully acknowledge the guest speaker.

The teacher could have primed the students so they could provide applause successfully the first time they were asked by saying "Please place your pen down on your notes."

When it was clear that everyone had set down their pen, he could say, "Now, please thank our speaker by giving her a big hand!"

With their hands now free, there is a much greater chance the students will be successful at responding to the request the first time. The key is to make sure that students have been properly primed, so they can easily follow the upcoming instruction.

Simply put, priming allows students to be prepared for the next instruction from the teacher. It helps avoid those brief but awkward moments during instruction when learners fully intend to respond, yet find themselves hindered in their efforts for a variety of reasons. We as teachers know what is coming next. If we correctly prepare our students for each subsequent direction, they should be able to transition smoothly from one activity to the next.

When specifying the response, the second thing to keep in mind is we must always be sure to *complete the action*. According to scientific theory, each action produces an equal and opposite reaction. In teaching, an identical principle applies. In this case, the "action" is the specific student response a teacher seeks. The necessary "reaction" is the completion of the original movement, bringing the action to closure.

Here are a few examples of situations in which it would be useful and productive for teachers to complete the action:

■ If you specify the response by asking students to raise their hands, complete the action by telling them to put them down.

- If you specify the response by asking students to give you a thumbs-up, complete the action by telling them to put their thumbs down.

- If you specify the response by asking students to wave their worksheets in the air, complete the action by telling them to put their worksheets back on their desk.

- If you specify the response by asking students to hold their pen high in the air, complete the action by telling them to bring their pen down or place it on their desk.

- If you specify the response by asking students to take a nice deep breath in, complete the action by telling them to breathe out again, then breathe normally.

While asking students to complete the action may seem almost silly in writing, in practice it is surprising how often a lesson charges forward while students are still engrossed and amused by the response they've been asked for, especially if is novel or enjoyable. Completing the action allows students to leave the response behind and fully focus on the next section of information.

ASSESS YOUR CURRENT USE OF GETTING RESPONSES

- When asking questions, I am very specific in telling students the response I am looking for.

- When asking questions, I specify the response occasionally; however, I have not been doing this deliberately.

- When asking questions, I rarely specify the response I am expecting.

Your Ideas

When deciding what response to specify, find some options that are appropriate for your students and comfortable for you. Some teachers may feel completely comfortable asking their students to give them a thumbs-up in response to a question, while others may not feel this is appropriate to their own teaching style, the age of their students, or even their content.

To find the best response mechanisms for you and your students, first list some responses you feel might work in your classroom. Include at least five to get you started, even if it means stretching your thinking to include some choices you may not have previously considered. As you get used to specifying the response during a lesson, add more ideas to your list, expanding it until you feel you have numerous, appropriate options to choose from during any lesson.

Appropriate Responses I Could Use

1. _____

2. _____

3. _____

4. _____

5. _____

6. _____

7. _____

8. _____

9. _____

10. _____

Now write down at least three places within an upcoming lesson where you could specify the response. Make sure to note which form of response you are going to use.

Lesson Topic 1: _____

The Question I'll Be Asking: _____

The Response I'll Specify: _____

Lesson Topic 2: _____

The Question I'll Be Asking: _____

The Response I'll Specify: _____

Lesson Topic 3: _____

The Question I'll Be Asking: _____

The Response I'll Specify: _____

Lesson Topic 4: _____

The Question I'll Be Asking: _____

The Response I'll Specify: _____

Lesson Topic 5: _____

The Question I'll Be Asking: _____

The Response I'll Specify: _____

H = High-Quality Responses

Quality student responses require quality preparation time.

In General

A teacher is giving a brief lecture. At the end of 10 minutes, she turns to the students. She now wants to start a classroom discussion. To do this she uses the classic words: "Any questions?"

Given that it is a classic question, frequently used in instructional situations, she probably gets the classic response to it—the blank, stunned stare from the students. If no one asks a question, she might wait through 10 to 15 seconds of silence, her impatience building, before saying something along the lines of "Come on, people! Weren't you listening? Don't you care? Listen, this is important material! It'll be on the test. You *must* pay attention!"

Finally, perhaps someone is brave enough to tentatively raise a hand and ask a question. The situation is strained, but at least the discussion has begun. Or perhaps she simply gives up on her quest for information and begins to lecture once again.

Neither result, of course, is the reaction the teacher was hoping to generate from the students. She didn't get her desired response because she didn't give her students *adequate time to prepare solid, well-considered questions.* When we want students to respond with quality responses and engage in a useful classroom dialogue, we need to give them time to organize their thoughts and prepare their answers. In education this is traditionally referred to as "wait time," allowing individual students the opportunity to consider their response. The primary distinction this strategy offers is the idea of allowing students the opportunity to discuss their ideas with others near them during the wait time.

The Connection

One of the most important—perhaps even critical—things we can teach today's students is how to reflect, consider, and respond to new ideas in a meaningful way. In a world that is changing so rapidly, it will not be the amount of information they know that will determine their successes as adults. Increasingly, it will be their abilities to respond to new situations and to adapt appropriately to change that will determine the quality of both their personal and professional lives.

While thinking skills are widely discussed in education, they are often thought of in terms of broad, far-reaching ideas and thought patterns. However, in this situation, as teachers we have the ability to—in a brief period of time—consistently reinforce the notion of students thinking through their reactions and organizing their ideas. This thought process, even when done in the very brief manner suggested here, almost always leads to higher-quality responses. It also supports students' development toward becoming productive, successful adult members of the dynamic world in which they will find themselves.

QUALITY STUDENT RESPONSES REQUIRE QUALITY PREPARATION TIME.

The Big Picture

In the opening example of this section, why might students be giving the blank stare, the "deer-in-the-headlights" look? How might the situation described in the opening of this section be handled differently? How might teachers open up a discussion with a class and generate the maximum possible interaction?

To answer this question, assume that this teacher has indeed given a clear presentation on the topic, and that the students might have some questions to ask or thoughts to offer. What might keep them from responding in those first few seconds? To understand better, take a slow motion look at what might be happening inside one student's head, when he is presented with the phrase "Any questions?"

Before responding, this student must make several mental adjustments. First, he must mentally switch gears. Keep in mind that, assuming he has been paying attention, he has been *listening* to the presentation, *processing* the information, and making his own mental connections to the material for the last 10 minutes (Hughes, Henderickson, & Hudson, 1986; Ruhl, Hughes, & Schloss, 1987). Now, suddenly, he must bring that process to a quick halt.

Next, he must sort through to material to see if he does have a question to pose or a comment to make. Suppose that something does occur to him to say. Now another step in the process must take place. He must find the words to express his idea. Finally, this student has to work up the courage to state his opinion in public.

Simply put, this process takes time! While the brain operates at a very rapid pace, it must still have a moment to prepare and organize itself (Calvin & Ojemann, 1994). The blank stare from students is often simply the external expression of the fact that they are doing some internal processing. (Not always, of course. Sometimes that blank stare is actually a fairly accurate reflection of what's going on inside that student's head—nothing! But we're talking about those other times.)

The key, then, is fairly simple—allow students a short period of time to organize their thoughts and prepare their responses. We can do this either by encouraging them to talk to other students about their questions or giving them a moment to review their notes and write down some questions. Even giving students a brief moment to process can astonishingly improve the quality of the next few minutes in the classroom.

One of the side benefits of using this technique is that allowing all students the opportunity to talk, even briefly in the small group, gives each person the time to process the information in a different mode than passive listening. And when students process information *actively*, even for a short period, they are more likely to remember the content. This is true even for those students who do not talk during the ensuing discussion.

One thing to watch out for is ending any lecture segment with "Any questions?" as an automatic reflex. Often, this phrase becomes an ingrained part of our teaching "patter." If this is true of you, here's something to think about: If you don't really want your students to interject at a certain point, don't ask for it! Then, when you actually do want them to ask questions, and set up the conditions for a successful discussion, the questions you receive will be much deeper and more thoughtful.

Of course, we don't have to use this technique in every situation! For example, if your students are quick to respond when given an opportunity to interact, or if they're already raising their hands to speak, they don't need time for mental preparation.

At the same time, this technique is useful even for extremely interactive groups for two reasons:

1. It allows slower students a greater chance of contributing to class discussions, because they "catch up" during processing time. Sometimes the insights of these slower processors are more profound than those of their quicker thinking peers.

2. These students will still benefit from the chance to actively process the material.

But if your students are reluctant to interact in a large-group discussion, give them time to prepare first by having a brief preparatory discussion in a pair or trio with other students. This provides them with the opportunity to clarify what they are thinking. It also helps them organize their words so they feel more articulate and more confident when the discussion begins.

Focus on Classroom Management

If a teacher does not offer students a way of dealing with this mental processing issue, a key classroom management problem can quickly emerge. Teachers who typically use only that form of the question will find that only those students who are verbally quick will be involved in the discussions, and they will come to dominate all class discussions.

In these situations, it's easy to create a pattern that is hard to break. The verbally gifted students will dominate classroom interactions, while students who are slower to respond will start to believe they shouldn't interact at all—and disengage from the discussion.

In Practice

We need to give our students a chance to *verbally prepare* their thoughts—in a safe way—before opening up the discussion to the large group. How can we do this? Here's one method for achieving this outcome. When the 10-minute lecture has concluded, the teacher might say, "Thank you. Now, turn to one or two people near you and briefly discuss this issue."

Wait approximately 60 to 90 seconds, then ask: "What thoughts or questions do you have about this topic? What comments would you like to make? What areas, if any, might I clarify?" In this situation, here's what tends to happen. Students begin by turning to someone near them. For the first few seconds they might be a bit hesitant, as they organize their ideas and focus on the other person, but then the conversation begins to pick up pace.

When it appears they are sufficiently talkative, the teacher can now move the group toward discussion, saying "Please thank your partners. Face back toward me. Now, what questions or comments do you have?"

In an ideal world, most students have now made the mental adjustment from listening to talking, briefly organized their thoughts, and prepared a question or comment to offer to the discussion. Of course, it's not always an ideal world. However, by using this approach, students at least have a *better* chance of being prepared to interact in the classroom by asking a question or making a comment.

How long might this process last? Interestingly, it should be fairly short. Perhaps no more than 60 to 90 seconds for the entire sequence. Remember that the purpose of the interaction is not to generate a lengthy discussion in the small groups. The purpose is simply to give students an opportunity to make some mental adjustments and prepare themselves to take an active part of the discussion. This may feel unusual at first, especially if your small-group discussions usually last five to ten minutes. The key is that the goal of the interaction between students has been changed. All they need is a minute or so to prepare themselves. At the same time, in certain situations, taking a more extended amount of time is perfectly fine—the purpose is to have them generate ideas, and occasionally they will need more time, given the depth of certain topics or the type of question posed.

Next Steps

If you're thinking this sounds like a waste of precious instructional time, remember that students will go through a stage of adjusting and processing whether we give them time or not. By controlling the process—and acknowledging the need for it—we win on several levels. Not only will the quality of classroom discussions improve, but students will get into the habit of thinking before they speak. Moreover, the slower and less verbally gifted students will contribute more and become more confident. And generally, all students will feel better prepared to join in—creating a positive atmosphere in which to conduct our classroom discussions.

ASSESS YOUR CURRENT USE OF HIGH-QUALITY RESPONSES

■ I frequently allow students the opportunity to talk to each other before I ask for their responses.

■ I occasionally allow students the opportunity to talk to each other before asking for their responses.

■ I rarely, if ever, allow students the opportunity to talk to each other before asking for their responses.

Your Ideas

Consider your own content area and a few upcoming lessons where you'll be teaching new information primarily by using lecture. Carefully plan for two to three places where you'll want to ask for deeper, high-quality responses. Remember the key to success here is to *proactively plan* for these brief moments of student-to-student interactions. Below, write down two or three different lesson topics, and in each case note *at least* two appropriate moments where this technique might fit. Then, carefully write out the words you'll use to explain to them what to discuss: Do you want to ask for questions about content clarity? Do you simply want to ask for their general reactions? Do you want to ask if they agree or disagree with what you've said? The goal in each of these situations is different, and the more clearly you explain to the students what you're looking for, the higher quality responses you'll receive.

Lesson Topic 1: _____

First Time I'll Ask Them to Prepare to Respond: _____

_____

How I'll Explain to the Students What to Do:_____

_____

_____

_____

Second Time I'll Ask Them to Prepare to Respond:_____

_____

How I'll Explain to the Students What to Do:_____

_____

_____

_____

Third Time I'll Ask Them to Prepare to Respond: _____

_____

How I'll Explain to the Students What to Do:_____

_____

_____

_____

Lesson Topic 2: _____

First Time I'll Ask Them to Prepare to Respond: _____

_____

How I'll Explain to the Students What to Do:_____

_____

_____

_____

Second Time I'll Ask Them to Prepare to Respond:_____

_____

How I'll Explain to the Students What to Do:_____

_____

_____

_____

Third Time I'll Ask Them to Prepare to Respond: _____

_____

How I'll Explain to the Students What to Do:_____

_____

_____

_____

Lesson Topic 3: _____

First Time I'll Ask Them to Prepare to Respond: _____

_____

How I'll Explain to the Students What to Do:_____

_____

_____

_____

Second Time I'll Ask Them to Prepare to Respond:_____

_____

How I'll Explain to the Students What to Do:_____

_____

_____

_____

Third Time I'll Ask Them to Prepare to Respond: _____

_____

How I'll Explain to the Students What to Do:_____

_____

_____

_____

I = Involve, Don't Tell

Involving students in learning instantly increases the impact.

In General

Within most lessons, there are central, essential pieces of information students most need to know. All the rest of the content usually flows outward from these vital beginning points. Unfortunately, teachers typically present these keys aspects of their lessons in ways that are fundamentally the same as the rest of the content. Nothing differentiates key points from other—still critical, but ultimately secondary—points within a lesson. However, when the things students most need to know stand out as significantly different from the rest of the content, they can provide a valuable foundation for student's comprehension of the entire lesson.

Our job then, as teachers, is clear. We first need to isolate these key points within the content we are teaching. Then, we need to decide how best to present them to our students. Instead of simply stating or explaining them, we need to create ways that students can truly be _involved_ in learning—and thus remembering—them.

The Connection

Today's students have access to an almost infinite amount of facts, figures, numbers, and statistics. They must learn to survive within this seemingly endless ocean of information. One of the most valuable tools we as teachers can offer them is a strategy for coping with large amounts of information. The idea of involving students in learning key ideas within a lesson is actually teaching a much more fundamental skill for being a lifelong learner.

When students both see and experience this process being modeled in the classroom, they don't just learn the content—they learn how to do it for themselves. They begin to understand the power of learning central ideas and connecting related information to central pillars within a topic. When this strategy for handling large quantities of information is a natural part of their skill set for learning any topic, they are better equipped for dealing with today's information-intense world.

INVOLVING STUDENTS IN LEARNING INSTANTLY INCREASES THE IMPACT.

The Big Picture

Involving students in learning the primary points of a topic improves learning, helping students not just remember these points, but quickly recall the entire lesson (Cusco, 1994). Once a student is able to recall the key points, related issues will be easier to locate around it (Berstein, 1994).

Memory researchers are convinced that students will remember only a vague impression of most things they hear and experience in a classroom (D'Arcangelo, 1998; Jensen, 1996). But, if we isolate and highlight the key points of our presentation through involvement, our students will have an easier time focusing on and encoding the main points. We will help them walk away from the classroom with more than just a hazy sense of the lesson.

This idea is supported by a theory of cognition that sees memory as a function of "nodes" and "subnodes" and the connections between them, known as a "knowledge network" (Anderson, 1990). But let's not worry too much about the theory. As teachers, we need to understand the practical applications that come from this conceptual idea about learning.

Focus on Classroom Management

Here's an important practical application: When students are *not* given central points within a lesson to mentally hold onto, they can easily feel overwhelmed by the sheer volume of information they are supposed to learn. When they are besieged by bewildering bushels of ideas, they rapidly lose concentration. If students are inundated by information, snowed under by substance, or flooded with facts, they quickly surrender. Mentally, students shrug their shoulders, saying, "I'll never learn this, so why try?" This negative attitude is a fertile breeding ground for all sorts of inappropriate classroom behaviors.

On the other hand, students who are able to clearly understand and connect with key points of a lesson pay attention longer. If we involve our students in pivotal ideas, these ideas function as the "mental struts" from which students construct an internal framework for understanding the rest of the related information. This increased clarity of understanding helps keep them on task, paying attention, and not falling into inappropriate modes of behavior.

In Practice

Involving students in learning key aspects of new information, instead of simply saying it, requires two distinct steps. The first is to isolate the central facts or ideas within a lesson. Sometimes this will be obvious, such as an essential formula in chemistry, a fundamental equation in mathematics, or a significant date in history. Other times, however, we must look closely at the material we are teaching and decide within this entire chapter—or within a specific lesson—what do we most want students to know? What things—if they know them well and can remember them easily—will help their overall understanding of the topic?

The second phase is deciding how to teach these key points in a different way from simply stating them. Can students be involved physically, by raising their hands or standing up? Can students be involved socially through a discussion or interaction? Can students be involved emotionally through seeing pictures that elicit strong reactions?

Here is an example of involving students in learning the central aspect of one particular lesson. The topic under discussion in this high school classroom was "Domestic Violence in the State of Arizona." The teacher's overall goal was to raise students' awareness of the serious nature of this issue within their state. At one point during the lesson the teacher stated, "Did you know that last year, of the number of women in Arizona who had to go to the emergency room, 36% were there as a result of domestic violence?"

Having made this statement, she then continued forward with the lesson. Here's our question: Has she maximized the impact of this key statistic? Has she *involved* her students in it?

The percentage she stated was actually shockingly high to many of the students. However, the statistic had been *told* to them—they were not involved in discovering it. Here's how she could have involved her students:

- She might poll them for what percentage they thought was accurate.

- She might ask a third of the students to stand up, point to them, and say, "That's approximately 36% of the people in this room—the same percentage of all women who went to emergency rooms in Arizona as a result of domestic violence."

- She might ask students to think of the answer and then raise their hands. Then she could ask, "What percent do you think . . ." and begin with 5%, then 10%, and continue on in 5% increments. The students would be told to drop their hands when she passes the percentage they thought was the correct answer.

These are just a few of her choices for increasing the impact of this statistic. The following year, she chose to use the final idea mentioned here. Using this approach helped her achieve her intended outcome at a much higher level. It even led to a useful twist in her future discussion on this topic. She observed that in the majority of her classes, by the time she had reached 25%, no one's hand remained in the air. In these groups she was then able to say, "And that's a big part of the challenge—very few people are even aware of the seriousness of this critical problem here in Arizona."

Here's another example concerning a related topic. A teacher used to ask her class if anyone had heard the term "rule of thumb." She would then go on to explain the term may have originated in 1800s, when a man could legally beat his wife if the "width of the bruise was no bigger than the width of his thumb." (Note: Other variations of this phrase included the idea that the "width of the stick could be no bigger than the husband's thumb.")

Despite the fact that this information should generate a strong reaction from the students, she felt she could do more. Could there were other ways she might use to create an even more effective moment than by simply stating a possible definition of "rule of thumb"? Over the years she experimented with several different approaches. After experiencing various levels of success with each of the techniques, she finally found the one that seemed to be the most effective. When she now teaches the subject, she involves her students by saying:

> "Please hold up your thumb. Now, compare the size of your thumb to those of your neighbors. Who has the largest thumb in this room? [After a pause for people to compare, she continues.] Please take your thumb and push it against the skin of your other arm. You should be able to make a visible impression on your arm. Try that now. [After everyone has tried it . . .] Please look back at me. The reason I had you do that was to demonstrate what was originally meant by the expression 'rule of thumb.' The size of that white mark you made on your arm was the size of the bruise that, if you were the man, you were legally allowed to inflict on your wife in the 1800s—something known as the 'rule of thumb.' We've come a long way since then, it's true, but we have even further to go."

As teachers we can help students to encode primary pieces of information and build a "knowledge network" by involving the class in discovering this information—instead of simply telling them about it. This creates a more active mental process, one that is more likely to generate longer-term memory.

Next Steps

No single involvement strategy is ever simply the *best* one to use. However, involving students in *some* way is almost always a better, more effective way to teach than simply saying it. Therefore our primary focus for future lessons should be on trying something, anything, to help our students grasp the central facts of our lessons.

Ask yourself—are you willing to try new ways to present your key ideas? Are you willing to take a risk one day, stopping to isolate a central point and making it totally memorable to your students by involving them in learning a key point? If you hesitate even slightly, consider trying some of the lower-risk techniques first. When you find yourself becoming comfortable with including these ideas, perhaps move forward to working with "higher" involvement strategies. Through everyday exploration and experimentation you will find the right ones that best fit your own teaching style, your content, and most importantly, your students.

ASSESS YOUR CURRENT USE OF INVOLVE, DON'T TELL

- ■ I often involve my students in learning key points, rather than simply stating the information.

- ■ I sometime involve my students in learning key points of the lesson.

- ■ I have seldom considered involving my students in learning the key points and tend to simply tell them what is important.

Your Ideas

List a topic you'll be teaching your students, then two or three key points central to the lesson. Write out how you plan to involve students in learning each key point.

First Topic:_____

Key Point 1:_____

How to Involve the Students: _____

_____

_____

_____

Key Point 2:_____

How to Involve the Students: _____

_____

_____

_____

Key Point 3:_____

How to Involve the Students: _____

_____

_____

_____

Second Topic: _____

Key Point 1:_____

How to Involve the Students: _____

_____

_____

_____

Key Point 2:_____

How to Involve the Students: _____

_____

_____

_____

Key Point 3:_____

How to Involve the Students: _____

_____

_____

_____

Third Topic:_____

Key Point 1:_____

How to Involve the Students: _____

_____

_____

_____

Key Point 2:_____

How to Involve the Students: _____

_____

_____

_____

Key Point 3:_____

How to Involve the Students: _____

_____

_____

_____

J = Jump Up

Movement enhances learning and keeps students alive and awake.

In General

The evidence is clear: We need to get today's students *moving* (Ratey, 2008). If they sit too long in their chairs, blood flow slows, and less oxygen is transported to the brain. And simply put, the brain needs oxygen to thrive, grow, and learn. Oxygen helps the brain function at its highest levels (Hannaford, 2005). In fact, stopping our students from moving may be the single greatest obstacle to them learning and recalling new material (Jensen, 2002). We need to find ways to get students to, at least occasionally, jump up, leave their seats, and be in motion—if for no other reason than to get their blood flowing.

The Connection

Movement provides natural stimulation on many levels simultaneously. For today's students with microsecond attention spans, it is a powerful means of engaging and keeping their attention. The massive success of "active" video games demonstrates this phenomenon. Once video games were largely static activities: The only movement in evidence was thumbs on buttons or joysticks. But now video games like Nintendo's Wii have wireless controllers that detect movement in three dimensions. Movement has become an integral part of the gaming world—just as it should be in our classrooms.

The Big Picture

In a High-Impact Classroom, students learn while standing—as well as sitting. While traditional teaching links learning to sitting, this idea is not based on science. The fact is, students do *not* learn better sitting, because sitting reduces the blood flow to their brain. The only reason we resist allowing students to move and are more comfortable with them sitting all the time is the fear of losing control.

While this is a reasonable fear, let us be honest with ourselves. If our students are uncomfortable, fidgeting, and incapable of concentrating on our lesson, making them sit still only gives us the *illusion* of control. So, let us surrender this illusion, and deal with the reality that student engagement requires them to move—frequently.

This is not to say that students can't be in their seats during certain moments in the course of instruction. It's usually easier for students to take notes while sitting. However, there are numerous other moments during most lessons when it really isn't necessary for students to remain seated.

Oddly enough, we often permit movement in classes with younger students. But there appears to be an unconscious rule in education that, once students are "old enough," they can and should be able to sit for extended periods of time. In fact the opposite might well be true: The older students are, the more movement might be needed to keep them attentive and awake.

So how can we introduce movement into our classrooms while still retaining classroom control? Consider the following four primary areas:

1. Movement during *administrative* tasks, such as gathering worksheets

2. Movement as a part of the *structure* of a lesson, such as small-group discussions while standing

3. Movement to help *teach* part of a lesson, thus making it more memorable (*see* U = Uniquely Memorable)

4. Movement purely to energize the learners, such as brief games purely for the purposes of getting the blood pumping, oxygen flowing, and muscles moving

In this way, we can include movement as a natural and normal aspect of the flow of our lessons.

Focus on Classroom Management

If we make students sit too long they become uncomfortable and find it difficult to concentrate. The first sign of this is students placing their arms on the desk. Next they gradually lean forward. It's only a short move now to rest their head in the cradle of their arms—and *boom*, they're asleep! When students are struggling to focus and unable to concentrate, their behaviors begin to fall apart as well. Even the most normally well-behaved student may start acting up once they are physically uncomfortable. As any parent knows, an overcontrolled, antsy child is the hardest to mange. And when they *are* finally given the chance to release, it may well result in an explosion of energy.

Consider the opposite situation. Imagine a classroom where students are given frequent—but *appropriate*—opportunities to jump up and move about the classroom. Once they come to understand that they *will* have at least occasional opportunities to jump up, move around, and stretch in the classroom, most students can actually focus better on the lesson, safe in the knowledge that their teacher will honor their need to be physically engaged in the learning process.

In Practice

When students can concentrate on our lessons, they learn better. Movement actually *enhances* learning, allowing students the chance to get reenergized and reinvigorated for the rest of the lesson.

Most of the activities described below should last less than five minutes, a length of time that most students are easily able to remain standing. Consider having students stand up while doing any of the following:

- Participating in general conversations with classmates

- Having small-group, content-related discussions

- Standing and completing a worksheet with a partner, using a clipboard

- Observing a short demonstration in the front of the room

- Standing to work on a worksheet at their desk

- Participating in any brief activity during the class session

- Congratulating others for successfully completing a project

- Gathering handouts, workbooks, or other resources

- Carousel activities in which students write on papers hung on walls at different locations throughout a classroom

These suggestions are merely a beginning point for the almost endless number of ways we can allow students to jump up and move. While not all of them will fit for all situations, finding a few that are appropriate for your classroom is critical to your success as a teacher working with today's students.

Next Steps

The comfort level of our students should be our top priority when designing and conducting a classroom activity. When we ask students to physically interact with each other, we need to be aware of their interpersonal dynamics and watch for signs of student discomfort.

Sometimes, it's easy to see this reaction—for example, if students choose not to participate in a particular learning activity. At other times, students' reactions will be more passive, evident only on a subtle level. While continuing to remain involved, they may mentally remove themselves from the experience. The result in either case is a fundamentally less effective learning experience.

At the very least, this feeling of unease might significantly decrease an individual's willingness to participate in future exercises. If students grow even mildly distrustful of a teacher who has made them feel physically uncomfortable, they stop engaging and learning.

However, when we handle those potentially threatening situations in a manner that reflects our concern for their comfort, students will quickly develop a bond of trust—allowing the boundaries of learning to be stretched even further (Maslow, 1968, 1970).

ASSESS YOUR CURRENT USE OF JUMP UP

- I use as much movement as possible in all of my lessons.

- I use movement sometimes, but could probably use it much more.

- I very rarely allow student movement and conduct most of my lessons with students seated at their desks.

Your Ideas

How are you going to add more movement to your learning environment? Keep in mind that the simple ways are the easiest places to begin. Perhaps you can find an appropriate moment for students to stand up and talk briefly with each other. Or perhaps you could place the handouts or resources they will need at the sides of the room and invite them to go get one for themselves. When you become comfortable with having students move about the room, begin to develop more ideas—possibly more advanced and involved ones—for how to keep students moving in your classroom.

The key is to find some way, somehow, somewhere in each lesson to have a few moments when students can be physically engaged. Below, decide how movement might fit into three upcoming lessons. Describe as many opportunities as possible to get them jumping up and moving.

Lesson 1: _____

Movement Opportunities: _____

_____

_____

_____

_____

Lesson 2: _____

Movement Opportunities: _____

_____

_____

_____

_____

Lesson 3: _____

Movement Opportunities: _____

_____

_____

_____

_____

K = Keen Visuals

Visual images—everywhere in life—should be everywhere in learning.

In General

Teaching usually relies, in one form or another, on *words*. Whether written or oral, words are the primary means by which students learn new ideas, concepts, and information. Language, of course, is an excellent communication tool. However, the learning process is more likely to be successful if we reinforce these ideas with visuals. This is because one of the primary ways human beings intake, process, and encode new information is through *visual imagery*.

Contrary to the idea of the traditional teaching mode of lecture, being told about something is not the only way we learn. In fact, it may not even be the *primary* way many of our students learn. Visuals will often jump more rapidly into our brains, help us organize information, and stay there longer than mere words. This is why, as teachers, we should use visuals wherever possible to increase the impact of our lessons and help our students learn more rapidly.

The Connection

With the amount of new information growing exponentially, Generations Y and Z will have to make sense of unimaginably large volumes of data. Visualization will play an increasingly important role in this process, because our brains process visuals and text/auditory input in separate channels. Therefore, adding visuals to words in the learning process has the potential to augment and accelerate understanding and improve recall. This is particularly true of digital natives, whose world is awash with images. Visuals have never been more important teaching aids to help our students grasp meaning, organize ideas, and remember concepts.

The Big Picture

Schools clearly recognize the critical nature of visuals, as evidenced by the fact that there are so many blackboards and whiteboards—and more recently, *interactive* whiteboards—in almost every classroom. Unfortunately, the tradition has been to use these potent tools merely to reinforce *verbal* communication—writing words, but avoiding images. Instead, adding relevant, engaging, and practical visuals to our lessons can greatly increase our students' potential to fully understand and memorize new content. Creating an appropriate visual image of the key content is a powerful idea for ending the lesson, cementing the central concept in students' minds (Baghban, 2007).

In some cases, not only do visuals communicate messages easily as well as words, they may actually make the point more effectively. As Mehrabian's studies showed, much communication is nonverbal (Mehrabian, 1981). We may miss spoken—or written—words, yet we only need a millisecond to intake information encoded visually.

To fully appreciate the power of this idea, imagine the following scene: You are a student in a classroom, listening well, concentrating intently, and furiously taking notes. At one point you get distracted, and end up doodling off to the side of page 6. Eventually you catch yourself and refocus your attention back on the lecture. Later, preparing for the test, you carefully review those endless pages of notes. Then, when you go to take the test, and . . . what's the *first* thing you can remember? What's the one thing that sticks out most in your mind? It's probably that doodle from page 6! In other words, even under pressure, our brains can swiftly process and recall images, often far more easily than words.

Because students can rapidly and easily assimilate visual information, lessons that use diagrams, icons, symbols, signs, illustrations—and occasionally even doodles—are highly memorable. Marzano (2004) refers to these alternate ways of learning, remembering, and notetaking as *nonlinguistic representations*.

Focus on Classroom Management

Students are often daunted at the prospect of learning "content-heavy" topics. They may perceive this endeavor as being similar to finding their way across vast, uncharted, unfamiliar territory. Without a map, they may begin to feel helpless. They refuse to put forth their best effort when studying and learning, simply because they believe—sometimes quite rightly—that they'll never get it. Many will simply surrender to seemingly inevitable failure, allowing their minds to waver off task to anything that catches their wandering attentions.

A great deal of this disappointment, aggravation, and ensuing bad behavior can be eliminated if we start students off with a visual "map" of the material, or even allow students to create their own map (Goldberg, 2004). If students can visually organize their thoughts, the topic instantly becomes more manageable. With a map in hand, they can formulate a proper plan for setting out on a successful journey of discovery and learning, keeping their attention focused in the direction we intend.

In Practice

The use of the word *visuals* in this section is deliberately broad, since we can employ them in so many ways to enhance learning. Visuals that help students to process, encode, understand, and recall new information include:

- Mind maps, concept maps, or other "mapping" devices

- Organizational plans for lecture notes, such as diagrams or flowcharts

- Creative layouts to visually organize primarily verbal information

- Cartoon images used on posters, in slides, or on handouts
- Graphic icons representing the content created by the teacher
- Graphic icons representing the content created by students
- Symbols, figures, or sketches that illustrate a concept
- Bumper stickers created by the students
- Posters created by groups of students to summarize key ideas
- Drawings or doodles created by the students, added to their notes

The mapping devices mentioned at the top of the list are useful tools for making sense of and learning large amounts of new material (Budd , 2004). They are particularly effective when we allow students to create their *own* visuals (Margulies & Valenza, 2005).

Next Steps

To increase the visuals in our classroom, we need to address two issues. First, we must give our students permission to use more visuals. Many students have been actively discouraged from using any form of visuals when studying. So we must give them explicit and direct permission— repeating the idea that visuals are excellent study aids so students can overcome their prior programming about using *only* words to take notes and study.

Second, we must show many of them *how* to create visuals. While some students at all ages are comfortable doodling, drawing, and creating flowcharts and diagrams, others aren't. Quite early on, many students latch onto the idea that they "can't draw." Therefore we need to devote classroom time to teaching students how to create useful visuals (Pineda De Romero & Dwyer, 2005). We can teach any student to draw. For inspiration and confidence see Wordtoons at www.wordtoons.com (Logue, 2007).

Many will need a little encouragement to push them into a willingness to draw (Heath & Wolf, 2005). We might help them along this path by avoiding potentially dangerous words such as *draw* or *sketch* and create a new phrases. Perhaps we could use expressions such as "study squiggles" or "lines for learning," or maybe even call it "the art of the deliberate doodle." Anything will suffice, as long as it gets them to put their pencils to paper and begin to create.

Remember: Helpful classroom visuals do not have to be museum-quality masterpieces! Our students don't have to be artists to create useful study aids. All they need is permission and encouragement.

ASSESS YOUR CURRENT USE OF KEEN VISUALS

- ■ I use as many visuals as possible in my lessons, both ones I create as well as ones students create, to teach and to create notes.

- ■ I use visuals to teach, some I create and some students create, but have not had the students use them to take their own notes.

- ■ I use visuals when I teach, but have never had the students create some to use in the lesson or to help them remember their notes.

Your Ideas

Successfully integrating more visuals into your lessons requires careful advance planning. Remember to consider your students' current skill levels. Once you feel you have an idea what they are capable of—and willing to do—you're ready to begin.

Below, list at least three upcoming lessons. Then choose at least one place within the lesson where you could ask students to create visuals.

Lesson 1: _____

Visual Image Technique: _____

_____

_____

_____

_____

Lesson 2: _____

Visual Image Technique: _____

_____

_____

_____

_____

Lesson 3: _____

Visual Image Technique: _____

_____

_____

_____

_____

Lesson 4: _____

Visual Image Technique: _____

_____

_____

_____

_____

Lesson 5: _____

Visual Image Technique: _____

_____

_____

_____

L = Labels

*We create the world around us with words—
choose yours carefully!*

In General

Labels are words that cause a reaction in us because we have had experience with them in the past. They can be both positive and negative and are context specific. Tell a classroom of 8-year-olds they're going to play a game, and they will jump for joy—probably literally! Now try it with 18-year-olds and watch the ripples of discomfort and disdain spread around the room. By using negative labels, we make our teaching lives harder. On the other hand, using positive labels can help our students achieve more than they believed possible.

The Connection

Generations Y and Z have already assigned their own labels to classroom learning, with many of them, even those eager to learn, labeling traditional schooling as "hard" and "boring." For them, if an activity proves to be easy and fun, it's not real learning. We can use positive labels to shake this perception. If we can get students to start an activity feeling positive and interested, they are more likely to enjoy and learn from the activity. Because the words we use to describe the activity set up this feeling, we must choose them with care.

The Big Picture

When teachers use a labeled term, students immediately call to mind past experiences they may have had related to that label. For better or worse, they mentally prepare themselves for what they *believe* the label means. If they have had a bad experience with this label in the classroom, we have added a heap of negative emotions to an already stressful situation.

Learning is a highly emotional process. By its very nature, learning new information requires students to explore the unknown. Thus, learning can be a risky endeavor, making it easy for negative emotions to come to the forefront.

As teachers, we must therefore work *consciously* to establish and maintain positive emotions. Without consciously avoiding words with negative connotations, we may unwittingly plunge a normally willing group of students into a negative emotional reaction. Our first task in setting up a High-Impact Teaching environment is to make our classroom emotionally "safe" for students (Qais, 2007).

If we carefully pick words that create the right emotional atmosphere, our students will mostly likely feel much more comfortable following our lead. The more comfortable students are in the learning environment, the more willing they might be to engage in lessons and to take the risks necessary to learn the material.

Focus on Classroom Management

If we use inappropriate labels to set up activities, we give our students an excuse to act out. Let's go back to our 18-year-old students. Imagine the teacher beginning the class by saying "OK, everybody, it's time to play a game!"

Already, some students are groaning in dismay or rolling their eyes. But the teacher plows ahead with the activity and the class grudgingly goes along. The truth is, many of the students secretly enjoy the activity. But it's been set up as a "game" and everyone knows it's not cool to participate in a game. The teacher ends up with reluctant, disengaged students and the behavioral problems that go with it.

Instead, in this situation, the teacher might simply have *framed* (*see* F = Framing) the activity differently. If a reason were given for the activity that students accept as valid and worthwhile, instead of shying away they will tend to step forward and engage. From this much different mental outlook they will usually also behave much better.

In Practice

Here are some words that, in some contexts, may trigger negative or unhelpful emotions in your students—and some alternative words or phrases. There are no rights and wrongs with labels; it's just a question of using words that your students will feel more comfortable with.

- Play: Action or involvement
- Sing: "A chance to share your musical abilities . . ."
- Game: Event, challenge, activity, or opportunity
- Fun: Enjoyment or pleasure
- Dance: Movement, action, or motion
- Homework: Studies, homeplay, or independent time activity
- Test: Assessment, analysis, or check-in time
- Draw: Doodle or create visual notes

Labels with *multiple definitions* can also be challenging to use in a learning context. For example, a teacher once turned to his group of middle school students and asked: "Who can tell me the definition of a *wave*?"

He was quite startled when no one responded. The room continued to remain silent as he glanced around at the students. Finally he said: "What? You've never heard of a wave? I'm amazed!"

To the teacher's way of thinking, he had asked a very basic question. In reality, however, the question was more complex than it appeared.

The teacher hadn't taken into account how many different definitions there are for the word *wave*. For example, a wave might refer to the hand gesture people make when leaving, a wave in the ocean, a radio wave, a sound wave, or even a wave created by sports fans in a stadium! The students didn't know which one he meant. They were confused and hesitant to ask for fear of looking foolish. Learning had come to a grinding halt. Instead, this question could be answered much more easily if it was stated in the *open* format (*see* B = Be Open), perhaps by saying: "How would *you* define a *wave*?"

Here another situation to consider: Imagine the potential risks in making the following announcement to a class:

"This is an activity called Speed-Warp Time Juggling!"

While the teacher who uttered it may have been looking to generate excitement for the upcoming activity, many of the labels within the statement may give students a reason to hesitate. Pick any of the following words: speed, time, or juggling. Each of these could have negative contexts. "I hate to be rushed," "I'm not good at doing things fast," or "I can't juggle," are all possible internal reactions from students. The key here is that there are *many* possible negative labels. If students are nervous about even *one* of these words they may become resistive and end up not learning anything from the activity.

Here's another example where a label is used too early. A large class of 8-to-12-year-olds were just coming up to a break. The teacher announced: "OK, everybody, in just a minute we'll take a break."

To those young people, the word *break* was a powerful label. In their minds they saw a chance to run around the room, play games, and have a great time. The instant they heard "break," they all raced for the door, not waiting for the teacher to announce the break. The teacher had meant to tell them a few quick things first. But once she had spoken those words, it took over two minutes just to get them quiet enough so she could be heard. Had she never actually used the label *break*, they would have remained listening while she finished the directions.

Next Steps

Labels are always *contextual*, meaning they vary from group to group. As we move between classrooms, we need to consider the vocabulary changes required to engage and not put off this next group of students. Of course, we may not always be aware of all the connections students might have with certain labels. However, if we monitor our classrooms for students reacting badly to certain words, we can gradually build a greater aware-ness of good and bad labels into our teaching. The result will be better motivated, more engaged, and increasingly positive students.

ASSESS YOUR CURRENT USE OF LABELS

■ I am very careful about the words I use and deliberately avoid any that might have a negative connotation to my students.

■ I am careful about using some words, but there might be others I should avoid to make my lessons go smoother.

■ I rarely consider whether my words are unhelpful "labels."

Your Ideas

Consider your students, their ages, and their maturity levels. Based on your own experience, what words are negative "labels" to them? In the spaces provided below, list five of these labels. Then note how you could phrase them differently next time.

Label 1:_____

Saying It Differently: _____

_____

_____

Label 2:_____

Saying It Differently: _____

_____

_____

Label 3:_____

Saying It Differently: _____

_____

_____

Label 4:_____

Saying It Differently: _____

_____

_____

Label 5:_____

Saying It Differently: _____

_____

_____

Label 6:_____

Saying It Differently: _____

_____

_____

Label 7:_____

Saying It Differently: _____

_____

_____

M = Music

Music is a magnificent motivator.

In General

Music is an extraordinarily influential teaching tool that should be a natural and consistent part of most classrooms. Music has a direct physical, emotional, and psychological effect on both students *and* teachers (Jensen, 2000). Properly employed, it can create a heightened social learning context, motivate students to engage more rapidly, and quickly establish a sense of safety. Each of these factors helps to create a powerful and positive learning environment (Burko & Elliot, 1997; Weinberger, 1998). Best of all, music achieves all this with very little effort from the teacher.

The Connection

Outside the classroom, today's students live with an almost permanent soundtrack. Plugged into MP3 players, they are accompanied by music on the way to school, between classes, and during lunch. In the foreground or background, on the road, in shops, in their bedrooms, music is an integral part of their universe. The only time it stops is in the classroom.

If life beyond the confines of the classroom reverberates with a constant barrage of sound, classrooms should do the same. Given its pervasive presence in every aspect of their existence, any place that does *not* have music will be perceived by Gen Y and Z students as odd, unusual, and inherently *wrong*. Therefore, music simply *must* be a part of every lesson, in every classroom, and every school—not just a "one-off" novelty. Once we accept this, we become free to explore how, where, and when to use music to enhance learning.

MUSIC
IS A MARVELOUS
MOOD MODIFIER

The Big Picture

Handled correctly, music can unleash the energy of any group of students and help guide them in a useful direction. By actively using music in the classroom, we bring our teaching space to life (Chapman, 2007). Interestingly, teachers who use music in the classroom actually expend less of their own valuable energy to build a dynamic, interactive, engaging experience for the students (Bucko, 1997; Jensen, 1996).

Here is just one tiny example of the power of music. One morning, the teacher asks students to move the tables and chairs to the sides of the room. As students stand up, the teacher turns on upbeat, lively music, with the volume fairly high. Students jump rapidly to accomplish the task, and move energetically onto the next activity. Now imagine what might have happened *without* the music. While students still accomplish the task, they are sluggish and reluctant. The task is tedious. It takes much longer to achieve the same objective. As the next part of the class begins, the teacher struggles to get students fully engaged.

The contrast between these situations easily demonstrates the simple productive, constructive, and ultimately *instructive* influence music can have on today's students. As teachers, we need to use appropriate music everywhere and anywhere we can.

Focus on Classroom Management

Music is a mood enhancer. With no effort from the teacher—other than hitting "play"—music will calm and cheer students who arrive stressed or grumpy. It will motivate reluctant participants and engage even the "coolest" nonconformer. The natural byproduct of this situation is that discipline issues decline—and often disappear entirely.

In Practice

We have an almost infinite variety of ways to use music in the classroom. However, here are six key places—beginning points—where you might consider adding it in your lessons:

- Music before class

- Music as a signal

- Music during movement

- Music to match a theme

- Music behind small-group discussions

- Music after class

Music before Class

Imagine a silent room on the first day of a new class. Students might not know each other and they are reticent about saying hello. Even if they *want* to introduce themselves, the silent room is a major deterrent. Suddenly, merely talking to one other person becomes an adventure in public speaking. Everyone can hear you.

Alternatively, by playing music in the background, we allow students to speak to each other without being overheard. Since there is already noise, adding to it seems natural. Subtly, we are inviting students to interact with each other. The music reduces the "threat" level of the room. Students can chat comfortably under the cover of music. Without realizing it, they have already begun the new class, independently moving to interact with each other—unprompted by the teacher.

Music at the start of any class—not just a new one—can also set the tone, create a relaxed auditory ambiance, and generate a positive atmosphere in the room. If the class is going to be activity based, or if lively group discussions are anticipated, it might be useful to play more up-tempo songs, to begin building energy in the room. In this situation, music may act to subtly bring to mind a party-type atmosphere, a useful mindset for delivering certain lessons. However, if the lesson plan calls for a more quiet, contemplative, or perhaps even emotionally challenging session, the choice of music might be softer songs or gentle classical and baroque selections.

Music as a Signal

Imagine music is playing at the start of a class. When it's time to begin, the teacher lifts the volume and then cuts the music. The loss of music causes students to turn their heads, knowing something is happening. We can then seize the moment and officially start the class.

This signaling mechanism saves us from using such phrases as "OK, could you all look at me?" or "Well, I guess it's time to begin," or "Everybody, could you please get quiet so we can start?" By using music as a cue for our students to stop talking and listen, we can move directly to the lesson with the first words we speak. And we don't have to raise our voices to get students' attention.

To further enforce this effect, we can start playing a particular song to indicate the lesson is starting. This cue lets students know our session is about to start, acting as a signal to find their seats. Early on, we can tell students, "This is your 'call in' song. When you hear it, please take your seats." Students of all ages quickly adapt to this approach to the start of the class. For regular classes, we can keep things fresh by changing to a new song as needed, perhaps once every week or two.

Some schools might want to work together to expand on this idea. Instead of a bell to signify the start of each new period, a song could be played over the speaker system. Students would know they must be ready for the class to begin when the song reaches its last note. Of course, this means playing the same song six times a day, so the song is changed at the beginning of each week.

Students can even own this process. Some schools encourage students to nominate songs, with a student body deciding on the one to be used the following week. As a final bonus, the name of the person who nominated each new song is announced as when the song is used the first time on Monday morning.

Using songs as a signal works easily with younger students in some additional situations. You might want to create a "line-up song" or a "clean-up song." Just choose a song; then explain to the students what it signals. If you can get the lyrics to match the activity, so much the better. When you start to use it consistently, sit back and watch the magic happen!

Music during Movement

Whenever movement is a part of a learning activity, we can use music to motivate the students to accomplish the task more rapidly, and with a sense of animation and enjoyment (Jensen, 1996). This works for longer periods of movement, for example, when students are rearranging tables and chairs, but also for 20- or 30-second bursts of movement, such as when students are forming groups or moving to get supplies.

Upbeat, bright, energetic music is best in these situations. Since our goal is to transition students rapidly to the next direction or activity, music provides an auditory stimulus to get them moving! We can then build on the sense of energy created by this type of music as we segue into the next section. It saves us from having to expend our own precious energy to get our students up and motivated.

Every time there is movement on the part of the students, turn on music that matches the mood you want to create.

Music to Match a Theme

Consider choosing music that speaks directly to the current lesson. Of the three basic learning styles—visual, auditory, and kinesthetic—often only the auditory students will truly catch the moments we use themed music. But when they do, it will bring their attention levels to a peak in the classroom.

We can use thematic music in a variety of ways. Content-specific songs can be found to match content areas. For example, for math—"ABC" by the Jackson 5 or "Heartaches by the Number" by Guy Mitchell for basic math or "I Walk the Line" Johnny Cash for geometry. For writing projects, "Paperback Writer" by the Beatles or "The Letter" by the Boxtops might be appropriate. Or, students studying earthquakes might listen to "Shake, Rattle, and Roll" by Bill Haley and the Comets or "I Feel the Earth Move under My Feet" by Carole King. Expanding this theme, perhaps, on the first day of the week, you could add some humor to the day by playing "Monday, Monday" by the Mamas and Papas, "Manic Monday" by the Bangles, or "Rainy Days and Mondays" by The Carpenters. Many more ideas for these types of songs can be found in *The Green Book of Songs* (Green, 2005).

With today's students, there's one more important opportunity— ask them for thematic music to match what they're learning. Simply tell them what next week's unit will be covering, and ask them to find you songs to match! With the easy availability of music these days, students will often find this an intrinsically exciting opportunity to help the teacher.

As the driving force in the lives of many students, music can bring a potent and positive energy to the classroom. Teachers who introduce music often find learners eagerly asking to help create this "auditory aspect" of their environment.

Music behind Small-Group Discussions

Whenever we introduce small-group discussions, there is a chance that conversation from one group may intrude on another. By playing music lightly in the background, we can lessen this sense of interference.

This effect is called a musical "pad." Physical padding is used to soundproof rooms in a home, walls in an apartment building, or a musical studio. In the classroom, the use of light background music effectively "pads" the room so sound from one group will not interfere with sound from another. In a silent room, if one group should break into laughter, the sudden intrusion of sound can be quite disruptive to other conversations. However, a pad of music reduces the effect of the interruption.

This pad can also *encourage* conversation within a group. In a silent room, it may be a bit intimidating for some students to speak up and voice their opinions—even in a very small group. With the protection and privacy created by a music pad, even timid students feel free to engage themselves in the discussion.

Since students will be talking during this time, be careful about using songs with well-known lyrics. Sometimes, songs with words may prompt people to listen closely to the song, which in turn causes them to tune out of the conversation in which they are supposed to be participating. In most cases, this is definitely *not* the effect you are trying to create.

Music after Class

As the class ends, students gather their belongings and begin to file out of the room. This is a wonderful opportunity to play music. The music we choose at this time should leave students with a positive impression of our class. Try using "Celebration" by Kool and the Gang, or "Up, Up, and Away" by the Fifth Dimension. Since this is the final image they take away from your classroom, it will frequently be the first thing they think about when they begin to organize their thoughts for their next class with you. It's helpful if our students begin our classes with a positive feeling about the last session they attended.

These six places are an excellent starting point when deciding how to use music in your classroom. However, if you've never used music in your lessons, organizing even these isolated moments might be a slightly over-whelming, given everything else that happens in most classrooms. Start with just one place and give yourself time to learn; experiment with a variety of music. As you become confident in one place, you can gradually add music to other areas of your lessons, until your classroom rocks!

Once you're confident about using music, consider allowing your students to be involved in running the music. Before rejecting this idea as completely insane, know that many people can focus quite well on two things at once. Also, in a situation such as a year-long class, you might run the music for the first few weeks. Then, once students have understood the role of the music, they could take charge of this aspect of the classroom.

This strategy is especially useful if there is one person—at any age level—that just can't seem to pay attention. Ask them to run the music, and watch what happens. While some people may argue that this student is no longer paying attention, think about it more closely. To run music properly, and get the timing right, this person must *follow your instruction very closely*. Perhaps, since they are now actually paying attention, they will pick up more of the information you are teaching. If other motivational strategies you've tried have not been successful, why not try this novel approach? The benefits of having students offer suggestions and ideas and even help run the equipment are enormous, especially given the *diversity* and *relevance* they will bring to the library of possible musical choices (Moore, 2007).

One of the keys to using music successfully is appropriately manag-ing the volume at which it is played. Know in advance that it will never be exactly right for every student. Some will always want the music louder, while at the exact same time other students will want the music softer. Similarly, some will like the song that is currently playing, while others will want it changed immediately. This is a natural by-product of any aspect of instruction where students have the opportunity to have input. Understanding that this is the case may help you maintain your sanity when these situations arise. As much as possible, aim for the middle. Adjust the volume so it maximizes the desired effect, while minimizing the number of people who are distracted or feel a need to complain. Alternate song choices so all students get to hear something they prefer at some point in the lesson. Continue to stay focused on the changing needs of the group and adapt as necessary.

On a final, more prosaic note, all the good things that can come from the proper use of music are frequently undone by a very simple logistical issue. Teachers whose situations require them to be mobile may not want to go to all the trouble of lugging a heavy stereo player around with them as they move from location to location.

Teachers who do have to occasionally—or perhaps frequently—switch classrooms should remember that the bottom line of most instruction is to add value to the lives of the students. Music is invaluable in helping achieve this objective. Therefore, find a way to make it work. Ask a student to carry the equipment from room to room if needed. Buy a more compact, powerful system that's lighter to carry. Or buckle down, carry it yourself, and simply enjoy the idea of bringing music into students' lives. Most of all, find a way to use music. It works.

Next Steps

Carefully consider what type of music to play. This should be based on the reaction you want from your students—not on your favorite music. For example, if working with teens, ask them about popular songs, and have some of these on hand. If you don't personally own any of these, you might want to ask your students to bring in some from their own collections. This request saves you money, and it also brings a sense of student ownership into the room.

When considering lyrics, there are three options: (1) none, (2) unfamiliar, or (3) familiar. Music without words is good as a pad of background sound. Songs with unfamiliar lyrics are useful in some cases, since the mere presence of words may encourage them to talk and interact. I occasionally use gentle Hawaiian music in these circumstances. This is partly because the melodies are a nice background choice, but mostly because my students don't speak Hawaiian! Finally, songs with familiar lyrics are useful for before and after class, or occasionally within lessons if the words relate to the content.

Teachers of teen audiences may also have to cope with one very specific issue: rap music. While its appeal as basic entertainment may be quite strong to some students, its usefulness to a teacher in a learning setting is limited due to its frequent reliance on bass and drums. The issue is that heavy, low tones are counterproductive for the needs of almost all aspects of learning and recall.

If your students ask to use rap music during class, you need to explain the purpose behind the music. Here's what I usually say:

> "I think rap music is perfectly OK. However, much of that form of music relies on a heavy bass notes. The wavelengths these notes produce do not encourage learning or long-term memory. We're only using music in our class because we want it to help everyone learn better. So here's what we'll do. If you're willing to let the class use music that is useful for learning when we're studying, I'll be willing to have rap on during a few of our breaks—provided, of course, that the lyrics are decent!"

Generally, with a clear enough explanation, most students are willing to compromise and go with the program. Interestingly, many of these students—even the most rebellious teens—often come to enjoy the other forms of music fairly rapidly. Their understanding that the presence of music is it not there purely to entertain them is frequently the key to making it work.

ASSESS YOUR CURRENT USE OF MUSIC

- I use as much music as possible—in as many ways as possible—and with deliberate purpose in my classroom

- I occasionally use music, but mostly as random background noise.

- I have not yet had the opportunity to use music in my classroom.

Your Ideas

How will you use music in your classroom? This section has offered a variety of possibilities. Below, some of these key areas are highlighted. In each case, try to write down at least three songs that might work for your students, your material, and . . . for *you*!

Music before Class

Song	Artist or Band
1. _____	_____
2. _____	_____
3. _____	_____
4. _____	_____
5. _____	_____
6. _____	_____
7. _____	_____
8. _____	_____
9. _____	_____
10. _____	_____

Music as a Signal

Song	Artist or Band	Used as a Signal for
1. _____	_____	_____
2. _____	_____	_____
3. _____	_____	_____
4. _____	_____	_____
5. _____	_____	_____
6. _____	_____	_____

7. _____ _____ _____

8. _____ _____ _____

9. _____ _____ _____

10. _____ _____ _____

Music during Movement

	Song		Artist or Band

1. _____ _____

2. _____ _____

3. _____ _____

4. _____ _____

5. _____ _____

6. _____ _____

7. _____ _____

8. _____ _____

9. _____ _____

10. _____ _____

Music to Match a Theme

	Song	Artist or Band	Theme to Match

1. _____ _____ _____

2. _____ _____ _____

3. _____ _____ _____

4. _____ _____ _____

5. _____ _____ _____
6. _____ _____ _____
7. _____ _____ _____
8. _____ _____ _____
9. _____ _____ _____
10. _____ _____ _____

Music behind Small Group Discussions

Song	Artist or Band

1. _____ _____
2. _____ _____
3. _____ _____
4. _____ _____
5. _____ _____
6. _____ _____
7. _____ _____
8. _____ _____
9. _____ _____
10. _____ _____

Music after Class

Song	Artist or Band

1. _____ _____
2. _____ _____

3. _____ _____

4. _____ _____

5. _____ _____

6. _____ _____

7. _____ _____

8. _____ _____

9. _____ _____

10. _____ _____

N = Novelty

When was the last time you did something for the first time?

In General

Students rarely arrive to the classroom in anticipation of being intrigued, fascinated, enthralled, and mesmerized. And yet, when this does happen—often by accident—an almost magical rise occurs in their attention and energy levels. Not surprisingly, an equal rise occurs in their learning and retention. Our goal as teachers, therefore, should be to have the unusual become the usual, the unexpected become expected, and the unanticipated become the eagerly awaited. Students who know their teachers use novelty in their lessons enter the classroom with a far different, far more productive attitude than those students who fully expect to be facing the same old thing every day in the classroom (Wolfolk, 2004).

The Connection

Outside our classrooms, fascinating images, devices, sounds, and possibilities vie for our students' attention. Compared with Gen X teachers—many of whom remember getting excited about color TV—Generations Y and Z have grown up with an unimaginably rich and stimulating array of toys. This ubiquitous availability of high stimulation has not just shortened our students' attention spans, it also makes it harder for us to access their sense of curiosity and wonder. Without a technology budget seriously beyond the capacity of most schools, how can the classroom compete with the marvels of the online world?

The answer is to do something—anything—that draws our students' attention away from distractions in the outside world and brings it sharply focused into the classroom. By surprising and intriguing, we gain their attention. And when we have their attention—even if just for a moment—we have a critical starting point for teaching and learning. We have a room full of students fully present with what is happening right there, right at that moment, in the classroom.

Consider this: In today's world, if you sign a contract to be a teacher, you're actually agreeing to—first and foremost—help students be in the right mindset to learn. While those exact words may not appear on your contract, they are the underlying, implicit truth in working with Gen Y and Z students. As teachers we truly share the responsibility for keeping this generation of students focused. While you may have worked hard to prepare the content they're supposed to learn, they will only be ready for it if you have their absolute, undivided attention.

The Big Picture

Students rarely come into the classroom truly ready to learn—they are distracted by a hundred different thoughts, events, conversations, and emotions. But if something is novel, they are captivated. Anything that is different, new, or unusual—even slightly—draws their attention. Novelty creates a critical shift in internal focus, drawing students quickly into the lesson—without us having to battle for their attention. So let us understand the dynamics of novelty and consciously exploit it to hook our students' interest in our lessons.

As human beings, we remember unusual moments over routine, typical, everyday events. We remember "firsts." Even though it may have been decades ago, many of us still remember the first time we felt snow falling, saw the ocean, or traveled to another country. We remember our first kiss, our first trip to the theater, our first time bungee jumping!

Students in our current educational system—especially those in middle and higher grades—are often jaded and cynical. They believe, frequently correctly, that there's nothing new to be found in the classroom. However, you can enthrall your students and help them remember material by consciously including novelty in your lessons. This is particularly important if your content is relatively abstract. If we can found abstract concepts on novel elements that are real and tangible, students are more fully engaged and usually learn quickly and easily (Lin, Chen, & Dwyer, 2006).

Focus on Classroom Management

It's easy to see how students' attention can wander in a traditional classroom. Wandering thoughts lead to wandering eyes. Wandering eyes tend to prompt thoughts to wander even further afield. Wandering thoughts eventually lead to wandering hands, idle conversations, and inevitably, trouble.

However, when the teacher does something different, unusual, or unexpected, a student's focus pours in on the subject at hand. When focused on a specific task, they are less likely to be distracted by their personal concerns or by their peers.

In Practice

We have a wide range of opportunities to include novelty in our lessons. On one side of the continuum, novelty might simply be a twist to an established format or sequence of instructions students have encountered previously. At the opposite end, it might be something the students have literally never seen or experienced before. Here are some broad examples of situations where you might consider using novelty as a part of your lessons.

- Introduce a subject in a novel way, perhaps by holding up an unusual object—one related to the new subject— and having students guess what it is.

- Create a sense of mystery, suspense, or surprise.

- Add cartoon images to handouts.

- Put supplies in a "mystery box" before distributing them.

- Use unusual music.

- Teach a lesson in an unusual location, such as the hallway or outside.

- Sit students in an unusual arrangement—perhaps at the front of the room while the teacher teaches from the back.

- Use unusual teaching props—especially ones students can touch or hold.

- Make novel connections between content they are learning and things they care about in their personal lives, such as an upcoming dance.

- When asking for a response, make it something novel, such as "Put an elbow up if . . ."

- Use students' bodies to teach, such as learning to measure something by using body parts like hand spans, arms, or legs.

- Create unusual memory aids—for example, songs, bumper stickers, or ads.

- Create competitive and cooperative games for teaching and reviewing information.

- Teach grammar dressed as a Victorian woman or gentleman.

- Teach using an accent.

- Do assessments in an unusual manner—for example, use a game show format (*see* E = Entertainment) or ask students to draw the answer.

These are merely a few of the many ways you might hold the interest of today's students by teaching in innovative and creative ways. Do something abnormal, strange, or unexpected and students will react by sitting up and paying close attention. With their attention levels elevated, students will be more likely to engage in the lesson at a higher level, process the information more deeply, and consequently remember the information better.

Next Steps

Novelty should become a standard tool for raising students' level of engagement. And yet we need to keep a balance between novelty and ritual. A ritual—the opposite of novelty—is any frequently repeated activity or teaching device students are familiar with. While we are deliberately emphasizing the importance of using novelty in the classroom in this discussion, we must remember that ritual also serves a useful—in fact, *vital*—function in many classrooms, since it helps to sustain student comfort levels. Examples of typical classroom rituals might include:

- Always sitting in the same location

- Always putting information about upcoming tests on the chalkboard

- Always giving students time to talk before asking them to answer questions aloud

Rituals are superb classroom devices because they frequently offer students a sanctuary for their emotions, a time when they know with certainty what is expected of them. Since so much of the learning process is testing unknown waters, having occasional benchmarks of normalcy can help students feel secure.

Yet while rituals are important, we need to use them with care. If done too often, *without sufficient variation*, they may be perceived as being boring. To strike a balance between ritual and novelty, we simply need to be aware of the power of each one, and combine them where possible to create a high-level impact.

ASSESS YOUR CURRENT USE OF NOVELTY

- I frequently add novelty to my lessons.

- I occasionally teach in a novel way, but only when it seems appropriate to a particular lesson.

- I rarely do anything novel in my classroom and stick more with established classroom rituals.

Your Ideas

How will you bring more novelty into your classroom? Below, list a few upcoming lesson topics. In each case, consider if there's anything, big or small, you might do to introduce the element of surprise, innovation, or originality to the way you teach it. Remember, if in any way you can bring freshness to the topic, it will come instantly alive for students, they'll focus better, and they'll remember better.

Lesson Topic 1: _____

Novelty Ideas:_____

_____

_____

_____

_____

Lesson Topic 2: _____

Novelty Ideas:_____

_____

_____

_____

_____

Lesson Topic 3: _____

Novelty Ideas:_____

_____

_____

_____

_____

Lesson Topic 4: _____

Novelty Ideas:_____

_____

_____

_____

Lesson Topic 5: _____

Novelty Ideas: _____

_____

_____

_____

_____

O = Ownership

Thinking is the hardest work; that's why so few people bother.

In General

Giving students *ownership* means finding ways for them to be personally involved in creating, presenting, and evaluating the content we are teaching. When students are briefly in charge of what happens in the room rather than the teacher, a subtle, although important, shift occurs in their perspective of the classroom. No longer are they simply sitting back and receiving information. While the moment may be fleeting, it serves the deeper purpose of giving them a new orientation toward the class, one of involvement, responsibility, and ownership.

The Connection

Ownership is a critical part of learning for today's students, whose lives are filled with so many more choices than previous generations. From TV channels to consumer products, forms of entertainment to flavors of ice cream, no generation has ever had so much choice. It's easy to think of the Y and Z generations as being spoiled by this cornucopia of choice, but according to psychologist Barry Schwartz, choice does not lead to greater happiness. In his book, *The Paradox of Choice*, Schwartz makes the compelling case that, while limited choice is liberating, having an unlimited array of choices and few constraints is actually a burden.

As teachers, one of our jobs is to help our students carry that burden: to take responsibility for their choices. We can model this by helping them take responsibility for their learning. Learning, like life, is a journey of change, where the ability to be flexible, think critically, and adapt to new circumstances are important skills. We can help a learner to take more responsibility for their lives by giving them at least some power and control in the learning environment.

Instilling or reinforcing the desire to learn may be the single most important outcome of all education—to have the students walk away from a class with an emotionally positive, rewarding experience, while simultaneously learning the necessary content (Sviniki, 1990). If learners develop a healthy regard for the learning process, they will be better prepared to deal with the realities of today's world. We can help our students to develop this outlook by deliberately empowering them as part of the learning process.

THINKING IS THE HARDEST WORK, THAT'S WHY SO FEW PEOPLE BOTHER

The Big Picture

When students first enter a classroom, they perceive the teacher as having all the ownership for the class. It is easy to see where they get this idea. After all, the teacher is the subject-matter expert who will control what, when, and how you learn about that subject. The teacher has probably even arranged the tables and chairs. Even on an unconscious level, students walk in knowing that we, their teachers, will have a significant impact on their experience.

We may not always feel like it, but by virtue of age, experience, and role, teachers are in the dominant, controlling position. By default, students are in a far less responsible, less involved role. Under these unavoidable circumstances, how do we create an environment where students have greater ownership? The key is using small but frequent opportunities to put students in control at *appropriate* moments, where their choices or actions won't disrupt the lesson's objectives.

For example, we can give our students choices around nonessential issues, such as the order we tackle the day's topics in, how they sit, where they sit, what color they make notes in, when we take breaks, and so on. This type of focused choice plays an important role in learning contexts. Too often, learners feel they are simply being *told* what to do—and naturally they resent this. Providing people with choice may open doors that release this energy so they can focus on the information.

Offered consistently, these tiny choices help all students feel as if it is *their* learning environment, rather than the sole domain of the teacher. This distinction can create a powerful shift in how students view their environment, and as a side effect, how they perceive and encode the information. When students feel personally involved in material, they tend to look harder to find the value in the information and how it might apply to them. This attitude toward learning in general, and specifically toward the broader applicability of content, will enhance students' overall ability to remember the information.

Choice moves learners toward taking responsibility. If we give our students more options while teaching them how to choose appropriately, we will lead learners to become better decision makers. Today, that skill may improve their ability to solve a math problem, deduce a scientific principle, or choose content for an essay. But later on, it may help them to make ethical, well-informed decisions about life. Learners always make their own choices, both in the classroom and in life. By giving them more options and encouraging them to take responsibility for their choices, we teach an important life lesson.

Focus on Classroom Management

If we support our students in becoming responsible and accountable, we also derail a large amount of negative behavior in the classroom. Moreover, we help students engage with the content, enhancing their learning and long-term retention of the material.

Each student comes into the classroom with a personal history of school experiences, some positive and some negative. Each student's history is an internal chronicle of how he or she behaved in previous similar situations. Over time, these patterns of behavior become deeply ingrained and can be triggered by associations with anything recognized from those previous scenarios. Now, imagine teenagers walking into class at the beginning of the year. As they sit in their chairs or desks, they look around the room. Everything seems familiar. They remember being seated at desks, looking at chalkboards, raising their hands to ask questions, and listening to someone else speak. It all seems so familiar, and suddenly, they are flooded with memories of being in other classrooms. Even though they may have been out of school for the summer, given the confluence of these readily identifiable stimuli, those memories exert a powerful influence on their behavior.

This quick stroll down memory lane can set up poor classroom behavior before the teacher utters a single word. The familiar, negative connotations of the classroom move students into a resistive frame of mind. Most importantly, this may not conscious! Students may not even be aware of this dynamic, but simply find themselves uninterested in the current class.

We must engage these students in the learning process by holding them as responsible as possible for the interaction that occurs in the room and inviting them to share in the process of assessing the applicability of the ideas to other parts of their lives. This same idea holds true for students in middle school and even those of much younger ages. Behavioral habits can develop quite rapidly, although we have known for a long time that they are much more difficult to change in later years (e.g., Yerks & Dodson, 1908). The idea of student ownership may be one of the most powerful tools teachers have available to counteract these potentially destructive feelings.

In Practice

Here are a few of the many places where we can bring more ownership into our classrooms:

- At the start of the school year, instead of a typical introduction, allow students to ask questions.

- Allow students to choose where they want to sit. If this is too radical, perhaps consider having a seating chart for the majority of the time, but occasionally allow them the freedom to choose.

- Occasionally, allow students to help set up the classroom. This is especially effective when the arrangement of the room is something out of the ordinary—simply explain what needs to be done and where tables, desks, and chairs need to go, and ask for their help.

- Whenever a lesson has a number of things to be covered, invite your students to choose the order. For example, if students need to know seven essential terms, instead of simply starting at the first one, ask them which one they want to discuss first. Or if a lesson has three distinct components that can be taught in any order, again ask for their opinions—where do they want to begin? In a situation like this, students now have a higher level of emotional investment in the class.

- If you are planning to write student responses on the board, turn this responsibility over to your students. One student can become the "teacher" and ask for the responses while one or two others can write these responses on the board.

- Let students choose how to process content, whether by writing, drawing, or perhaps even using the Web.

- Let students choose from a list of "starter phrases" and then summarize their learning from a lesson using that phrase as a jumping-off point.

- Invite students to teach some portion of a particular class to the other students. This could be anything from a simple one-minute comment to taking over the entire lesson while you provide additional details and explanation as needed.

- If your students have resources that are theirs to keep, allow them to "own" it in some manner. For example, if they are given a packet of materials, give them 30 seconds to decorate the cover with some doodles. If they have a text, allow them to cover it in their choice of design.

- If the room is arranged so that young students have their desks in groups of four, get them to create name markers for each other's desks.

- Use student-created visuals to decorate the classroom.

- Allow your students to develop visual reminders of the content and use them as posters around your room.

- Suppose some students missed yesterday's class. The next day, you want these two students to know what was covered. Ask the students to come to the front of the room and ask the rest of the class to fill them in. You then can ask the absentees to repeat back what they think they have heard. Finally, give the class a chance to fill in anything they missed. This ownership approach to the review process will both update your absent students while simultaneously reviewing the material for the whole class.

Everyone appreciates feeling valued for what they can contribute. Students enjoy feeling they are an important part of the learning process. We need to constantly communicate this message to our students—either blatantly, by asking students to help in arranging a room, or less obviously, by giving them the opportunity to shape the lesson format. We create a sense of ownership and responsibility when we invite students to be part of their own education, growth, and development.

Next Steps

The profession of teaching is fraught with potential illusions. These educational myths are tricky because they may be true in the majority of situations, while they may be false in other, perhaps less obvious, cases. For example, some teachers may believe that a focus on content is always the most important consideration. Other teachers may hope that the push for grades will always motivate students to achieve higher levels of success. Many teachers believe a final exam is an accurate reflection of a student's understanding of the material. True or false? We tell our students a college education will lead to a higher-paying job. (Come on, be honest, you heard that one somewhere too, didn't you? Think about it: Is it necessarily true?) But of all these "illusions," perhaps none is so powerful as the belief that teachers can truly control their students.

As frightening as this may seem to some of us, effective instruction boils down to the simple concept of *influencing* the choices our students make. The weight of this influence can affect choices made both in the present and in the future (Cialdini, 1984). This leads us to an important idea: "Given all they know, people *always* make the best choice available to them."

At first glance, this idea may seem to go against common sense. Consider, however, the student who gets labeled as the "class clown." The disruptive behaviors exhibited by this student may appear to be negative choices, since they constantly result in trouble with their teachers. On closer examination, however, it might become apparent that the individual's need for attention clearly outweighs his desire to learn. From this perspective, the best choice of behavior is to make off-the-wall comments and play around during class. This way, their primary need is being served.

If we accept that, in general, people make the best choice available to them, then we also need to consider the first part of the previous statement: "*Given all they know . . .*" Now the goal of the teacher becomes clear. If they want learners to make effective, powerful choices, they must increase their awareness of the choices they have available to them. This creates the statement: "Awareness leads to choice."

Making our students take ownership for their choices is not *just* about us running an effective classroom. There is much more at stake. Our students will need this skill to be successful adults. By occasionally offering

them choice and control in the classroom, we help our students develop a
critical lifelong learning skill.

ASSESS YOUR CURRENT USE OF OWNERSHIP

- I give my students as much ownership of the classroom experience as possible.

- I occasionally allow my students to take ownership of what is happening in the classroom.

- I tend to be in charge most of the time, and only rarely allow students to take ownership.

Your Ideas

How will you bring more ownership into your classroom? What choices
can you allow your students to make? How can they have more input into
the flow of a lesson? Below, list some topics you'll be covering in the near
future. In each case, see if you can find some "opportunities for ownership" for your students.

First Topic:_____

Opportunity for Ownership: _____

_____

_____

_____

Second Topic: _____

Opportunity for Ownership: _____

_____

_____

_____

Third Topic:_____

Opportunity for Ownership: _____

_____

_____

_____

Fourth Topic:_____

Opportunity for Ownership: _____

_____

_____

_____

P = Pause

Pausing for processing improves understanding.

In General

When we give our students new visual information, we must also give them time to process it. We need to allow students to become fully comfortable with an image before we start explaining it or adding other information that builds on it. Depending on the complexity of the visual, this may take only a few seconds, or as much as a minute. Regardless, we always need to make time for students to organize a mental image of the material and get used to it.

The Connection

Visuals are an enormous part of the learning world of Gen Y and Z students. On the Internet, for example, they scan site after site rapidly and easily, visually processing an enormous amount of information in a brief period of time. Given that visuals play such a natural and frequent role in their normal experiences, they rightfully expect them to be present in other aspects of their lives, such as the classroom.

However, even with this level of experience with visuals, we need to give them enough *time* to process the information, without interference of any kind. Only when they have had sufficient time to fully intake the new information will they truly be ready to move forward with the lesson.

The Big Picture

To see this issue clearly, examine the following situation.

The teacher is busy delivering a lesson using PowerPoint slides. The students are busy copying the information down in their notebooks. When the teacher is ready to move on to the next overhead, he clicks over to a new slide and keeps right on talking.

What's the first thing students do when they see the new slide? Naturally, they'll want to understand it, so they take a moment to study it. And here's the problem. If they are concentrating on the visual, then they are *not* concentrating on what the teacher is saying. Or if they are furiously trying to copy down the information, they are more focused on getting it all down than on understanding what it means, while paying absolutely no attention at all to the teacher's commentary.

However, the teacher in this situation does not appreciate the difficulty his students are having, and he plows on full steam ahead. He is blissfully unaware that he has just left most of them bobbing helplessly behind in his enthusiastic wake. He is then amazed to discover that the students failed to remember most of what he was talking about! He is shocked that they don't remember the material, because he *knows* he said it! He reprimands them for not paying close enough attention to the material.

As students ourselves, we fully understood this problem. We've all been in the situation where the lecturer is talking and we're still desperately trying to understand the slide. It's simply not conducive to effective learning.

The good news is, there's a simple solution. *Pause whenever you present an important new piece of visual information.* It's that easy. Simply don't talk for a moment. Give your students a chance to put all their attention into understanding the visual. Don't speak again until you think everyone has seen and feels comfortable with the new visual information. Then, after they have had time to construct a mental picture, they will be able to concentrate more fully on what is being said.

The first time you use this approach, it may feel awkward. It might not seem natural to simply stop speaking while you're in the flow of teaching.

Yet the longer you use this technique, the more you'll see it working for your students. You will reduce the incidence of "notetaking panic," since your students no longer have to try to capture everything simultaneously. They are free to focus on only one thing at a time. In this more relaxed, stress-free learning environment, their ability to retain information will increase immediately.

Of course, in many situations students *can* have their attention divided and still be able to learn effectively. One of the most common examples occurs when students are listening and taking notes about what they are hearing at the same time. The key to the idea explained here is based primarily on the complexity of the visual being shown. If students' attention is going to be so distracted that it reduces their ability to concentrate simultaneously on other relevant information, then pausing to help them concentrate is very helpful.

Finally, don't pause too long or too frequently during a lesson! The constant interruption of lengthy, unnecessary silences would get tedious very quickly. Pause only when it's necessary to assist your students in concentrating on new, complex visual information.

Focus on Classroom Management

The primary goal in these situations is to avoid splitting the students' focus. If we simultaneously show a new visual while continuing to speak, we are asking students to pay full attention both to what is being shown *and* to what is being said. What happens? The students end up putting only half of their focus in each direction, reducing their understanding of both. This can be intensely frustrating for students and makes it hard for them to keep up. And we all know what happens to the behavior of frustrated students who get left behind. They give up and act out.

In Practice

There are a number of places where pausing for a new visual might come in handy. Here are just a few of the many situations you might apply this idea.

■ **When Using PowerPoint Presentations:** Using PowerPoint or similar programs as visual aids is becoming increasingly popular in many classrooms. Despite these useful advances in technology, the underlying ideas of learning still apply. Each new visual shown is similar to a new slide, flipchart, or overhead. As dictated by the density of the information displayed, we need to pause long enough to allow students to understand and process the image before proceeding.

■ **When Distributing Handouts:** Even though each person will have their own copy of the visual, the same idea applies. Give students a moment to glance completely through the handout before providing any comments or explanations about what they have received.

■ **When Demonstrating the Solution to a Math Problem on the Chalkboard:** Since our back is often turned to the students, part of the information may be obscured from some of them. Once the solution is complete, turn around and step aside so everyone can clearly view it. Remain silent while the students study the steps in the solution.

■ **When Writing Ideas on a Chalkboard:** The same idea applies. Depending on the complexity of your information, students might find it useful to have a moment to process and organize the information in their own minds.

■ **When Using Flipcharts:** Some teachers prepare paper flipcharts in advance, then tape these on the wall for use during the lesson. If you have more than a few flipcharts, consider asking students to walk around and review them in preparation for the upcoming discussion. Perhaps it might even be useful to do this in pairs. As they walk, your students can discuss each chart—helping them to process the information in an engaging way.

Next Steps

Written notes are another critical part of the visual aspect of learning. The idea of pausing for visuals should also apply here. If you are speaking and suddenly see many students taking notes, then perhaps you've said something worth remembering! So don't interfere with the notetaking process; stop your commentary and let them gather your pearls of wisdom for future reference.

We need to recognize these precious learning moments and do our best to respond to them by pausing, even if we're in the middle of a sentence. When students have written whatever it was that caught their attention, they generally look back up. So when most of the room is looking expectantly at you, you'll know it's time to continue.

There's another way we can honor students as they take notes. Students often experience a sensation of panicked energy when trying to take down what the teacher is saying. When in this frantic state of mind, they rarely take the time to glance back over what they have just scribbled on their paper. They are rushing to get the next name, date, or statistic written down correctly. They may not look back over what they have written until that night, the next day, or perhaps even the following week.

But if they fail to return to the information until a much later point in time, they will miss a golden opportunity for long-term learning. The images, ideas, or stories that were connected to the few words they had time to jot down will quickly fade from their memory. We can help ensure this does not happen. Here's a suggestion for how to increase student recall when they have taken notes.

Give them classroom time to briefly review what they have just written in their notebooks. Perhaps you could pause every ten or fifteen minutes and give them two minutes to look over what they have written so far. During this time, encourage your students to add other notes to help them remember the information. You might suggest they draw symbols, diagrams, or doodles to help trigger their memories through visual cues. Finally, give them a minute to ask clarifying questions about the information they've just taken notes about.

Taking the time to do things like this can help students avoid that moment later when they are studying, as they stare at their notes in amazement, wondering "Why did I write that down?" If this has ever happened to you as a student, you'll be familiar with this frustrating, hair-pulling experience. Your students' retention will increase immediately and dramatically if you give them even a brief moment in the classroom to review and reflect on their notes.

By supporting your students when they take written notes—either by pausing or helping them to build long-term memories—you will make learning the material faster and easier. Making sure your students have sufficient time to build the mental connections between the information they are hearing and the notes they are taking encourages their natural learning process. It may also remove some of the panic and alarm students often experience in class and fill them, instead, with increased levels of confidence and optimism.

ASSESS YOUR CURRENT USE OF PAUSE

- I carefully and consciously pause during lessons and allow students to process new information before moving forward.

- I occasionally pause at key moments, but could probably do this much more frequently during my lessons.

- I only pause when there is a natural break in the way the lesson has been designed, perhaps to ask the students a question.

Your Ideas

Plan carefully when you'll be using visuals in the near future, so you'll know when and for how long to pause. For at least three upcoming lessons, note what kind of visuals will be a part of the lesson. Then, decide on a "Pause Plan"—simply meaning how long you'll pause, given the amount of content being shown, the complexity of it, and whether or not your students have seen it before.

Lesson Topic 1: _____

Visuals Used: _____

Pause Plan: _____

_____

_____

Lesson Topic 2: _____

Visuals Used: _____

Pause Plan: _____

_____

_____

Lesson Topic 3: _____

Visuals Used: _____

Pause Plan: _____

_____

_____

Lesson Topic 4: _____

Visuals Used: _____

Pause Plan: _____

_____

_____

Lesson Topic 5: _____

Visuals Used: _____

Pause Plan: _____

_____

_____

Q = Questions

Effective questions are the key to deeper learning and understanding.

In General

As teachers, when we ask students questions during lessons, it allows them to interact with new information at a more profound level than simply listening. However, *how* we ask these questions is a key aspect of making this part of learning successful. In particular, the *question-clarify-question* format (Q/C/Q) offers us a practical, powerful, and precise three-step sequence for creating focused, thoughtful, and animated student conversations. It helps us achieve the highest possible impact when we align students' thoughts in the proper direction during these discussions.

The Connection

Seeking answers has always been a key component of how students learn. Yet now, more than ever, students' ability to focus their search for understanding *in the proper direction* is important. With the amount of information available today, the skill of unearthing the necessary details—while simultaneously seeing the global picture—has become increasingly critical.

This dual learning modality is not just important while Gen Y and Z children are students; it will continue to grow in significance when they become adults. The students in today's classrooms will emerge as adults in a world where the amount of information available will dwarf today's apparently information-saturated environment. We must teach our students to sift through mountains of facts and figures while holding onto the central theme of their inquiry. By encouraging their development in this area of learning as students, we will also support their long-term success as adults.

The Big Picture

The question-clarify-question sequence comprises three distinct phases:

1. Ask the general question.

2. Provide details that clarify the question.

3. Repeat the original question.

Each component plays an important part in achieving our desired result:

- In the first phase, we state the question clearly to allow students to see the overall picture.

- In the second phase, we provide details to help students understand the type of responses we expect.

- Finally, we repeat the original question—usually slightly rephrased—to serve as a springboard for the group to jump into the general discussion.

Without this clear, linear setup, students' responses will often be hesitant, vague, or accidentally off purpose. However, using this three-step sequence will guide students in our intended direction.

Once you begin to use this idea consistently, you'll see how powerful it is at helping your students to both (1) rapidly engage in the conversation and (2) be able to generate answers that focus on your intended line of instruction.

Focus on Classroom Management

The idea of precisely focusing students' attention in an intended direction keeps them on task and responding appropriately. However, it can also have other equally important benefits. By adapting this questioning technique slightly, we can avoid a number of potential distractions.

For example, a teacher is leading a class in which a vocal minority tend to dominate by frequently making sarcastic, off-the-wall remarks. Every time the group is given an opportunity to share their thoughts, these individuals make distracting, silly comments. At first the teacher laughs along with the rest of the group, hoping it will cease as the class continues. When it doesn't, the teacher tries to simply ignore this pattern of behavior, but to no avail. Finally, the teacher realizes something must be done about the situation.

Here's an idea for dealing with this situation, based on the Q/C/Q principle. The basic idea is quite simple: Give those jokesters a brief forum in which to play. Focus their energy, while acknowledging the humor they bring to the situation. For example, we might say something along these lines: "Why do you think we include a section on this particular topic in this course? Discuss this with your neighbor. See if you can generate at least three possibilities. However, at least one of these *must be a sarcastic response*! So discuss with your group—what are some reasons why we might have included this section?"

Then, when the time has come for the small groups to share their thoughts with the whole class, you begin by asking for sarcastic responses only. After these have been enjoyed by everyone, you state: "Those were great. Thanks. Now, let's move to the other point of view. In a more serious vein, why do you think we might include this topic in this course?"

Now the group sees the clear shift in our expectations. Indirectly, we have identified the sarcastic responses as having had an appropriate time and place, while having set some parameters to limit their use. We've now also established that this is not the appropriate time to make another sarcastic response. In a subtle manner, peer pressure has stepped in to help us keep the class focused in the appropriate direction.

Offering students the opportunity to express their humorous, sarcastic, off-beat responses achieves several objectives simultaneously. First, it takes the energy away from the potentially disruptive nature of the remarks—they can no longer be disruptive if they are exactly what the teacher is seeking! Second, since humor now has the official "stamp of approval" at clearly designated times, these dispensers of sarcasm often no longer find the same joy in it as they did before. It has been legitimized. Oddly enough, many will stop making those comments altogether. Indeed, handled correctly it can provide light, relaxed moments that further enhance the learning environment by creating a contrast that highlights more serious moments.

In Practice

Here are three examples of different areas in the classroom where the
Q/C/Q technique is particularly useful.

■ **Small-Group Student Discussions:** A history teacher might say, "As
a group, discuss what you think were some of the most significant factors
that resulted in the Great Depression of the 1930s. For example, do you
think it was primarily overspending by the public, or was it a sudden lack
of jobs, or the government's failure to provide sufficient regulation of certain industries in the preceding years? What do you think were some of the
most significant causes of the Great Depression?"

■ **Providing Clarity:** A math teacher might say, "What aspects of this
chapter would you like me to talk more about? Do you want more information about the theory, more practice on the problems, or is there one
particular aspect of the problems that always seems to be difficult? Check
your notes for a minute, and see what points you'd like me to explain
further."

■ **Responding to a Lecture:** A science teacher might say, "I've been talking about the ongoing search for other planets in the galaxy that might be
inhabitable by mankind, what we've done, and what we've found so far.
What do *you* think? Do you think we should be doing more? If so, what?
And do you think it's important that we find other inhabitable planets, or
is this just a wild goose chase that really has no purpose? I'm interested;
what are your reactions to what I've been talking about?"

Next Steps

The key to the question-clarify-question format is that it provides specific
guidelines for where students should focus their discussions, questions,
or general responses. If you're not getting the quality of responses you're
seeking, consider thinking through how you originally set up the question. Perhaps the Q/C/Q format might provide more precise and valuable
responses.

Equally important, remember humor is not necessarily a negative quality, and a variation on the basic Q/C/Q approach often allows us to maintain a comfortable level of humor. Individuals who bring humor to a group
can be highly valued if their energy is focused in an appropriate direction.
People who are quick-witted are often quite intelligent, and if guided correctly, have the potential of becoming powerful, positive parts of any learning situation. Instead of attempting to shut them down, consider using this

strategy to guide their humor so it can be acknowledged for the positive energy it brings. Doing this will simultaneously clearly delineate the times where humor is *not* the appropriate choice.

ASSESS YOUR CURRENT USE OF QUESTIONS

■ I often ask questions using the Q/C/Q format to help students more clearly understand what I am asking.

■ I occasionally use the Q/C/Q format, but could probably do this much more often to help students better understand what I'm asking.

■ I tend to ask traditional questions and have not had the opportunity to try the Q/C/Q format.

Your Ideas

Consider some of your upcoming lessons. Select a few where you know you'll be asking the students for input, questions, or ideas. For at least three of these lessons, first clearly identify where you'll be asking for student responses. Then, carefully write out how you'll use the Q/C/Q format to elicit the best possible responses.

Topic 1:_____

Moment for Questions: _____

_____

Question: _____

_____

Clarify: _____

_____

_____

_____

_____

Question: _____

_____

Topic 2:_____

Moment for Questions: _____

_____

Question: _____

_____

Clarify: _____

_____

_____

_____

_____

Question: _____

_____

Topic 3:_____

Moment for Questions: _____

_____

Question: _____

_____

Clarify: _____

_____

_____

_____

_____

Question: _____

_____

Topic 4: _____

Moment for Questions: _____

_____

Question: _____

_____

Clarify: _____

_____

_____

_____

_____

Question: _____

_____

Topic 5: _____

Moment for Questions: _____

_____

Question: _____

_____

Clarify: _____

_____

_____

_____

_____

Question: _____

_____

R = Revolutions

Open loops result in revolutionary levels of learning.

In General

The circular nature of expectation and discovery is often the driving energy behind successful teaching. When students become fascinated with solving a puzzle, intrigued by unraveling a mystery, or simply want to know what comes next, they begin to take a high level of ownership for their learning. We can create this effect by introducing an *open loop*, which we then close as the learning comes full circle.

By definition, an open loop is any statement, action, visual device, or other event that tells our students what is coming or arouses their curiosity and invites them to know more. As teachers, we can use open loops to set the stage for what is about happen, inciting anticipation and curiosity in our students.

The Connection

For today's students, open loops are a constant part of their online learning experience. They are used to new elements popping up in online games—

new characters, new gadgets, new traps. These things don't come with a formal introduction—they just appear, and the user knows they will find out about them in the course of the game. By using this same technique in our classrooms, we can trigger in our students this same "Oh, cool, something interesting is about to happen" feeling—not a bad emotion with which to start a lesson!

The Big Picture

Open loops create a sense of expectation. We can make them through a simple statement, a sign, a poster, or a sentence on the board. A guitar placed in plain view, even though never mentioned, may serve as an open loop if it is used later. Or perhaps we put a box with colorful supplies sticking out of the top in plain view of our learners. All these events are open loops: They serve the purpose of arousing learner curiosity (Berlyne, 1965; Keller, 1987).

Closed properly, open loops create a sense of accomplishment, leading students to want to know more. The student experiences a sense of "Aha! Now I see!" This sense of success is an extremely powerful learning dynamic—one that can be used on many levels to help students succeed.

To gain a clear perspective on how open loops help learners, try the following experiment for yourself:

> "Wherever you are as you read this, follow along with the instructions. First, right now, notice the feeling in the bottom of your feet. How do your toes feel? Next, check out the feelings in your legs. How about your back? Your arms? Your fingers? OK, relax!"

So now you're aware how your feet feel. But what about before you were given these instructions—was there still feeling in your feet, even though your attention wasn't directly focused on it? Of course there was; you were just unconscious of it—your attention was focused elsewhere. In fact, our five senses (touch, sight, sound, taste, and smell) guide stimuli from the environment into our brains all the time. We aren't aware of it, but our senses are in *constant operation:* scientists estimate a human brain receives thousands of different bits of information every waking second (LaBerge, 1990).

Given all that incoming information, how does our brain know what to focus on? How do we sort out the chaos of incoming stimuli and locate the key bits of information we need to pay attention to? Fortunately our brain has an amazing focusing mechanism called the *reticular activating system,* or RAS.

The RAS is the sorting mechanism that makes decisions about which stimuli are important to *consciously* focus on and which can be processed on an *unconscious* level (Driscoll, 1994, pp. 262–268). The RAS allows the brain to concentrate on what is most important, while moving the other information to the background.

If you've ever been in one of the following situations, you've probably experienced this RAS phenomenon for yourself.

You're hungry, but you decide to walk to a restaurant three blocks away for lunch. As you walk along the street, what do you notice? Signs about food, pictures of food, restaurant signs advertising food. What do you smell? The sandwich in the hand of a man walking past you. Fresh bread from the bakery. Fresh coffee being brewed in the corner deli. Suddenly, food is everywhere!

Or, have you ever decided on the make, model, and color of the new car you want? Once you were very clear about what you wanted, what happened? Did you start noticing that exact car everywhere around you, passing you on your way to work, behind you on the freeway, and parked at the grocery store? Suddenly it seems that car is coming at you from every direction.

Why do these things happen? The answer is actually quite simple. It's because you "programmed" your RAS to become acutely aware of the food or the car. Once it became clear to your brain that these were the most important elements in your environment, the RAS focused on finding them and registering them in your conscious mind. By the way, did you feel a little hungry just now while reading the food example? If so, that's another demonstration that your RAS is functioning quite well.

In the example where you were asked to focus on different

REACH THEM...
THEN TEACH THEM

parts of your body, your RAS was directing you to experience certain sensory inputs at that moment, though you had been unconsciously aware of them all along. The instructions you were reading directed your RAS where to focus your thoughts.

As teacher, we can use the RAS mechanism to great effect. We can direct learners' unconscious attention to focus on the most important aspects of the information.

And if we do this appropriately, the learner is more likely to retain the information on which they have been directed to focus.

Focus on Classroom Management

Open loops create a dynamic that drives students to find a way to "close the loop." In the classroom when we focus students' attention on seeking answers, their attention is less likely to wander into unsuitable and potentially unfortunate areas. Their desire to close these loops will help keep both their conscious and unconscious attention levels pointing in an appropriate direction, thus minimizing the potential for behavior problems.

Our students, like all human beings, have a strong desire to close loops. For instance, have you ever been in a car, listening to one of your favorite songs? You're enjoying this tune as you cruise on down the road, happily singing along. However, right at the very end of the song, the DJ fades it out and fades up an ad. How do you feel? Cheated and almost irrationally irritated? That's because the loop didn't close. The longer you were listening to this song, the stronger the loop, and the greater your irritation that you didn't get to hear the end lyrics.

What creates this effect? It's the desire within each of us to bring things to completion. Look at this figure; what do you see?

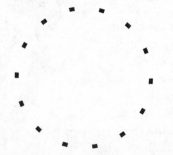

Most people see a circle—not a series of arcs. We mentally join the lines. Even our visual field has a desire for closure! In the classroom, we can use this natural human phenomenon as one more tool in our instructional toolkit to focus and maintain attention in the proper direction, resulting in a better learning environment for everyone.

In Practice

Here are some examples of open loops. Each is followed by a brief explanation showing one situation where you could use it.

Example 1: "We found three elements during this analysis . . ."

A loop consisting of three elements has now been created. To close the loop, we must cover all three elements. What happens if class ends and we've only introduced two elements? There is an open loop still out there, and we'd better close it at the start of the next class or half the class will come at the next bell asking about the third element. The use of a specified number in an open loop is sometimes referred to as a *framework*. The following statements are further examples of frameworks:

- "I'd like to make eight points tonight."
- "There are really only two ways to look at this issue."
- "Four primary factors led to this decision."
- "Five distinct issues led to their downfall."

In general, if we have a set number of points to make, it helps learners if they know this number in advance. Now they can mentally prepare themselves to receive and organize the appropriate amount of information.

Example 2: "In 30 seconds, when I say *go* . . ."

This phrase, used when giving students directions, creates a very short open loop that informs precisely *when* the action is going to occur. The brief duration of this loop demonstrates an important factor in using loops. Open short loops early in a class and close them fairly quickly. This builds confidence with learners that all loops will be closed. Now the teacher can create larger and larger loops, and the impact of these loops on learners' attention will be increased. For example, suppose we announce something will happen in 10 minutes, and it actually does. This builds our credibility. Now when we tell learners they will have mastered this new skill by the end of the week, they will be more inclined to believe us.

Example 3: "Next week we'll be taking a look at . . ."

This is a phrase frequently used by teachers across many contexts. It opens a loop by indicating the topic will be covered the following week. It is included here exactly because it has that familiar ring to it. Familiarity may be useful in some situations. However, if students have heard a particular phrase quite often, they may not pay attention to it, thereby reducing the effect when the loop is closed. Instead, try to be as creative as possible with language to maximize the reaction from the learners. In this situation, we might instead say: "Let's end here, so when we return next week your minds can be focused on the most critical aspect of this entire unit . . ."

With these slightly different words, the learners may be listening more closely. The more carefully they are paying attention to the loop, the more the RAS will be engaged, and the more powerful the effect will be when the loop is closed.

Example 4: "Here are my final two ideas, and then we'll take a break."

Suppose this statement were made in a setting where the learners were beginning to get restless. The intention of the statement is to let them know that a break is definitely going to be happening soon. Now they are aware they only have two more ideas left, they will be able to fully engage all their remaining attention and stay with the material being delivered. However, if we use this phrase, we'd better be sure to get to the announced break fairly soon. If not, students may begin to doubt our integrity—a definite distraction.

Example 5: "This next piece could be the most valuable hour of the entire year for some of you."

With these words, the teacher is focusing the student's RAS mechanism intently on the value of the next piece of information. They will want to pay close attention to the content being delivered, on the chance that *they* are one of the people for whom this would be a useful piece of information! Clearly, we can't use open loops like this too often—they really do have to be about the single most important piece of information. Used too often, they lose their effect.

Example 6: "You don't have to believe me now; you'll see evidence of this tomorrow."

This statement actually serves a dual purpose. In terms of open loops, students will now be watching carefully for the purported "evidence" in the next day's session. However, it also allows them to pay attention to the information without getting caught up in evaluating whether or not it is true. This "mental editor," as it is sometimes called, can stop our students from even considering information if they have a negative initial impression. The first half of the statement allows the teacher to at least temporarily filter out some of the possible negative aspects of the student's internal editor.

Example 7: "Please take about two minutes to walk around the room with your group and discuss the posters on the walls. Which concepts have you already encountered, and which are new to you?"

In this situation, new posters had been placed on the walls of the room that morning before class began. By giving the students two minutes to obtain an overview of the information, the teacher is creating a huge open loop. Students now understand the general direction of the upcoming lesson. They will also be bringing to mind any information they know related to these concepts, which could then be brought into future discussions. This validates them as people and acknowledges the work they have done as students so far in the class.

Example 8: "For you folks on the left side of the room, I'll have a question for you in a few moments. For those of you on the right side, here's your question . . ."

When used correctly, this type of open loop creates a wonderful effect. The following example came from my observation of an actual class. Here was the situation:

The room was divided into two halves, separated by an aisle down the middle. The class was going to break for lunch soon. The students appeared slightly restless, and the teacher wanted to do something a little extra to keep them paying close attention to the content. She turned and created the open loop exactly as it is stated above.

The right side of the room got a question. However, it was a simple, fairly innocuous question which those students easily answered. When the interaction was complete, the teacher continued teaching. She made no mention of the fact that the students on the left side of the room were still expecting a question. What effect did this have on the audience?

As I watched from the back of the room, there were two reactions. Both, however, served the same purpose. The students on the left half of the room that had not yet answered a question were watching the teacher closely, anticipating that their question could be coming at any moment. On the right side, students who had already answered a question were also watching the teacher, knowing that she still had to ask a question of the other side of the room. In other words, *both sides were paying careful attention* to what the teacher was saying!

This teacher was excellent at the game of keeping them attentive. Twice during her subsequent instruction she paused, looked at the side of the room that had yet to receive a question, and smiled knowingly before going back to teaching! This both entertained the class and kept them tuned in. In fact, she was able to go almost *15 minutes* before turning to the left side of the room and saying "Now, I've got a question for this side of the room . . ."

What was their reaction when she finally said this? As you might guess, there was an audible sigh of relief as they realized it was finally their turn! This occurred even though this second question also added very little to students' understanding of the material! It was not the question itself that mattered, rather it was *how the question was used in the course of the instruction.*

Notice that unless we have a good relationship with the students, this situation could potentially cause an unwanted backlash. The class could easily end up paying close attention, but not be listening to the material. However in this case, the teacher was quite animated and able to maintain interest during those 15 minutes using humor, body gestures, vocal changes, and her gift at storytelling. The use of the open loop was simply one more tool to further the cause of instruction.

To summarize these examples, here are some of basic structures of open loops teachers might consider using:

- A numbered list, such as "There are three main points . . ."

- A short time frame, such as "In 30 seconds . . ."

- A longer time frame, such as "Next week we'll look at . . ."

- An indicator when something will be changing, such as "After we finish this we'll be taking a break . . ."

- An indicator of value, such as "This is the part you might find most useful . . ."

- A creator of curiosity, such as "You may not want to believe me right now, but you probably will by the end of the week."

- A signal that something new is happening, such as "There are some new posters in the room . . ."

- A creator of expectation, such as "I have a completely different task for the girls, which I'll get to shortly . . ."

Next Steps

The concept of open loops is not limited to teaching environments. They are everywhere around us. Recognizing their universal appeal helps us realize the incredible potential of this tool in a classroom.

From now on your RAS will prompt you to notice open loops in marketing and advertising. You'll hear the first few notes of a jingle and picture the product. You'll notice them in every novel: One large loop contains the plot of the book, while numerous smaller loops are opened and closed as the story moves forward, drawing you onward.

ASSESS YOUR CURRENT USE OF REVOLUTIONS

- I use frequent and deliberate open loops to help keep my students engaged and in a state of anticipation.

- I occasionally use open loops, but it has been more by accident then design.

- I only use open loops when they are obvious, such as when students can expect to be tested.

Your Ideas

Open loops come in a variety of forms. However, they all share one common objective: To alert the students to what is coming and its potential value to them. Providing this perspective makes learners more receptive to new information and better able to remember it. Make sure you close all the loops you open. This will help your students lock away the information for later recall.

Consider some of your upcoming lessons. In at least three lessons, decide how you'll create an open loop, and how and when you'll close it.

Lesson 1: _____

How I'll Use an Open Loop: _____

_____

_____

_____

How I'll Close This Open Loop: _____

_____

_____

_____

Lesson 2: _____

How I'll Use an Open Loop: _____

_____

_____

_____

How I'll Close This Open Loop: _____

_____

_____

_____

Lesson 3: _____

How I'll Use an Open Loop: _____

_____

_____

_____

How I'll Close This Open Loop: _____

_____

_____

_____

Lesson 4: _____

How I'll Use an Open Loop: _____

_____

_____

_____

How I'll Close This Open Loop: _____

_____

_____

_____

Lesson 5: _____

How I'll Use an Open Loop: _____

_____

_____

_____

How I'll Close This Open Loop: _____

_____

_____

_____

S = Socialization

Friendship is one mind in two bodies.

In General

For teaching to be effective, students need to *talk* about what they are learning. This is because, when talking about a topic, they must first think about and mentally process the information. As they discuss the content, they verbally process the ideas. As a result, they come to a better, deeper, and more complete understanding of what they are studying. In addition, while talking, they will practice using new vocabulary, take a higher level of ownership for their learning, and better recognize connections between new concepts, terms, and ideas. When all these things happen, students are more likely to truly comprehend and retain new information.

In many cases, through conversations with their peers, students can often discover the core of the lesson on their own. Moreover, working together in a social situation allows students to grasp material far more rapidly than merely listening to it and taking written notes (Fernandez-Berrocaal & Santamaria, 2006). Thus, if we want our classes to have the strongest possible positive impact, we should not only allow, but even *encourage*, students to talk to each other frequently during our lessons (Myhill, Jones, & Hopper, 2005).

The Connection

Because of advances in technology, today's students are in constant and consistent contact with each other—far more so than any generation has ever been before. Through cell phones, email, text, or chat, they remain in close, regular contact with family, friends, and classmates. When this connection is severed—even for the short time in a traditional classroom where talking is not permitted—it can be disorienting and disconcerting. Indeed, anytime we remove something integral from our natural order, it disrupts our natural rhythms and rituals.

At first, of course, students will think of talking to their peers as merely an opportunity to ramble aimlessly from thought to thought, as they might do in their typical interactions outside the classroom. However, once they have been shown how they can apply their natural conversational desires in the classroom to become a focused mechanism for learning, most will pounce on the idea joyfully and grab tight to this lifeline to their lives beyond the walls of the classroom. They will relish the opportunity to do what they do naturally, often, and *well*—and learn more easily while doing it.

The Big Picture

The truth is, intuitively most teachers seem to recognize talking as an essential component of effective instruction. However, in a traditional classroom, the primary way students are given permission to talk—often the *only* way—is by responding to a question posed by the teacher (Pontefract & Hardman, 2005). In this situation, students are indeed talking when responding to a question. However, a closer look at this typical classroom moment can be quite revealing.

Within this seemingly innocuous teaching strategy lurk a number of hidden dangers. What if a student doesn't know what to say? What if the answer they provide is wrong? What if a student begins to respond, yet stumbles on the words and feels embarrassed? Traditional classrooms—where students are only allowed to talk *publicly* in response to the teacher's questions—are high-threat learning environments. The sort of talking these classrooms permit is unlikely to assist the learning process.

High-Impact Classrooms, on the other hand, provide students with numerous opportunities to talk within the context of a lesson. These discussions allow students to learn through peer-to-peer social interactions, absent any of the dangers that lie in wait in typical question-and-answer sessions. Whenever we give students a chance to work together, they will likely feel more connected to the core content, leading to a deeper understanding—and a higher level of comprehension—of the new concepts (Williams, 2007).

Lecturing is often falsely accused of being all that is wrong with teaching. In certain situations, it is a perfectly reasonable means of giving students key content. It allows the teacher to explain, clarify, and elaborate on the information as needed. However, it can't go on for too long. While lecturing can serve an important function in delivering information, it is only *part* of the much greater learning process.

After approximately 10 to 15 minutes of lecturing, students will mentally overload (Ruhl, Hughes, & Schloss, 1987). *Student-to-student* discussions offer a wonderfully effective way to break up lecturing into manageable segments. However, pausing in the middle of a lecture to allow students to talk to each other is only one of many ways of bringing more social interaction into the classroom. For social learning to be most effective, students need to interact in a variety of formats (Moura, 2006).

That said, we need to be cautious of the way we set students up to work together. "Peer coaching," for example, can be an excellent teaching strategy (Cropley, 2006). However setting up these peer-coaching situations can create problems. For example, we must avoid the feeling that all the smart students are helping all the stupid ones. If we don't handle the setup appropriately, we can accidentally create a negative emotional tone that will undermine any value gained by the students' interaction. This can make students on both sides of the equation resentful. However, if we set up peer-coaching moments as friends helping each other learn, students will enjoy these sessions, remaining focused and on task.

Focus on Classroom Management

Tapping directly into students' natural interactive mode and guiding it to become a useful teaching technique can turn a potential classroom disruption into a positive force for teaching. Moreover, allowing students to talk helps avoid information overload. When students are bombarded with too much information their concentration wavers, interest diminishes, and the quality of their notes suffers. When students begin to slide down the slippery slope of a mental meltdown, behavior problems frequently ensue. They're bored and they simply can't take any more, so they begin to act out.

Student conversations effectively allocate "brain breaks" for these struggling students to discuss the new information with their peers. This allows them to "download" the information, process it, make connections, and prepare for the next wave of input. These brief conversations essentially allow them to breathe for a moment. Ultimately it makes the lesson more effective and students become more focused learners during lectures, because the segments aren't long enough for them to disengage.

Perhaps the most important point about student conversations and classroom management is that if we *don't* allow these moments to occur frequently, students may very well end up doing them anyway. Unable to resist the urge to talk, they begin side talking, whispering, or passing notes. When their focus wanders like this, they definitely aren't paying attention to the lesson! The key is to read what your class requires, and if they need to talk, let them do what they need to do (Mercer & Sams, 2006). Then, as needed, gently guide them back into a discussion about the content.

SMILES
ARE CONTAGIOUS

In Practice

We have numerous opportunities for social interaction at our disposal. The key is to find which ones fit your teaching style, your students, and the content of each lesson. Remember, one of the essential ingredients to being an effective teacher at any level is to take a fundamentally successful teaching strategy and discover *alternative application options.* This is especially true when finding ways to incorporate more social interactions in your classroom. Keep that in mind as you look over the following possible ideas:

■ As has already been discussed—but is absolutely worth mentioning again—stopping in the middle of the lecture to allow students to discuss the material is one of the primary ways of introducing more group conversations.

■ The idea of "mismatching" can be an effective approach to generate productive student conversations. Normally, we ask students to work together to find the right answer. When we use mismatching, one student in a group deliberately makes a mistake, and the goal of the others is try to find the mistake. Many students love the opportunity to do something wrong, especially when it is on purpose! While students think they are merely having fun, we know that the only way to know they are wrong is if they know what is right! Without realizing it, when mismatching, students are actually cementing their understanding of the content.

■ For some lessons, we can create a matching social situation where the content might be used in a conversational role-play. For example, if young students are learning to count change, perhaps they could play out becoming a store owner and a customer. During this interactive play, they will learn to add and subtract basic numbers. If learning vocabulary, perhaps they pretend to explain the meaning of words to a younger sibling. Any content that will be used in a social context should be taught—at least partially—in that context. This brings the content to life and makes it real. Learning a concept within the borders of its matching social setting will increase students' ability to recall it later when that situation actually arises.

■ Group conversations can often be stimulated by physical objects. If you have physical objects related to your content, give them to a group to examine up close. Perhaps you could ask each group to explain the object to the rest of the class: what their object is and how it relates to the unit they are studying. Or the group could use the objects to create a story about where it came from, who owned it, and how it was used. The dynamic combination of objects and small groups coming together can offer many unique teaching strategies.

■ Could students occasionally be the "teacher"? When we give students the opportunity to become the teacher for a particular lesson, or part of a lesson, the amount they learn and remember increases exponentially. Telling the other students about the material, combined with the heightened emotions involved in this process, dramatically increases levels of learning.

■ If the idea of one student talking in front of the entire class is too overwhelming, perhaps the same process could be done in small groups. For example, each member of a group could be responsible for teaching the other members of their group a particular part of a lesson. Or one group could be responsible for teaching another group a part of a lesson.

■ Many review situations are perfect for allowing student conversations. Students could test each other within their own group, or perhaps as a group they could prepare some questions to pose to the other groups. The key here is that students are often unaware of the amount of effort they are expending when they work in groups to review content. Since their conscious focus is on something else—the social interactions they are having—they are often distracted from thinking, "I don't want to review again, that's so boring!" The social dynamic of working together allows them to engage fully in the lesson.

High-Impact Teaching offers frequent opportunities for social interaction. We need to give our students regular opportunities to process new information through peer-to-peer conversations. These conversations will open the door to improved understanding, better questions, and sharper recall.

Next Steps

Often, when we first try out the idea of allowing students to talk to each other, the biggest challenge is that we simply . . . *forget!* Meaning, we are so caught up in the normal teaching modes, we forget to take that moment to pause and—briefly at least—put the lesson in the hands of the students. If you struggle with this, find a way to "remind" yourself to allow your students to talk to each other—especially in lecture situations—at select times throughout a lesson.

You could even ask your students to remind you to pause for conversation. Get them to tell you when 15 minutes have passed, even if they need to interrupt you in the middle of a key point. This strategy allows student ownership (*see* O = Ownership)—a powerful tool for involving students in the learning process at a higher level.

If the idea of encouraging students to interrupt you is too much, use an old-fashioned hourglass designed to time 15 or 20 minutes. As class begins, show the hourglass to the students and tell them, "When the sand runs out, it will be time for you to work briefly with each other." Turn over the hourglass and begin the lecture. If you don't notice when the sand runs out, your students certainly will! There are also a number of timers available that are filled with bright-colored liquids that flow from one compartment to another. The bright colors, of course, add an element of novelty (*see* U = Uniquely Memorable) to this idea!

ASSESS YOUR CURRENT USE OF SOCIALIZATION

- I frequently allow students to talk in the classroom, about a variety of things and for a variety of purposes.

- I occasionally allow students to talk in the classroom, but only about the information they are learning.

- I rarely allow my students to talk to each other in my classroom.

Your Ideas

Consider how you can build more social interactions in your classroom. For at least three upcoming lessons, write the name of the topic you'll be teaching and indicate at least one—perhaps two—places where you'll allow students to talk about the material.

Topic 1:_____

First Opportunity for Socialization: _____

_____

_____

Second Opportunity for Socialization: _____

_____

_____

Topic 2:_____

First Opportunity for Socialization: _____

_____

_____

Second Opportunity for Socialization: _____

_____

_____

Topic 3:_____

First Opportunity for Socialization: _____

_____

_____

Second Opportunity for Socialization: _____

_____

_____

Topic 4:_____

First Opportunity for Socialization: _____

_____

_____

Second Opportunity for Socialization: _____

_____

_____

Topic 5:_____

First Opportunity for Socialization: _____

_____

_____

T = Tiers

Teaching in tiers takes students rapidly to the heart of the matter.

In General

The concept of *tiers* refers to teachers using carefully regulated, sequential steps during an interactive lesson that build deliberately and distinctly on each other. Properly employed, this tier structure helps students understand ideas in the fastest manner possible, without unnecessary diversions and distractions. Using discrete tiers to segment an instructional sequence maximizes students' ability to pay attention at each point, creating a more lasting overall impact and consequently a better learning result.

The Connection

There is no special reason why teaching in tiers is particularly important to the current generations—and none is needed. It is simply fundamental to the way human beings of any generation learn. Most things we learn successfully in life, we learn in tiers. When we fail to learn, the reason is usually not that we are "dumb," but that we tried to learn to learn too much, too fast. The trouble with biting off more than we can chew is that we develop an aversion to trying it again. Our reaction, then, is simple: "I can't do it."

As teachers, this is one reaction we want to avoid at all costs. Instead, we need to maximize the chances of our students succeeding. One important means of doing this is to carefully control the chain of events that lead from one idea to the next.

If we present too much information all at once, numerous problems arise immediately. Students become confused, overwhelmed, and perhaps most importantly, they tend to focus on the wrong thing at the wrong time. However, if we break content down into sufficiently simple steps and explicitly show students how to memorize information, the truth is *anyone can learn anything.* One of the secrets for making this statement true lies in the sequence of the tiers we use as a part of the learning process.

To create the highest possible impact, we must consciously control the amount students learn at each tier and choose the right moment to proceed to the next level. When we create a balanced, ordered progression in the learning process, student success levels rocket skyward.

The Big Picture

The concept of "tiers" is essentially a technique for clearly subdividing activities or lessons into distinct, learnable components. It assists students in understanding the activity or lesson through deliberately adding new elements on top of what students already know. Tiers keep students' attention focused in the appropriate direction, creating the strongest outcome in the least amount of time. (Note: The way *tiers* is used here is distinctly different from its use in Response to Intervention [RTI]. That said, it works similarly in sequential steps that let the teacher know what to do or teach next to meet the needs of the students.)

Here's a simple example: Before moving into the learning activity, the teacher gives students a chance to warm up—to help them get the most value out of the lesson (Ormond, 2000; Vygotsky, 1987). To accomplish this objective he uses a basic three-tier sequence:

■ First, students organize themselves into groups of four or five people. Each group receives a hacky sack, a small round object commonly used for passing between people with only their feet. In this case, however, the teacher invites them to try *hand hacky,* meaning they are to pass the ball to each other by using their hands to bat it in the air. Music plays and the members of each group begin passing the ball to each other by batting it with the palms of their hands.

■ After a minute, the teacher stops the music. He then introduces the next tier in the warm-up activity. Each time the hacky sack hits the ground, the group is to vigorously applaud their efforts before picking it up and continuing to pass it to each other. Groups add this component and the activity continues.

■ After another minute, he introduces the third tier of this activity. Each time a person hits the hacky sack they are to count out loud. The objective is to see how long they can keep it in the air before it hits the ground, at which time they will applaud their efforts, pick it up again, and start back at one. The groups reform, begin again, and add counting into the activity.

After another minute, they acknowledge each of their group members with a high-five or a thank you and are ready to engage in the primary activity.

The entire sequence lasts less than four minutes, including time spent giving instructions. After this activity students are alive, energized, and ready to learn. The activity was incredibly successful because the teacher used these three specific and distinct *tiers*.

The point is, the teacher could have led the same exercise completely differently. He might have given all the instructions at once, including batting the object with their hands, applauding when it hit the ground, and counting each hit. At first glance this may appear to be a simpler, more efficient method of leading the activity.

However, the primary reason for using these three tiers—presenting it as three individual components—has to do with the ability of a group to fully remember each component of the exercise. If, for example, the teacher presented the entire activity at once, groups might forget one of the three steps, and the exercise could end in confusion—not a good mindset for going into the learning activity. Instead, by introducing each step in turn, the teacher allowed his students to succeed at this warm-up activity—giving them a springboard from which to jump into the key learning exercise with confidence.

Focus on Classroom Management

Information taught all as one enormous "chunk"—lacking any distinct tiers or segments—can easily be overwhelming. Without tiered information, students can easily become frustrated and feel crushed under the sheer volume of "stuff they need to know." This sense of "I can't do it" is often followed by an attitude of unconditional surrender. After all, it's impossible, so why try? And the sense of defeat is fertile breeding ground for misbehavior.

Yet on the other hand, success often leads to more success. Students frequently react to their mastery of one tier with a sense of pride, which makes them think, "What's next?" Now they are emotionally engaged with the lesson in a positive way, and ready to move forward to the next tier. In this mindset there's no time for misbehavior, and classes proceed smoothly.

In Practice

You can use tiers at any point during brief interactive games or engagers, longer learning activities, and of course during regular lessons. Below are a series of examples showing how tiers might work in each of these three areas.

Tiers in Interactive Games or Engagers

Warm-Up Questions

1. The teacher asks the class several questions.

2. The teacher chooses individual students to ask questions to the rest of the class.

3. Open season, where anyone can ask a question, without being invited or prompted.

Each tier requires a different level of attention and focus.

Getting to Know You (groups of 5 or 6 people)

1. Ask a general question that everyone in each group answers. The questions might be along the lines of "How many brothers or sisters do you have?" or "What's your favorite color?"

2. Give each student in each group a turn to ask a question.

3. Anyone in the group can ask a question, in no particular order.

General Engager (large group in a circle of chairs; one person without a seat in the middle of the circle)

1. The person in the middle makes a statement beginning with the words "All my neighbors who . . ." and completes it with anything they choose, such as " . . . are wearing tennis shoes" or " . . . have something blue on" or " . . . ate breakfast this morning." Those people who fit the stated category must leave their present chair and find a new place to sit. At the same time the person in the middle finds a seat, meaning that someone new will not have a chair. That person now comes to the center of the group and makes a new statement beginning with those same first four words.

2. Add the words "have ever" to the original statement: "All my neighbors who have ever . . ."

3. Add "stealing," where two students can steal places, meaning any person can exchange seats with another seated individual while the person in the middle is thinking of the next idea.

Wake-Up Energizers—Frisbees (good after lunch!)

1. Stand in a circle, throwing the Frisbee from student to student.

2. Add "creativity," where students toss or catch the Frisbee creatively, with others applauding the unusual ideas they see.

3. "Star in the Middle," where several students are brought to the middle of the circle, and if they intercept a Frisbee thrown by someone else they can trade places with that person, who now becomes the "star" until they catch one and trade places with someone else.

Acknowledgment

Many teachers energize students by allowing them to *physically* thank each other using common acknowledgment actions such as high-fives.

1. Regular high-five.

2. Use the *opposite* hand, which may feel strange to some people.

3. Give "low-fives," where instead of raising their hands they lower them.

4. Give high, low, and behind the back "tens"—using both hands.

5. Get creative and doing high or low "sevens," "threes," or "nines."

6. Allow 30 seconds where each student has the opportunity to give and receive as many different kinds of high fives or tens as possible from the other students in the class.

Tiers in Longer Learning Activities

Memorization Techniques

This example focuses on "Linking," where students memorize items by creating a story, using them in the order in which they appear on a list.

1. Tell the class a story and have them tell the story to someone else. Then tell them there are a certain number of items contained in the story, and see how many they can recall. This opening demonstrates the validity of the method, as in most cases students will be able to recall every item.

2. Give the students a different list of items, and ask them to create their *own* story to memorize it.

3. Give students a list of items relating to the lesson they are currently learning, and will soon be tested on. They must then create a story

for memorizing these items. For example, in science class one list that could be used is the "mineral hardness scale," which is a sequence of ten minerals from nature, ranging from the softest mineral (talc) to the hardest (diamonds).

Tiers in Regular Lessons

New Vocabulary Words

1. *Only* teach the words and their meanings. This initial tier focuses solely on knowing the definition of each word. Once all students are completely comfortable with the vocabulary . . .

2. Explain how these terms relate to what students have already been studying that year.

3. Show where these concepts can be seen in literature they are studying.

Biological Process

1. Teach the five basic steps. While there is much more to actual process, this first tier is an important step to student's overall, eventual success in the unit.

2. Introduce two steps that precede the actual process.

3. Expand and elaborate on the details within some of the initial steps.

4. Focus on after-effects of the process.

Social Studies

1. Concentrate on knowing only six major people from an era—and perhaps just the basics about each person, such as where they lived and what they were famous for.

2. Explain how these key figures knew each other and the nature of their relationships—were they friends or enemies, lovers or bitter rivals?

3. Introduce minor players from that era in history and their connection to the key players learned in tier 1.

If we only move students on to the next tier when they are fully confident and comfortable with the present tier, they should never feel burdened by an unnecessary excess of material.

Next Steps

One of the keys to truly making the idea of tiers work at the highest possible level is to complete each one with some type of *positive acknowledgment*. When students successfully master a particular section of a lesson, it is an important moment to them, and we should duly recognize it as such. A sense of accomplishment is full of positive emotions. Harnessed correctly, this uplifting energy can provide the impetus needed to launch students forward into the next tier of the lesson.

ASSESS YOUR CURRENT USE OF TIERS

- I frequently use tiers when teaching, allowing students to fully grasp one step—no matter how small—before continuing the lesson.

- I occasionally use tiers during my lessons, although I could probably use more of them and make each one smaller.

- I mostly deliver an entire lesson as an intact unit, then ask students where they need more explanation or clarification.

Your Ideas

Look at lessons you are planning and consider which ones might be taught using the concept of tiers. Below, write the name of the topic, then list the distinct sequence of tiers you'll use. You won't always need five tiers—you might need more! This is just a starting point for your thoughts.

Topic 1:_____

First Tier: _____

_____

Second Tier:_____

_____

Third Tier: _____

_____

Fourth Tier: _____

_____

Fifth Tier: _____

_____

Topic 2: _____

First Tier: _____

_____

Second Tier: _____

_____

Third Tier: _____

_____

Fourth Tier: _____

_____

Fifth Tier: _____

_____

Topic 3: _____

First Tier: _____

_____

Second Tier: _____

_____

Third Tier: _____

_____

Fourth Tier: _____

_____

Fifth Tier: _____

_____

U = Uniquely Memorable

Imagination is intelligence at play.

In General

If our students sit through a lesson and don't remember it, did we really teach it? One of the most fundamental—indeed critical—issues for truly High-Impact Teaching is to somehow make lessons *uniquely memorable* to our students. And that means using explicit memorization strategies as we teach. In other words, it's not enough to teach our students content—we also have to teach them how to *remember* that content.

Teaching our students memory strategies is the equivalent of giving them the key to learning success. Once students discover they can remember lessons easily and effortlessly, they also find a new enthusiasm for learning. You'll see them start to use memory strategies by themselves. When they do, you can sit back, confident that you have laid foundations for lifelong learning by empowering students to understand that, if they know how to, they can remember anything.

The Connection

For years, a large component of education examination has required to students to memorize large amounts of information. And for years, many otherwise perfectly bright students have failed tests, because they simply didn't know *how* to remember the content. This issue is coming to a head with our current generations of students, who cannot see the point of remembering facts when, outside the exam room, all they need do is google to have a million facts at their fingertips.

Requiring these generations to memorize vast amounts of information—without showing them how—is unlikely to achieve good learning outcomes.

Not only will they find it incredibly hard, but they have more reason than any previous generation to question the necessity of such an unreasonably arduous task. Instead, let us show our students the miraculous workings of the human memory—and teach them to take control of this amazing learning tool.

The Big Picture

Many classrooms are underpinned by a pervasive, powerful, yet primarily unconscious guessing game between teacher and students. The parameters of the contest are clear from the beginning, despite never being openly stated: The teacher will present a vast quantity of material, and students must intuit what is most important and will appear on the test. Those who guess the best, win! This incredibly silly setup, still widespread in education, is totally unproductive and ultimately runs counter to our goals in teaching.

Instead, we should openly show our students how to remember new information, since few will have ever been specifically taught these skills. We should explain to our students exactly why they remember certain things, while forgetting others. Most importantly, we must show them how to apply these ideas for themselves.

We can do this by intentionally designing lessons that help students encode information along redundant retrieval routes—in multiple memory pathways.

Verbal recall—remembering what was simply *said*—on its own can be a challenge for many students. Therefore, the central question becomes "How can teachers make information easily memorable for all students?"

The answer is actually fairly simple: Our lessons must not only be verbal, they must be *multidimensional*—taking into account how different people learn—and they must include explicit memory strategies.

To address your question, yes, students *do* have responsibility in remembering information. However, we too play a key role in the ease with which this can be accomplished (Hansen, 1998). We must present information in a way that directly helps students to encode the material—both at a broad level and by using specific memory strategies.

We have countless methods for making information memorable. To begin the discussion, here are several examples at the broad level. One way to facilitate recall is by attaching emotions to the material. High levels of laughter, joy, or celebration can cause students to review those moments at a later point in time. While mentally reliving those pleasant experiences, students also revisit any key points demonstrated during the activities.

Involving the students in presenting the material also makes it highly memorable. This plays on the idea that, if you want to know something well, teach it to someone else. When students teach—to the whole group or just one other person—they become deeply involved in the material. Explaining to someone else assists them in understanding it for themselves. Also, beginning a teaching section by allowing students to share what they already know about the subject may serve to engage them. Even simple group conversations about the material will involve the students and help them remember the material at a deeper level.

Another method of making a lesson memorable might be to limit all discussion of a topic until the students have learned the key ideas. For example, suppose 20 new terms will be an integral part of a two-hour session. We could spend the first portion of the lesson focusing specifically on learning what these words mean. During this time, we present no other information that might possibly interfere with the process of memorization. Only when our students have mastered these key terms will we progress to the next part of the lesson.

Here's another, very specific way of make a lesson memorable. A high school mathematics teacher was starting a new chapter. As the first class of this new section began, he welcomed the students by saying:

IMAGINATION IS INTELLIGENCE AT PLAY

"We're beginning a new section of the book today, and I have a story to tell you. You see, there was this really negative bee flying along. He flew up and down until suddenly he ran straight into a square root sticking up out of the ground. He looked inside and saw a really square bee. This square bee was dragging along behind him four AC batteries. He looked down and realized that he and the root were being balanced on a seesaw that had two apples holding it up at the middle."

As he told this story, students were staring at him, wondering what in the world he was talking about. However, he wasn't done yet.

"That was so fascinating, let me tell it to you again."

He repeated the exact same story a second time. When he had finished the story this time, he asked each student to find a partner and sit facing them.

"Now, one person is going to tell the other person this same story, as exactly as you can. When they are done, the other person will tell that story back to them."

Although thoroughly puzzled, students did as they were told. The entire process to this point took approximately five minutes. When each person had completed telling their partner this strange story, the teacher picked up a piece of chalk and turned to the black board.

"Now, for the final time, let's look at that story. What was the first line in the story? There was a negative bee [as he said this, on the board he wrote "–b"] who was flying along. He flew up and down ["+/–"], until suddenly he ran straight into a square root sticking up out of the ground. [He drew the mathematical symbol for a square root.] He looked inside and saw a really square bee ["b squared"]. This square bee was dragging along behind him four AC batteries ["–4ac"]. He looked down and realized that he and the root were being balanced on a seesaw that had two apples holding it up at the middle ["all over 2a"]."

On completing the story, he had written the following formula on the board:

$$\frac{-b \pm \sqrt{b^2 - 4ac}}{2a}$$

This is the quadratic formula, which was the basis for the chapter he was introducing. For the next two weeks, each class session began with the students first telling that same story to someone near them, then writing the formula down on their paper. Knowing the formula rapidly became second nature to all students in the class.

Why did this teacher start class in this way? In previous years, he had noticed that, even after two weeks of concentration on learning how to *use* the quadratic formula, students were still struggling to *remember* it accurately. Somehow, this initial step in the learning process had been passed over. The teacher realized that before students ever learned to apply the formula, they needed to be able to simply remember it and write it down. Now, by memorizing this story, students were quickly able to remember the basic formula. When these students had to solve any problem where they needed to use the quadratic formula, the first thing they did was to tell the story in their mind and write the formula down. From that point on it became a simple matter of filling in the numbers for the variables and completing the mathematical calculations.

In this situation, knowing the quadratic formula was the key to solving the related problems. In many lessons, there are several basic elements our students must know. These nuggets of information are the basis for all remembering, the building blocks on which all other information is built (Johnson-Laird, 1988; Ormrod, 2000). Unless this base is solid, any new information runs the great risk of crumbling, falling through the gaps, and being forgotten.

Recently, students in one high school class made up their *own* story to remember the quadratic formula. The story they made up was:

"There was a very *negative* boy (–b). He was *undecided* (+/–) about going to a *radical* party (*radical symbol*). He was such a square boy (b²) that he *lost out* (–) on 4 awesome chicks! (4ac). The party was *over* by 2 am (2a)."

Making up their own story instead of using one created by the teacher to remember the equation was an even more powerful memory device for many of these students.

Interestingly, simple memory techniques such as these may be familiar to you but considered appropriate only for use with young students (Bower & Clark, 1969; Bulgreen, Schumocker, & Deshler, 1994; Higbee, 1997; Pressle, Levin, & Delancey, 1982; Scruggs & Mastropier, 1987). However, techniques such as these frequently work very well regardless of the age of the student. Most learning sessions, from academic classrooms to corporate seminars, have at least one key concept to which all other material is related. Easy access to the central ideas within any lesson opens the door to related concepts and connections. Teaching students a simple method for recalling the material may make learning the rest of the material a much simpler matter.

Focus on Classroom Management

In traditional classrooms, students are never actually taught how to encode and attach recall prompts to the information they need to learn. Instead, they are simply given the direction "Learn it!" without any instruction on *how* that process actually occurs. But this presumes that students somehow know how their memory works, how information is encoded along different memory paths—audio, visual, kinesthetic, emotional, and so on—

and how to create recall prompts that trigger the process of retrieving the information.

Of course, most don't. This lack of information leads to frustration and a sense of failure. Success, on the other hand, is exciting to students. When information is taught in a memorable way, most are fascinated and intrigued—many even shocked—with their level of achievement. In this state they transform into remarkably focused, interested learners. The behaviors they exhibit match their interest levels, and classroom management becomes a breeze.

Indeed, one of the greatest injustices of our education system is that students who stumble across good memory strategies make great leaps forward in education, while equally capable students who do not stumble across these techniques often decide, because they find recall difficult, that they aren't "smart enough" and begin a downward spiral in their learning process. How can we allow students to think they're stupid when they simply lack an understanding of how to remember information? It seems disgraceful to leave them to fend for themselves in this crucial aspect of learning.

Instead, if teachers show students how easy it is to achieve a sense of success by using and applying simple, practical memory strategies, these experiences will prove to students that they *are* smart and they *can* learn anything if it is taught to them properly. If students experience frequent success, they will develop the inner drive to succeed—both in school and in life.

In Practice

There are many specific ways of making information *directly* memorable. Here are a few ideas to get you thinking.

■ **Acronyms:** An acronym is a word made out of the first letters of the key ideas to be remembered. For example, the word HOMES is often used to teach students the five Great Lakes—using this device, can you name them? (Huron, Ontario, Michigan, Erie, and Superior.) Do you know what SCUBA actually stands for? In fact, did you even know it was an acronym? (Self-Contained Underwater Breathing Apparatus.) Similarly, ROY G. BIV represents the colors of the spectrum, in order! Given this memory device, could you guess what they are? (Red, orange, yellow, green, blue, indigo, and violet.) Acronyms "chunk" data so students don't have to remember a great deal of information all at once.

■ **Acrostics:** An acrostic is a series of words in which the first letters of each word form a useful word or phrase. For example, an acrostic to remember the Great Lakes might be *Happy Old Men Energetically Swim*. One well-known acrostic from music class is *Every Good Boy Does Fine*—representing the notes on the lines of the treble clef. Another one from math class is *Please Excuse My Dear Aunt Sally*, representing the order of operations to be done in a math problem—parentheses, exponents, multiplication, division, addition, and subtraction.

■ **Association:** Association is the idea of connecting two things together, where seeing—or remembering—one thing triggers the memory of the other. It means relating something we want to learn to something we already know. Teachers can apply this idea in countless ways, such as having students connect key concepts to objects around the room or pointing out an object that is somehow tied to a subject—so seeing it again will bring back classroom discussions about that topic.

In fact, association is happening whenever you hear someone say, "That reminds me of . . ." You've probably even experienced yourself it when someone asked you to do something for them and then, having said yes, you completely forgot. However, seeing them triggered the memory of what you were supposed to do! You probably said, "Whoops, I forgot!" Actually, the truth is that you didn't forget; you just remembered at an inconvenient time! What you needed was a trigger that would help ignite your memory at the right time. If we can associate new content to things our students already know, they will be able to recall the new content more easily.

■ **Stories:** Telling a story is another easy way to make key information easy to recall—as demonstrated in the quadratic formula example shown earlier. For a variety of reasons, stories seem to be easy for many people to recall (Alna, 1999). A story can became a mnemonic device—also occasionally referred to as the "linking" strategy—in which the teacher weaves the items students need to recall into a simple story. In the classroom, stories serve multiple functions simultaneously, such as acting as a memory device while also increasing other critical skills, such as literacy (Brand, 2006).

Formulas, processes that have distinct steps, and specific lists all lend themselves easily to this storytelling memory device. Simply take a series of concepts, terms, or ideas like these and link them in an unbroken, integrated sequence that creates a chain of connections. Building visual imagery into the story will make it even easier for your students to remember.

■ **Body Location:** For younger students we can use the *body location* method. In this strategy, young students learn 10 positions on their body. First, teach students 10 locations on their body connected to different numbers. Once these connections have been established, students can "locate" material—make connections—to these locations.

Here are ten basic body locations you could teach:

1 = top of the head

2 = eyes

3 = nose, shaped like a triangle

4 = forearms (crossed in front of you)

5 = fingers

6 = shoulders (hold three fingers up over each shoulder)

7 = seventh heaven on the back

8 = what I . . . ate (rub the stomach)

9 = knees

10 = toes

Now, to teach the eight planets, students simply connect each planet to its appropriate location on the body, such as imagining dirt being on their nose to remember that the earth is the third planet from the sun.

■ **Novelty:** Novelty, discussed earlier in this book, is also a possibility for remembering key information better. We tend to forget things that are usual, things we've seen many times over and over. Right now, try to remember what you ate for dinner exactly two weeks ago. If you can't remember, it's probably because there wasn't anything special or unusual about it. If you can, most likely there's something that stands out in your mind, such as the location, someone you ate with, or perhaps something that happened during the meal. If a lesson is novel, intriguing, or fascinating, students will focus on it and pay attention at a high level. This higher level of attention gives them a better chance of remembering the information.

■ **The Peg System:** The peg method of memorization requires learning a given "peg" connected to the numbers 1 through 20—or even higher. For example, the students' pegs might be 1 = Sun, 2 = Eyes, 3 = Triangle, and so on. To learn content, students then connect an idea, concept, or fact to the already established peg for that number. Those pegs stay the same in any situation; what changes is the subject matter. Students might use pegs to remember key concepts from a unit on the rainforest; a Shakespearean monologue (by pegging the first word of each line); and facts from ancient history.

■ **Rhyming:** As every English child knows, "In 1666, London burned like dry sticks." The date of the great fire of London is indelibly printed in their memories by the use of a simple rhyme. American children, on the hand, would recall, "In 1492, Columbus sailed the ocean blue." You probably still remember many of the rhymes you learned in your elementary school days. The point is that rhymes can be used in multiple ways to easily remember key information.

Songs also use rhymes and can be used just as easily for remembering information. You could have students write new lyrics to a well-known song using key words from a lesson. They would then be able to remember the content by only humming a few bars from the song!

■ **Activity:** Movement engages our *muscle* or *procedural memory*—literally a memory learned through movement. Procedural memory is one of the most lasting forms, meaning if we learn a task by physically doing it, it tends to stay with us for a long time. In fact, learning by doing seems to last a lifetime! Current research (Paulin, 2005) suggests this may be because muscle movement triggers glucose production and engages far more neurons than simple cognitive tasks such as adding. Thus, literally acting out information significantly increases the chances the lesson will be recalled.

■ **Repetition:** Repetition helps recall. However, repetition is not a very well-liked technique for remembering information because most people think it's boring, tedious, and mind-numbingly dull. The basic thought is, "I've already gone over this before, why should I have to do it all again?"

So while repetition does indeed work, for it to be a truly useful memorization strategy, the key is to utilize it in different and unusual ways. Instead of simple, straightforward repetition, the material can be revisited in unique ways to avoid the feeling of "been there, done that." Examples of variations on review might include students questioning each other, students creating practice exams for each other, or playing game shows with the content. Any of the alternate means of going over the material again should avoid the negative emotions commonly associated with review that reduce the effectiveness of the strategy.

While there are many ideas listed here, there are many more you could consider. The key is to keep in mind that if students simply hear the information, the chances they will remember it are actually quite small. Our job, then, is to do something, *anything* else to help them remember it.

Next Steps

Primary pieces of information should be easy for students to remember if they are presented in a memorable fashion. However, we don't need to use memory strategies with all information that is being delivered. Instead, we simply need to isolate those elements central to the overall theme of the session and make them memorable. In general, the question, "How will my students remember this?" should be at the forefront of our thoughts when preparing classes.

Bear in mind, none of these strategies are meant to replace the actual teaching process. They only *support* students' ability to retain and recall the information.

ASSESS YOUR CURRENT USE OF UNIQUELY MEMORABLE

- ■ I teach my students specifically how to memorize information, since one of my goals is to create successful lifelong learners.

- ■ I occasionally use memory strategies, although mostly they are ones I learned when I was in school.

- ■ I mostly just teach the lesson and expect my students to know how to learn and remember the information.

Your Ideas

The key is to make your central points memorable. So how will you do this? For at least three of your upcoming lessons, decide how you will assist your learners by doing this clearly and deliberately. In each case, write the name of the topic, then describe what strategy you'll be using to make it memorable.

First Topic: _____

How to Make It Memorable: _____

_____

_____

_____

_____

Second Topic: _____

How to Make It Memorable: _____

_____

_____

_____

_____

Third Topic: _____

How to Make It Memorable: _____

_____

_____

_____

_____

Fourth Topic: _____

How to Make It Memorable: _____

_____

_____

_____

_____

Fifth Topic: _____

How to Make It Memorable: _____

_____

_____

V = Vocal Italics

Vocal emphasis allows key words to bask in the spotlight of understanding.

In General

New lessons frequently bring new terms, phrases, and ideas as students venture into the uncharted waters of a fresh topic. When students come across these new words, they often need time to fully understand them before moving forward to related new thoughts and ideas. In these situations, giving our students a well-timed, brief moment of focus will allow them to understand and remember the new term.

Thus, when we either (1) introduce a new word, or (2) use a term that may be unfamiliar to some of the class, we need to make that word stand out in some way. This process is referred to as applying "vocal italics" to the word, phrase, or expression. It simply means emphasizing the words vocally and pausing briefly to let our students digest this new term.

The Connection

Vocal italics are particularly important for introducing new terms into the short attention spans of Generation Y and Z students. As teachers, most of us know our content well. And while this is a good thing, it does mean we tend to forget our students are hearing it for the first time. In these situations, if we say the new word at our normal speaking rate, students who aren't paying attention will completely miss it. By emphasizing a word vocally, we can draw students' attention, ensuring they notice the new term.

Without this initial understanding, our students may well lose everything else we say about this new word. Failing to grasp a term the first time it's mentioned leaves students nothing to hold onto as the incoming storm of related information descends on them.

The Big Picture

The term "vocal italics" is drawn from the similar concept of emphasizing written words using *italics*—as occurs occasionally throughout this book. Just as there are many other options for drawing attention to written words—underlining, bold print, quotation marks, and so on—we have numerous options for creating this effect in our verbal delivery. Options might include pausing before saying the word, slowing down when actually saying the word, or pausing after saying the word—or perhaps all of these together.

Here's why these actions are so important: Consider in slow motion the mental sequence of a student encountering a new word.

1. A double-check to verify that they don't already know the term.

2. A search for related meaning with similar sounding words they do know (roots, suffixes, etc.).

3. A quick check to see if they can extrapolate the meaning of the word based on the context within which it has been presented.

If none of these steps yield a likely meaning, most students will return their attention to the lesson and hope that the meaning becomes apparent later.

The issue is *those steps take time.* And while our students are focusing their attention on making meaning out of this word, they are not focusing on what we are saying. Thus, they miss words, phrases, or even whole sentences in our teaching—reducing their recall at the end of the lesson because they miss a key word that many subsequent ideas are connected to.

Here's a real example of that process in action. The student was in the final months of a high school honors class on economics. She had a unique opportunity to attend a lecture on international economics in the European Community presented by a prominent speaker from an Ivy League school. Given the nature of her current class and its relevance to the lecture topic, she was looking forward to the presentation with considerable interest.

During the course of the presentation, the speaker naturally used a number of specialized words. Fortunately, the student was familiar with most of them. However, the speaker also used a number of expressions and phrases she'd never come across. As she encountered each new word, she observed an interesting phenomenon. She seemed to experience a "mental pause" as she sorted through her knowledge to see if she had any understanding of the word. When her attention returned to the presentation, she found she had missed the next few words, or even entire sentences. These gaps in her understanding became disconcerting: They were like holes in a dam. As the holes increased, more knowledge leaked through, and at an ever-increasing pace.

The session lasted slightly over two hours. As she left the room, she was disappointed at how few important details she could recall right then. If this was true even in the first few moments following the presentation, in spite of the careful notes she had written, what would her memory be like tomorrow? Or within a week? This student had just had a "swiss cheese" experience—one riddled with holes!

Now we know why this happened: Whenever she encountered a new term—but had not been given time to process it and make meaning for herself—she had significant difficulty in recalling the related information. Even with her strong internal motivation to grasp the content of the presentation, her learning had been hindered by her mental pauses to try to find meaning in an unknown word. If she, an honors student, had experienced this phenomenon, what about other students who hadn't had the information from her class as background information to rely on? How much of the presentation would they be able to remember the next day? Probably very little.

Focus on Classroom Management

Despite our best efforts, students can often perceive a learning situation as a challenging, even threatening environment. Missing the understanding of one, then two, then possibly three key words could quickly create a negative mindset in learners. Their ensuing frustration can start a downward spiral where students quickly lose motivation to try to learn at all. On the other hand, students who are clear regarding each key word used in a lecture may feel they are "really understanding this material," which increases their confidence and enthusiasm about participating and engaging in the lesson.

In Practice

We have a number of options for placing vocal italics around key words and phrases. Here are a few of them:

■ **Pause** before you say the word, then again after the word. The initial pause informs listeners that the next word requires special attention. The second pause following the word allows students time to process it, time to remember both the word and its definition. Here's an example:

> "When we consider the overall . . . pedagogy . . . of a particular teacher, it's necessary to include a discussion of their classroom management techniques."

Note that pausing and vocal inflection could be combined together in this example by simply adding vocal emphasis on the word pedagogy.

- **Use vocal inflection,** changing the tone of your voice. This may be most effective if we're going to define the word. For example:

> "Government hunters in Africa are said to be *culling* a herd of elephants, meaning they kill certain ones to bring the size of the herd down to a number that can live on the available food and land."

When we place significant vocal emphasis on the word *culling,* we allow students to focus on it, separate it from the other words, and encode it for later recall.

- **Use repetition,** as in the following statement:

> "This is known as . . . oxidation. Oxidation is the process in which oxygen causes some metals to form rust."

Repeating the key word allows it to become more familiar to the student, enabling them to practice recalling it. Further repetition of the word would be useful to allow them to verify its meaning for themselves.

These are just a few of the options for placing vocal italics on new words or key expressions. As in writing, we can combine these, and other options, to greater effect.

Next Steps

Have you ever had the experience where you're reading along and suddenly realize that you have no idea what that last paragraph was about? Sometimes this is because our mind needs time to process the material it has already absorbed. While the eyes continue to move forward, the mind

ASSESS YOUR CURRENT USE OF VOCAL ITALICS

- I deliberately and consciously make key words stand out vocally to help my students process them and learn better.

- I sometimes make new words stand out vocally, particularly if they are extremely unusual or complicated.

- I rarely make key words stand out vocally, other than through my natural inflection.

is busy organizing the material, processing it, and making meaning and connections between it and other related concepts you may have read. As a related idea, you might want to suggest that students occasionally *pause during reading,* allowing the mind to process the most recent material.

Your Ideas

Consider some of your upcoming lessons. What are the new words, phases, or ideas you'll be introducing? In advance, identify and isolate these and decide how you'll use vocal italics to make sure students can stay focused on the lesson without getting lost or distracted. Below, write the name of the topic, the new words, and how you'll use vocal italics.

Lesson 1: _____

New Words: _____

_____

How I'll Use Vocal Italics:_____

_____

_____

Lesson 2: _____

New Words: _____

_____

How I'll Use Vocal Italics:_____

_____

_____

Lesson 3: _____

New Words: _____

_____

How I'll Use Vocal Italics:_____

_____

_____

Lesson 4: _____

New Words: _____

_____

How I'll Use Vocal Italics:_____

_____

_____

Lesson 5: _____

New Words: _____

_____

How I'll Use Vocal Italics:_____

_____

_____

W = Walk Away

Step back so students speak up.

In General

When a student speaks as part of a lesson, it is important that everyone can
hear him clearly. If we obey our conversational instincts and move closer
to students while they are speaking, they will lower their voices, whereas,
if we move in the opposite direction, we will have the opposite effect: Our

student will speak louder. Thus, we can make it easier for the group to hear by positioning ourselves far enough away from the speaker to make him or her speak louder.

The Connection

In the course of a personal conversation we tend to move toward people who are speaking. As we do so, most speakers will instinctively lower their voice and reduce the size of their hand motions—the conversation becomes intimate.

But in a High-Impact Teaching context, where we're encouraging students to contribute in a large group, this instinctive reflex is unhelpful. In most cases, we want all the other students to be able to hear what the speaker is saying. If we push our students into an intimate conversational mode, the students furthest from the speaker are unlikely to hear what is said. Missing out on even a few words may cause these students to become frustrated and lose their concentration on the discussion.

The Big Picture

In many teaching situations, students project well and everyone can hear what they have to say. However, other circumstances may require us to deliberately encourage students to raise their voices. For example, our class size may be fairly large, the acoustics in the room may be less than optimal, or a particular student may have a naturally quiet voice. In these cases, we should avoid our natural tendency to move toward the person speaking.

Instead, we should keep our focus on the person speaking, but take several steps *in the opposite direction*. We can do this quite subtly, without distracting anyone from the person speaking. When we move away, the person speaking will instinctively raise her voice and increase the size of her hand gestures.

Focus on Classroom Management

We can use an extension of this "walk away" idea as a classroom management tool. A technique called a "step down" is especially useful in situations where there is a low level of conversation in the room. Perhaps students are chatting with each other, and we'd like to move forward to the next section. Rather than saying "OK, everybody, would you please be quiet so we may continue?" we could instead glide gently into the next section without appearing to be a disciplinarian—using a step down.

A *step down* is a gradual reduction of speaking volume over the course of a single sentence. We begin speaking at a volume slightly higher than the volume level of the class. Gradually we "step down" the volume until, by the final few words of the sentence, we are talking at the same level as we would during normal conversation.

Examine in slow motion what occurs next. Some students in the room immediately realize we are speaking again. They know they should be listening, so they cease their conversation and turn to face us. As these people become quiet, the level of sound in the room is reduced. Here is the key. As the sound level in the room drops, *we also lower the volume of our voice.* We vocally step down along with them. While our volume of speech always remains slightly above that of the class, it follows their cue and gradually decreases.

Since the sound level in the room has dropped, our voice becomes more obvious. Other students realize we are speaking. As they become quiet the situation repeats itself. Each time the level of sound in the room goes down, our voice steps down with it. By the end of the sentence, the room has fallen quiet and we are speaking at a conversational level. We have prompted the group forward into the next section of conversation without conspicuously interrupting their discussions.

While we do this, we can also take a step or two backward, thus unconsciously signaling to everyone that they are moving into a different section of the lesson, where someone—either the teacher or a student—will be talking to the entire class.

Used properly, this approach to class management allows us to simultaneously bring our students to silence while seamlessly moving the class forward into the next section.

In Practice

To make the "walk away" technique work successfully, we need to pay attention to a few small, but critical, points. One important detail is keeping our attention focused on the speaker while moving away. We should maintain constant eye contact while taking the necessary few steps, and perhaps even nod our head a few times. If we look away, the speaker, or even the other students, may mistake this for lack of interest. Also, we only usually need to take a few steps to create the effect. The greater the size of the room, the more steps we need to take. However, we wouldn't normally need to completely cross to the other side of the room. Finally, after moving, come to a complete stop and maintain focus on the speaker.

Knowing when to initiate the movement is also useful. The most natural times to move are either when first indicating it's time for the student to talk or at the start of the student's comments. These moments work best for several reasons. They are transitional moments, since a student is now speaking, and movement at this point supports the transition. It's certainly more natural than if it were to happen in the middle of the student's comments! Also, if we wait too long, the speaker will only raise their voice halfway through their comments.

Walking away prevents the need to say: "Could you please speak a little louder?"

This does nothing to boost the speaker's confidence and can interrupt their train of thought. It's far more supportive and productive to use the walk away strategy to get students to speak louder without interrupting them in the middle of their comments.

With practice, these walk away and step down techniques will become natural components of your teaching style—supporting interactive learning and keeping your students engaged.

Next Steps

It is often challenging to get students to speak at a volume level sufficient for everyone in the class to remain involved in what is being said. The key to accomplishing this is to always remember that there is a difference between interactions that take place between two people in a normal conversation and the interactions that occur in a classroom. In personal interactions, it is only necessary that one other person hear what is being said. In a classroom, however, while it is certainly important for the teacher to hear what is being said, it is equally important that the other students also be able to hear.

ASSESS YOUR CURRENT USE OF WALK AWAY

- I frequently step back to prompt a student who is speaking to raise his or her voice and use more expansive gestures.

- I occasionally step back from a student who is speaking, but have not been doing this consciously.

- I tend to remain in the same place I have asked the question when a student is speaking, and sometimes move closer.

Your Ideas

Consider the size of your classroom, the number of students in your class, and how loudly your students normally talk. To begin building this skill as one of your teaching strategies, decide in advance how you will use the walk away technique—and how you'll use a step down. Will you actually take a step or two backward? Will you do both? Below, write down what you plan to do in your situation.

How I'll Use Walk Away: _____

_____

_____

_____

_____

How I'll Use Step Down: _____

_____

_____

_____

_____

X = X-Ray Vision

Most people see what is and never see what can be.

In General

The human brain is constantly creating mental images. It's one of the primary ways we orient ourselves to the world. When we hear a sentence, certain words will always stand out—ones that we can most easily *see* in our mind. This is because a portion of the brain processes that "sensory data" as an image. It is as if we have X-ray vision and see directly through any extraneous words and focus directly on those that can more easily help us form mental pictures. The issue here is that the words we focus on may not reflect the speaker's intended meaning. For example, of the two words "Don't run!" only one creates a picture—"Run!" Thus, the picture formed by these words is actually the opposite of the speaker's intention.

As teachers, we want to avoid mental images that accidentally direct students' focus toward *negative* actions or consequences. Instead, we need to consciously create images of *positive* actions or consequences in our students' minds (Bayor, 1972).

The Connection

The generations in today's classrooms have grown up with history's most prolific array of visual stimulation. Plugged in to online and electronic games, their experience is primarily visual. While all human beings instinctively turn words into pictures, never has this been more powerful than for the highly visual Y and Z generations.

The Big Picture

One of the most curious words in the English language is "not," because, in terms of visual imaging, the brain *cannot process the word "not."* It is as if, within the human mind, the word doesn't exist. When presented with "not," the brain will immediately create the picture that the person speaking meant to avoid. For example, right now, try to follow these instructions: "Do NOT imagine a huge pink gorilla!"

Most people have a very difficult time following these directions. When they read those words, the very first image that pops to mind is that of a pink gorilla. Once there, it's difficult to remove. Go ahead, try it right now. Can you erase the image of the pink gorilla? If you're having trouble with this, don't be surprised. It takes a while to clear the image from our mind. And, if you successfully avoided imagining the gorilla, you probably first had to see it, then replace it with another picture, and focus all your attention on it instead. The instant you stopped thinking about the other image, what happened? Usually, that big pink gorilla came walking right back in!

Here's another classic example of this situation. A mother has just handed her 2-year-old daughter a glass of milk. She says to the child: "Now honey, don't spill your milk!"

Based on the discussion so far, what image is instantly created in the child's mind? The child immediately sees . . . spilled milk! Now that the image is clearly embedded in the child's mind, what happens? Of course, she *tries* to keep the milk in the glass, but that picture of milk all over the table keeps coming back to her! Suddenly, apparently without warning, the little girl's arm flies out and knocks over the glass of milk. The mother, horrified, rushes over and says, "I told you not to spill your milk! Weren't you listening to me?"

Actually, the child was listening quite closely to her mother's words. However, the choice of words created an image that influenced the child to spill the milk! The mother would have got a better result by deliberately using language to influence more positive behavior. For example, she might say, "Honey, please be careful to keep the milk in the glass."

Now the child has a picture of the milk in the glass and she is much more likely to replicate this picture in reality.

Not isn't the only word that may create an opposite effect from our original intention. Here are some commonly used negative words:

- Can't
- Shouldn't
- Avoid
- Won't
- Couldn't
- Stop
- Don't
- Wouldn't
- Never

To avoid accidentally directing our students in the wrong direction, we need to become aware of when and how we use these words. The more aware we become, the more our brains will trigger useful alternatives.

Focus on Classroom Management

Suppose we say, "Don't make a lot of mistakes, or you'll fail the test!"

What images are we creating in our students' minds? We're highlighting mistakes and failure—probably not the images we were intending to create. Instead, we might say, "Be sure to get as many correct as possible, so you have the best chance to receive an excellent score on this test." With these words we can focus our students' minds in a more useful direction.

The same idea applies to appropriate classroom behaviors. As teachers our goal is to maintain positive attention and focus. We can achieve this by using words that direction a student's attention toward these actions. Instead of telling them what *not* to do, if we use words that clearly indicate what *is* expected of them, we have a far better chance of seeing that behavior.

For example, if we say "Stop throwing that ball around the classroom," we are telling them what not to do. Instead, we might say, "Please place the ball back in the toy box, and return to your seat." Using these words we've created a clear picture of the behavior we expect.

In Practice

Consider each example shown here. If spoken as originally shown, the statement may have some unintended, potentially negative results. The examples then offer one possible option for rephrasing so the message has a better chance of registering in the mind of the listener—you can probably think of many others.

Example	Possible problem	Rephrasing option
"Don't look over there."	Where do a student's eyes immediately turn? Right to where we don't want them to look.	"Look over here" or "Keep your attention focused in this direction."
"Try not to be late to class."	These words create a picture of being late.	"Be on time" or "Be early."
"Be careful at recess. We don't want sprained ankles or broken bones."	Students' attention is now firmly focused on spraining their ankles or breaking their bones!	"Play safe" or "Be safe, healthy, and whole" or "Take care of yourself."
"Please complete this assessment without looking at your notes, at the board at the front of the room, or at anyone else's paper."	Now there are three things the students are thinking about, any of which may be strong enough to distract them. Suddenly they find their eyes wandering over to the paper nearest them, or discover that they are fixated on peeking at their notes.	"Please complete this assessment with only the information in your head" or "Keep your attention on your paper as you complete this assessment" or "Keep your eyes on your own paper at all times."
"Be aware of the danger of losing your patience."	This focuses students' attention directly on the danger of losing their patience.	"Stay patient" or "Maintain your cool at all times."
"At no time during an emergency should you allow panic and emotions to overwhelm you."	Look at all those negatives carefully compressed into a single sentence. Scary.	"Stay calm at all times" or "In an emergency, remain calm and focused."
"Avoid exiting this room by that door because you might set off the fire alarm."	These words prompt an awareness of the fire alarm. The second image stays with the students longest. If we have to talk about setting off the fire alarm, we should end with a more positive image.	"Everyone look toward this door. It is connected to the fire alarm and should only be used in an emergency. Now, would everyone please point toward this other door. This is the door we will be using at all other times."

In this final example, students are now fully aware of the fire alarm connected to the first door. They have also been shown a clear image of the door to be used during normal operations. Since the more important image came second, it will tend to remain the longest in the students' minds.

Next Steps

Here's an interesting example of how a biology teacher incorporates this idea into the classroom, but *in reverse.* When students are going to be studying dissection, he sets the materials out in advance. For this lesson, they arrive at the classroom and find placed on their lab tables real pigs' hearts. One of the first things this teacher says is, "It's very important that you *don't* squeeze the pig's heart."

Of course, as he expected all along, very soon one of the students (not surprisingly, it's usually a male) squeezes the pig's heart, and the blood squirts out all over everything. When this happens, the teacher is not upset. In fact, he calmly responds by saying,

> "What you've just done is shown the rest of us how a heart works. When it contracts it forces the blood out and into the circulatory system. Thank you for that very visual demonstration. Now let's all open one up and take a closer look at how it operates."

With that as an introduction, the lesson in dissecting a pig's heart has officially begun. The teacher's clever reverse use of the idea of mental images has served to begin the class with a bit of a surprise, and the students are now fully focused on the key points of the lesson.

MOST PEOPLE SEE WHAT IS.... AND NEVER SEE WHAT CAN BE

- I deliberately and consciously choose my words with the intention of having students create a useful mental picture.

- I sometimes use words that will create the best positive mental image, although this is more by accident than deliberate choice.

- I frequently use words that may accidentally be creating a very different mental image in the student's mind than the one I intended.

Your Ideas

Try this idea for yourself. In each case below, change the original, negative statement into one that creates a more positive, useful image in your student's brain:

Negative Statement: "Don't drop your pencil."

Positive Statement:_____

Negative Statement: "Don't forget your library books tomorrow."

Positive Statement:_____

Negative Statement: "Stop leaving your litter on the playground."

Positive Statement:_____

Negative Statement: "Never use swear words at school!"

Positive Statement:_____

Negative Statement: "Try not to color outside the lines."

Positive Statement:_____

Now, try some on your own. First, write a sentence in the negative, perhaps something you either hear often at school, or maybe even remember saying yourself! Then, adjust the words so that it creates a more positive mental image.

Negative Statement:_____

Positive Statement:_____

Negative Statement:_____

Positive Statement:_____

Negative Statement:_____

Positive Statement:_____

Y = Yesterday Lives!

Life must be lived forward, but can only be understood backward.

In General

Our lives are full of stories. Some of them are positive, some are negative, but all of them can teach us something. Stories can help our students to gain insight as to how to apply what we are teaching them and make connections for themselves. Bringing high levels of storytelling into the classroom is not only a High-Impact Teaching Strategy, it is basic common sense.

The Connection

Long before there were computers, before there were movies, and even before there were books, there were stories. The collective wisdom of ancient cultures—medicine, crop rotation, hunting strategies—was encoded in myths. Before books, these metaphorical tales were the primary means of passing on the accumulated knowledge of the elders to the younger members of the group. It was through stories that young children learned the essential skills of survival, from hunting techniques to which plants were safe to eat. It was also a way of maintaining the group's rituals and traditions. The storyteller in a tribe was looked upon as one of its most revered and venerated members (Campell, 1983).

Today, stories still serve much the same role and hold the same fascination for audiences of all generations. No matter how technologically sophisticated the current generations in our classrooms, announce you're going to tell a story and even the most cynical student settles in happily.

The Big Picture

Stories can be anything, from simple jokes to real-life situations you have personally experienced. They can be television or movie plots, popular myths, fairy tales, or fables. Each of these gives learners a different slant on the material, a different way to understand and process the ideas. You'll probably have noticed numerous stories, metaphors, and examples running throughout this book—they are included precisely to show how this particular idea plays out everywhere.

Certain areas of instruction, such as creative writing or history, may appear to lend themselves more readily to including stories and metaphors. However, we can actually include storytelling in almost every subject from math to philosophy. As teachers, we need to find relevant stories for our material to help our students learn.

Focus on Classroom Management

Stories are simultaneously educational and entertaining. Entertainment (*see* E = Entertainment) holds students' attention in multiple ways, allowing them to learn at multiple levels. Even a very basic story will capture our students' focus as they listen to discover what happens.

Of course, the primary benefit of using stories in the classroom is that stories lay down powerful memories. If we can relate the current content to something the students are already familiar with, we reduce the effort needed to recall the material later. When learning and remembering feel easy to students, attention levels soar while discipline issues fade.

In Practice

Here's an example of the use of a story in the classroom. It was a session on communication skills. The material had focused primarily on how much even a single misunderstood word could affect the outcome of an interaction. At the end of class, the teacher told the students the following story:

> "A man was driving on a winding mountain road. As he approached a sharp turn, a car came around it swerving wildly. It narrowly missed sideswiping his car. As it raced past him, a woman leaned out and yelled at him, 'HOG!'
>
> The man was completely startled. He thought to himself, 'Wait a minute, I'm not the road hog here—she is! She's the one swerving all over the place!' With that he leaned out of his car and shouted back at her, 'SOW!'
>
> He grinned in satisfaction to himself, rounded the corner, and ran promptly into a hog standing in the middle of the road."

This story illustrated the central concept the teacher was trying to teach to the students: that words are open to interpretation.

In this case, the story used was a joke. Jokes are particularly good at helping students to retain information. Here's why: If our students enjoy a joke, there's an excellent chance they will retell it later to their friends. When retelling it, they are *unconsciously reviewing at least one idea from the material.*

The teacher in this situation told the story at the end of the class. This is a wise timing choice, especially if we can find a story or metaphor that sums up the essential point of the lesson. Since it is the last thing the group will hear, it is often the image they will most remember when they walk away. We can also *open* a class with a story to set the stage for the content that is to follow—and connect our students to the material.

Next Steps

Where do we find good stories? They happen to each of us every day. People often say, "But nothing interesting ever happens to me!" The truth is that many interesting things are always happening around us. We simply need to look at them from the perspective of a storyteller. What message is contained in the moment? What could be learned? What is this situation similar to?

As well as looking for possibilities in the day-to-day, deliberately collect jokes and stories from your friends, emails, newspapers, and books. You'll find some great stories in *Chicken Soup for the Soul*, edited by Jack Canfield (Canfield, 1993). Another excellent source is the children's section of the library, where countless books have very short stories that we can use to emphasize a particular point of instruction. And finally, you'll find several stories included in the Appendix of this book to help you develop as a storyteller in the classroom.

ASSESS YOUR CURRENT USE OF YESTERDAY LIVES!

- I use stories as often possible—it is one of my most frequent teaching strategies.

- I sometimes use stories to make a point in a lesson, although this is the exception rather than the rule.

- I rarely use stories in my classroom and tend to teach mostly by simply telling the students what they need to know.

Your Ideas

Some teachers are natural storytellers. If you're one of those lucky people, go have fun using more and more of them! If, however, you find that stories don't easily pop into your mind, it's a good idea to plan your use of stories carefully. Below, write down some of your lessons and find a metaphor, example, news story, or personal experience you could use to illustrate the key point of the lesson.

First Lesson: _____

A Story I Can Use: _____

_____

_____

_____

_____

Second Lesson: _____

A Story I Can Use: _____

_____

_____

_____

_____

Third Lesson: _____

A Story I Can Use: _____

_____

_____

_____

_____

Fourth Lesson: _____

A Story I Can Use: _____

_____

_____

_____

_____

Fifth Lesson: _____

A Story I Can Use: _____

_____

_____

_____

_____

Z = Zones of Instruction

Instructional zones set the stage for learning.

In General

Using instructional "zones" builds on the psychological idea that similar stimuli generate a consistent emotional response. In other words, when we find ourselves in circumstances we recognize, we actually relive our previous emotional experience of those circumstances. As teachers, we can use this phenomenon to create a predictable learning environment in our classrooms by deliberately and consistently giving different types of instruction from particular locations in the classroom. Additionally, by moderating our voice, gestures, and posture to delineate these different zones, we can give our students predictable cues for transitioning from one type of learning to another.

The Connection

The generations in today's classrooms are intuitive learners, with hours of experiential learning gained from computer games and electronic toys. We can replicate this natural learning style by using predictable environmental clues to generate behavioral changes—rather than giving commands. Once our students know that when we move to a certain location in the room a particular type of instruction will ensue, they will automatically start to prepare for that type of instruction. When our students instinctively know what is coming, they feel safe and comfortable. At a subtle level, they take ownership of the next segment of the lesson.

The Big Picture

Imagine the scene: George is concerned to see his good friend Jake sitting in the corner, visibly upset. George hurries over and offers comfort by gently patting Jake on the shoulder. George stays sitting down beside his friend, with his hand on Jake's shoulder, until Jake feels better. The next day, Jake is much happier. He and George are chatting and, in the course of the conversation, George pats Jake's shoulder again, congratulating him. Shortly afterwards, Jake finds his good mood slipping away. Why? What triggered this emotional reaction?

The original interaction between the two friends established a powerful connection linking George's hand touching Jake's shoulder with the emotion Jake was experiencing at that time. In Jake's mind, the two were connected. The next day, when George's hand touched the shoulder again in the same manner, the connection rekindled Jake's original emotions.

This somewhat simplistic example illustrates a powerful psychological and physiological concept (Dastoor & Reed, 1993)—that similar stimuli can generate a consistent emotional response. The field of neurolinguistic programming (NLP) refers to this as "anchoring" (Grinder, 1988).

As teachers, we can use this human response to connect certain physical locations, or *zones*, in our classrooms to different types of instruction. The more clearly and consistently we establish these connections, the more effective they can be in guiding our students' internal responses.

Focus on Classroom Management

If students misbehave while we are teaching, we generally stop immediately and correct their behavior. However, this may unintentionally cause students to connect being in that location in the room with being disciplined. We don't want our students left with this unpleasant connection when we resume teaching. So how could we handle discipline differently?

Here's how a sixth-grade teacher in California deals with this situation. The very first time her students misbehave, she says, "Let's stop for a moment. Please turn your desks so they face toward the left."

At that point she has all students turn their desks ninety degrees to the left. When everyone has their desk turned in the new direction, she walks over to that side of the room and disciplines them as necessary. She takes whatever time is needed to complete this task. Finally, when the situation has been handled, she says, "Thank you. Now please turn your chairs back to face the board."

Then she moves back to the normal front of the room and continues teaching.

Using this strategy, she eliminates the potential negative connections students might have made had she disciplined them from her presenting location. Also, as the weeks pass, she repeats this pattern. All discipline is delivered after the students turned their desks in that certain direction. What the students come to realize is that while facing the blackboard they are *never* disciplined, never made wrong. Consequently, they feel safe facing that direction, and thus became more involved and interactive when she presents the lesson.

In Practice

We can create at least three distinct zones of instruction in our classrooms.

1. **Instruction Zone:** This is the area nearest the chalkboard or whiteboard, the space furthest from our students. This is the location from which we deliver content and usually place any supporting visuals. When we move to stand in this location, students will know that information is about to be presented. In some cases, simply moving to this location may alert them that it's time to take notes. This might prompt them to organize their materials for what is coming (Lozanov, 1979).

2. **Interaction Zone:** This is closer to our students. It is used for more casual conversation or interaction with the class, such as responding to questions. When we shift into this area, students know immediately we expect a different level of interaction and adjust their thinking accordingly.

3. **Direction Zone:** This is the heart of the class, which we step into when giving directions. Our proximity adds impact to the strength of these instructions.

We can help our students differentiate between these locations by changing both our tone of voice and gestures when moving between the different zones, as shown in the following diagram.

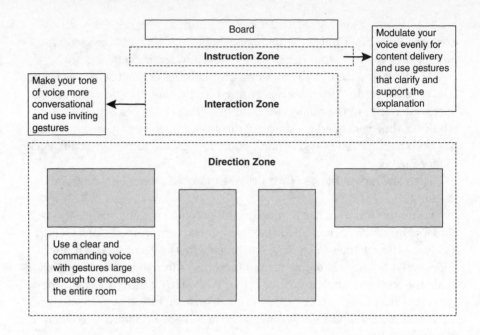

Next Steps

Once you've got the three basic zones working in your classrooms, you can add more locations where appropriate. For example, some teachers establish a storytelling zone in their rooms. This is the place they choose to stand every time they begin a story. Each time the teacher moves to that location, their students realize they are about to hear a story. This knowledge triggers a positive emotional response, as students settle down and prepare themselves for storytelling.

ASSESS YOUR CURRENT USE OF ZONES OF INSTRUCTION

- I deliberately delineate zones in my classroom for different types of instruction.

- I instinctively use a couple of different zones, but I don't employ this as a conscious strategy.

- I tend to stand in the same place most of the time when I teach.

Your Ideas

Map out one of your regular classrooms and add in the three main zones, and any special zones you'd like to create.

Identify three lessons where you'll use this idea and the places in these lessons where you'll move into your new zones.

First Lesson: _____

Instruction Zone: _____

_____

Interaction Zone: _____

_____

Direction Zone:_____

_____

Second Lesson: _____

Instruction Zone: _____

_____

Interaction Zone: _____

_____

Direction Zone:_____

_____

Third Lesson: _____

Instruction Zone: _____

_____

Interaction Zone: _____

_____

Direction Zone:_____

_____

Lessons in the Language of Learning

This section offers a series of High-Impact Lessons contributed by real teachers, in real classrooms, working with real students. Each lesson shows why the teacher developed a new approach, how the lesson is currently taught, and the result of teaching it this way. At the end of the lesson, the High-Impact Strategies being used are highlighted. A brief discussion then follows, illustrating how other teachers might consider using the central idea(s) in the lesson for students of different ages, with different content, and in different circumstances.

How do we create dynamic lessons that maximize the effectiveness of High-Impact Teaching Strategies? This is a tricky question, since it doesn't have a single answer. It will depend on many factors unique to your teaching situation:

- The age of your students
- The personality of your class of students as a group
- Your personality
- The amount of time you have for the lesson
- The physical aspects of your classroom—how much space you have, how many windows and doors, and so on

The temptation is to design a template into which the various techniques and any content can be neatly slotted. Yet this is simply not possible. As most teachers with even a limited amount of classroom experience will attest, there is rarely a perfect lesson plan template that will adapt into any and all teaching circumstances.

Instead, to help you understand how to apply the ideas in this book in your classroom, what follows is a showcase of how other teachers are using High-Impact Teaching Strategies in their classrooms—explained in their own words. These demonstration lessons are unlikely to fit *exactly* into your teaching situation. You will probably have to adapt them to all of the conditions unique to your situation listed above—and probably more! However, hopefully what you see here will show you what's possible, triggering your own creative thoughts about using the strategies with your content and your students.

Lesson 1: The Presence of Chlorophyll in Leaves

Students:	Kindergarten and First Grade
Submitted by:	Tiffany Reindl
School:	Jefferson School for the Arts, Stevens Point, Wisconsin

Ask the Teacher

■ **Why Did You Develop a High-Impact Lesson for This Topic?** Why leaves change colors in the fall is a difficult concept for young children because they can't see that the fall color was there the whole time the leaf was green. I wanted to develop a lesson that illustrated the concept visually for the students.

■ **How Do You Use High-Impact Strategies to Teach the Topic?** Using water and food coloring, I fill three baby food jars each with a solid color—red, yellow, and orange—and seal it closed with the lid. Then I take three slightly larger glass jars and place the baby food jars inside. I filled the remaining space in the large jars with a deep green food coloring and water mixture. When the large jar is held up, only green color is visible.

I tend to do a lot of hokey magic tricks with my class (I'm going to be magician when I grow up) and the children love to make lots of hypotheses to explain how I do it. We test their hypotheses to see if they work; if they don't we make adjustments and try it again. (We are true scientists.)

When studying trees in the fall, I put on a magic theme song and present my green jars. Voila! I ask them to share some observations about my jars. They can see the little jars inside but the liquid appears *all green*. I tell them that I am about to perform an amazing trick—I am going to change the color in the jar before their very eyes. I have them turn and talk to their neighbor to see if they can predict how I might accomplish this. Will I have them turn around and quickly switch the jars? Will I add something to them? Hmmm. Nothing up my sleeve, but . . .

I pull a bowl from under my top hat. (You have to have the hat if you're a magician.) Show time! Slowly I pour the green liquid out of the jar, revealing the color that is in the smaller, baby food jar. Ta-da! What? It was in there the whole time? They figured it out. Simple child's play . . . or a strategic seed of knowledge planted for a future discussion?

■ **What Is the Result of Teaching the Lesson This Way?** Later that day, when we began to discuss how plants make food and connect that knowledge to the seasonal weather changes we've been charting, students realized that the trees don't have enough ingredients to make enough food anymore. So when the green chlorophyll goes away, the other colors in the leaves can show through. Sound familiar? It does to them! Magical, isn't it? And they love it when the understanding falls into place . . . and stays there!

High-Impact Teaching Strategies Used in This Lesson

- *Entertainment.* The teacher acting as a magician.

- *Involve, Don't Tell.* Students actually seeing the colors change.

- *Keen Visuals.* The color changing dramatically.

- *Music.* Use of a magic theme song.

- *Novelty.* The surprise of a magic trick!

Expansion of the Central Idea

Entertainment comes in many forms. Our willingness to use it as a teaching strategy can often dictate the success—or lack thereof—of our lessons. In the hands of a more traditional teacher, the key idea in the lesson may well be lost by the students if they are merely listening to a simple verbal explanation. Just being told the idea will certainly not make it stand out in any way in a student's memory.

Instead, this teacher has chosen to employ a playful sense of drama and excitement, which brings the lesson to life. While play-acting as a magician, with a flourish of her hand, the teacher unleashes students' imaginations and emotions, from anticipation to curiosity, from surprise to understanding. In this heightened state of engagement, students learn better.

The key, though, is the teacher's initial willingness to step forward and present the lesson in a unique way. Are *you* willing to do this? Are you willing to—at least occasionally—step into the role of the entertainer while teaching? As this lesson shows, it's well worth the effort. Entertainment leads to engagement, and engagement leads to better learning.

Lesson 2: Natural Resources

Students: First Grade

Submitted by: Abbey Stodghill

School: Academy at Nola Dunn, Burleson, Texas

Ask the Teacher

■ **Why Did You Develop a High-Impact Lesson for This Topic?** My students have to memorize the natural resources in the community, state, and nation for the Texas state test, called TAKS. In the past, this has been a challenge for them, so I knew I had to find a new, High-Impact Strategy for teaching it.

■ **How Do You Use High-Impact Strategies to Teach the Topic?** Before introducing the natural resources and their uses the students needed to know, I taught them 10 "pegs" [discussed briefly in the Uniquely Memorable section]. One by one, we practiced these pegs—all together, in twos and threes, and individually. In line, we practiced. During bathroom breaks, we practiced. Any short transition was ideal for practicing our pegging. The amazing thing about young students is they did not need too much explanation about why we were doing this—they enjoyed it simply because it was active and fun! I did, though, explain that this would help them remember "other stuff."

Next, I showed pictures of the natural resources and their uses:

■ Plants = paper   ■ Water = drinking   ■ Oil = electricity

■ Animals = food   ■ Coal = heat

We then connected the natural resources to the pegs the students had learned earlier:

- Number 1, *sun*, became plants because sun makes the plants grow.

- Number 2, *eyes*, became tears, which are made of water.

- Numbers 3, *triangle*, turned into an oil derrick because it looks like a triangle.

- Number 4, *stove*, is for animals because you cook them on a stove.

- Number 5, *fingers*, is for coal because you have to pick up the coal from the ground.

■ **What Is the Result of Teaching the Lesson This Way?** Since teaching my students how to learn the natural resources by using the "peg" method, they have been able to remember them easily. Even much later in the year, students were still able to tell each other—and write down—the natural resources and their uses. Using the pegging method helped my students both remember the central information as well as make connections between the motions and the related information they later learned regarding each natural resource.

High-Impact Teaching Strategies Used in This Lesson

- *Being Open.* When practicing in "twos and threes."

- *Frames.* Explaining that the pegs will help them remember information.

- *Jump Up.* Doing movements with the pegs.

- *Novelty.* It's a different way for them to learn!

- *Uniquely Memorable.* The use of the peg method.

Expansion of the Central Idea

This lesson demonstrates the power of using a specific memory strategy. It teaches students an easy way to remember the *key points*—the natural resources. These key points then serve as "triggers" for students to recall other content they have learned regarding these central points.

EDUCATION DOESN'T COST... IT PAYS

On a broad level, this is what all memory strategies offer students. Lacking easy access to a clear starting place, their memory of what they've studied can often be scattered, random, and chaotic. However, through the use of a memory strategy—whether an acrostic, an acronym, the pegs, or any other device—the swift recall of the central ideas becomes a jumping-off point to recall related information.

In education, this is sometimes referred to as "schema theory," meaning that students have a scheme, or plan, on how to organize, sort, and recall the information. Memory strategies of any kind provide this much-needed structure and immediately promote significantly better learning and increased levels of recall. They offer our students a ladder to learning success.

Lesson 3: Using Question Marks Appropriately

Students: First and Second Grade

Submitted by: Tamara Hughes

School: Trip Elementary, Grayson, Georgia

Ask the Teacher

■ **Why Did You Develop a High-Impact Lesson for This Topic?** Many of my students had difficulty determining when to use a question mark at the end of a sentence. I created this lesson to provide a resource for students to use throughout the year. However, because they learn the idea so well when I teach it this way, by the middle of the school year most students do not even have to use the resource because they will remember the words on the poster we create.

■ **How Do You Use High-Impact Strategies to Teach the Topic?** At the beginning of the year we talk about how punctuation marks are used at the ends of sentences. I empathize with them that it is sometimes difficult to determine which one to use. I then tell them that today is the day they are going to learn how to make it really easy to know when to use a question mark. I show them a huge question mark that I have cut out of posterboard. Then I produce a little colored bag and tell them there's a secret item hidden in it, and they have to guess what it is—by asking questions!

When someone asks a question, I write the first word of their sentence on the chalkboard. After many questions have been asked, I then take the item out of the bag. This "item" can really be anything, because it's not the item that's important, but the questions they ask about it. I then allow them to talk to each other and come up with more questions to ask, although this time they are challenged to come up with *different* first words for their questions.

Finally, together, we organize the words they have generated and write them on the posterboard. I always put the *wh* words at the top. I explain that whenever a sentence starts with one of these words, then they know it is a question sentence and it ends with a question mark. Finally, we put the poster question mark on the wall, and I tell them that it is now a resource for them to use this year. Sometimes I even hang the little bag with the poster to remind them of the questions that they asked!

■ **What Is the Result of Teaching the Lesson This Way?** This lesson is highly successful because, when in doubt, students have a visual resource they can use on their own to remember when to use a question mark. If they forget to use it, I can easily prompt them by pointing to the big question mark. This creates independence and self-confidence. However, throughout the year my students become less and less dependent on the poster—ultimately becoming responsible for their own learning. This sense of ownership for what they are learning and their success in knowing what to do, often becomes a driving energy that positively influences many other lessons.

High-Impact Teaching Strategies Used in This Lesson

- *Frames.* Explaining that what they are learning today will help make it easier to know when to use question marks.

- *High-Quality Responses.* Talking to a neighbor to think of more questions to ask about the item in the bag.

- *Involve, Don't Tell.* Getting them to ask questions about what's in the bag.

- *Keen Visuals.* The use of the big poster question mark.

- *Novelty.* A big question mark made out of a piece of posterboard!

- *Ownership.* Reminding themselves of when to use a question mark simply by glancing at the visual.

- *Socialization.* Again, when talking to their neighbor in preparation for asking questions about the item.

Expansion of the Central Idea

The key to this lesson is that it results in a student-created visual that reinforces learning throughout the year. We need to remember that the pos-

sibilities for using visuals go well beyond images on a PowerPoint slide
or worksheet. While these visuals can certainly play a useful role in many
effective lessons, if they are the primary way in which we use visuals to
teach, then we are missing out on a critical pathway through which many
students learn.

Once we introduce a creative visual to our students, we can use it in
numerous ways to reinforce the original learning. In this case, with the
large question mark posted on the wall, it could be partially covered, and
students could be asked what you've covered up. Or you could ask students to tell you three words from the poster without looking at it. For
testing, of course, the poster would be covered up or taken down. However, because students have looked at it many times, simply looking at that
place on the wall will often be enough of a prompt for them to recall the
information.

Visuals—especially original, imaginative, and innovative ones—will
often become the easiest way for some students to learn certain ideas.
Knowing how important they are in the learning process, when preparing
for a class we should always pause to consider how we might add a visual
component to the lesson. If we can create one, students will often learn
faster and remember better.

Lesson 4: Know Your State

Students: First and Second Grade

Submitted by: Lisa Johnston

School: Midway Park Elementary, Bedford, Texas

Ask the Teacher

■ **Why Did You Develop a High-Impact Lesson for This Topic?** My students were struggling with geographical locations in Texas. We were expecting a few days of rain, so I came up with a structured activity in the gym for
recess. I wanted to keep the students moving, but also academically engaged.

■ **How Do You Use High-Impact Strategies to Teach the Topic?** I
created an obstacle course by setting up the gym as a miniature version of
Texas. I put the names of the different geographical locations around the
gym on posterboards with a real picture to help identify its location on a
map of the state. Then I used gym equipment—jump ropes, carpet squares,
and cones—to physically represent the geography of the state. (For example, the mountains were represented by the orange cones.)

For the lesson, the class was divided into small groups. Each group was given a large blank map of Texas and told to start at a certain location—for example, one group started at the Guadalupe Mountains. Once they arrived at their starting location they had to add something to their group map related to that area of the state. For example, the group that began at the Guadalupe Mountains was told to color the mountains green on their map. Once each group was finished with their task at that location they celebrated by cheering or high-fiving each other and then took their map to another location to do another task. To reinforce that they were learning our geography, I played Texas music in the background while students were working—one of the songs I used was "The Yellow Rose of Texas." They continued rotating until all groups had completed the task at every area.

When all groups were done we came back together in the middle of the gym. Using scissors, each group cut the areas of the map they had been working on into individual pieces and then practiced putting them back together and naming the areas. I also asked them to tell me what gym equipment had been at that area to help reinforce their memories. To end, every group contributed one or two of their cut-out areas and we created a collective map of Texas!

■ **What Is the Result of Teaching the Lesson This Way?** Later, when I gave my students a blank map of Texas for their assessment, I could see them picturing the gym in their heads. They were thinking of the movement activities and recalling what equipment was used. I even heard some of my students humming songs that were played while they were in a certain location. The students all enjoyed this lesson and scored 100% on their assessment!

High-Impact Teaching Strategies Used in This Lesson

- *Acknowledgment.* Cheering when completing a particular task.

- *Crest of the Wave.* The brief time spent at each task before moving on.

- *Keen Visuals.* The use of the gym equipment as a memory trigger for these young learners.

- *Music.* Playing Texas songs to learn about Texas!

- *Socialization.* Students talking to each other in the groups.

Expansion of the Central Idea

Understanding locations on a map is primarily a *visual–conceptual* skill, one these young students are only beginning to understand. However, something even very youthful students are good at doing naturally is learning by *doing*. By creating a physical map of Texas on the floor and by using the gym equipment to represent certain areas of the state, this teacher is building a link between a learning strategy that is innate to them and the skill they are trying to develop. Instead of continuing to be taught using only a visual approach, the bridge from kinesthetic to visual will help many of these students comprehend the geography of their state much more rapidly.

Students who struggle in any subject area are often simply not being taught in the way they learn best. Many teachers, on discovering a student who is not fully grasping new material, with the best of intentions will often attempt to help them by simply doing more of the same. This approach is rarely successful. Instead, perhaps the most important thing a teacher can do is to consider an entirely different—sometimes completely radical—approach to teaching the same topic. The specific strategy of taking a visual concept and making it physical—as demonstrated in this lesson—is a wonderful approach that can be used very effectively in many subject areas, with students of all ages.

Lesson 5: Sentence Types

Students: Third Grade

Submitted by: Dana Hand

School: Thalia Elementary School, Virginia Beach, VA

Ask the Teacher

■ **Why Did You Develop a High-Impact Lesson for This Topic?** I use High-Impact Teaching to introduce types of sentences because this topic could easily be perceived as boring. Instead, I wanted my students to enjoy learning about it. Also, because this topic is important on a long-term basis, I wanted my students to have ownership of their learning, so they would remember it better.

■ **How Do You Use High-Impact Strategies to Teach the Topic?** Initially, two students placed at opposite sides of the room are responsible for distributing materials. The materials are a small tablet and a pen. Students must pay each distributor a compliment before they are given their materials. Once students have the materials, they are organized into groups of four. Now, one student from each group remains in the room and music plays as all of the others are sent into the hallway.

The students in the room now stand and gather around me. I prime them by letting them know they will have the responsibility of teaching their missing classmates—those in the hall—the information I am about to share with them. I ask them to take a few bulleted notes that they will be able to use and will guide them as they become the "teachers" when the students in the hall return.

In a quiet voice, so those in the hall won't hear, I teach these students the points I want them to know about different sentence types. They always get excited, as if I'm letting them in on a secret. They look like a bunch of little journalists taking notes for a newspaper article. When I'm done explaining the content, the other students return from the hallway.

Then, the students begin teaching each other. I play quiet background music as the teachers explain what I have taught them. I move around the room listening to the teaching that is taking place. Often, "teachers" add their own examples and even quiz one another to make sure their "students" understand what they are learning.

One of the big keys to the success of this approach is that I repeat the process four times, giving each student from each group an opportunity to become the "teacher." I give each new "teacher" a new piece of information to teach the other students in their group.

■ **What Is the Result of Teaching the Lesson This Way?** All students are engaged in the lesson and in the learning. They also take great pride in being responsible for making sure the rest of their group learns the material. They all finish the lesson with notes on all aspects of the topic. The entire class finishes with a feeling of accomplishment, each knowing that they have taught someone else something brand new.

High-Impact Teaching Strategies Used in This Lesson

- *Acknowledgment*. Given to the students distributing the resources at the start of the lesson.

- *Entertainment*. Whispering creates a sense of drama.

- *Music*. Played when students were leaving the room and when working in small groups.

- *Jump Up*. Movement used when gathering their resources, when going outside the classroom, and when discussing the information in groups.

- *Ownership*. Students doing the teaching.

Expansion of the Central Idea

Using students as teachers can serve to increase the impact of many lessons. While clearly not all content is suited to this approach, whenever it *is* possible, teachers should actively seek to exploit this idea as much as possible. Simultaneously and on many different levels, it dramatically increases the overall impact of the lesson.

However, using this technique will frequently require additional prep time on your part. In addition, while temporarily being a teacher, students may not cover all of the necessary and important details. This means you'll often want to conclude these lessons by reclaiming the reins of command and doing a follow-up section to ensure that all students have learned all of the necessary material. For these reasons it may appear that valuable classroom time is being wasted, and some teachers will simply choose to avoid using the idea of student-teachers entirely.

However, because student engagement is incredibly high during these moments in the classroom, time is often saved later in the unit. Traditionally, a certain amount of classroom time is always set aside for review. Yet when the original lesson is taught using High-Impact Strategies, review time is often significantly reduced, since students have learned the material at a higher level the first time around.

Many High-Impact Teaching Strategies function in this way—at first glance they may seem to require slightly more time than simple "chalk-and-talk" methods. Yet on closer inspection, if students learn the original material more clearly the first time around, we often save precious time later. Using High-Impact Strategies successfully requires a careful consideration of this idea: More investment of energy and focus up front frequently leads to faster—and better—learning in the long run.

Lesson 6: ABCs on the Move

Students:	First through Fifth Grade
Submitted by:	Kim Cooke
School:	Marvin Ridge High School, Waxhaw, North Carolina

Ask the Teacher

■ **Why Did You Develop a High-Impact Lesson for This Topic?** I created the lesson "ABCs on the Move" to integrate academic subjects into the gymnasium, and to allow for student movement (and enjoyment) to help improve reading and socialization skills. The students even benefit physically from having a great cardiovascular workout!

■ **How Do You Use High-Impact Strategies to Teach the Topic?** Using index cards, I made over 500 flash cards with letters on them. I made more index cards for the vowels. I even included some "bonus" cards with stars on them to be used as wild cards. Before the students arrive I spread these cards upside down on one-half of the gym.

Students are then divided into relay teams of three or four people. Each team is assigned to stand behind a colored cone with a file folder hanging from it with four words printed on it. The words come from spelling lists for the week.

When the music starts—I like using the song "ABC" by the Jackson 5—the first person in each team runs down to the scrambled index cards and picks up only one card. If it is a letter they need to create the target word they bring it back to their team and place it in front of their cone. If it is not a letter they need for one of their words they put it back upside down and return to their cone empty-handed, and the next person in line takes their turn. A student choosing a wild card can choose any letter for that card.

When a team has completed all their words, they perform the Celebration Dance (the famous "Stayin' Alive" pose) to inform me that they have found all the letters, and then cheer on other teams until they are complete. When all teams are done, we replace the cards face-down on the floor and the teams move to a new cone—new words—and off they go again!

■ **What Is the Result of Teaching the Lesson This Way?** Students beg me to do this lesson! My ESL (English as a second language) students especially derive great benefit by looking at the index card and then looking at their cone to see if their letter matches any of the letters in the intended word. And while I am primarily a health and PE teacher, other classroom teachers appreciate how I am "teaming" with them to help improve all students' reading skills.

High-Impact Teaching Strategies Used in This Lesson

- *Acknowledgment.* Cheering their success, and cheering for other teams.

- *Jump Up.* Students running to get various cards.

- *Music.* Playing songs while students perform the activity.

- *Novelty.* An unusual way to practice spelling words.

- *Socialization.* Students working together and talking to complete the task.

- *Tiers.* Repeating the activity with new words, as time allows.

Expansion of the Central Idea

Combining a potentially tedious subject—in this case spelling—with a novel teaching method allows students to engage in the learning process at a much higher level than might traditionally be expected. It's easy to imagine this lesson happening with great enthusiasm, energy, and excitement on the part of the students—all while building their understanding of critical information.

As with the previous lesson, some preparation is required. However, once students have participated in this activity several times and understand the basic procedure, it's easy to see how the teacher could involve them in preparing for the activity. Students could help make the letter cards and prep the spelling words on the file folders. They could even assist in creating the physical setup by taping the file folders to the cones and then laying out the cards on the floor. Their excitement and anticipation about the upcoming lesson, coupled with their participation in the physical preparation for the activity, would further increase their sense of ownership for their own learning.

Lesson 7: Photo Journal Review

Students:	Third Grade (8- and 9-year-olds primarily, but could be used at any level)
Submitted by:	Shelley Deneau
School:	White Oaks Elementary School, Virginia Beach, Virginia

Ask the Teacher

■ **Why Did You Develop a High-Impact Lesson for This Topic?** Every year we are expected to spend two or more weeks reviewing material learned during the year to prepare for high-stakes testing. To me this seems like an incredible amount of instructional time to devote to review, especially since it's my belief is that if it's taught right the first time, only a little review is truly necessary before testing. Since I think paper-and-pencil review can often be boring and impersonal, I wanted to do something different—something that would stick with the children!

■ **How Do You Use High-Impact Strategies to Teach the Topic?** I love photography and have a good deal of experience in this area. I decided to use that experience to create a dynamic, unique, and useful project for my students to help them review their material in a creative, ongoing way. I begin by laying the foundation for the project during the first few months of the school year, as we occasionally talk about what a photographer does, where they work, and tools they need.

In November, I become an "editor." I distribute a letter to my "staff"—my students—and a small notebook. They are given an assignment, due in January, which is to take a picture of each topic in my letter. The letter is basically a summary of the major topics and concepts that will be assessed on our state testing. Of course I haven't taught everything by then, so in some cases this is the introduction to the concept. I also attach a letter to the parents explaining the intention of this photo journal project.

Simply taking pictures, however, is not enough. Over the next two months, as pictures are taken and added to their scrapbook, students must also decorate the page with additional drawings, key ideas, and at least one paragraph about how we use this concept in our lives. As a class we touch base every two weeks and discuss what is complete in their journals and talk about any places where they'd like more information to help them continue developing their journals.

The students are allowed to be as creative as they choose, and I've seen some pretty interesting representations of concepts! The most important issue, however, is that since they are the ones creating the unusual connections—taking the photographs, finding real-world examples of "big ideas," and building background and discussion points—they take real ownership of their learning. Treating them like photojournalists gives the assignments authenticity and a level of excitement not seen in many classroom projects, and they remain fully engaged in the activity whenever we revisit their journals.

■ **What Is the Result of Teaching the Lesson This Way?** The results have been extremely positive from both the students and the parents. On one level, everyone involved believes it is a novel and unique way to achieve the goal of maintaining an ongoing review process during the year. Parents often say that they especially appreciate the unique interaction time they have with their child, since it is not merely yet another paper-and-pencil activity they must look over.

On a pragmatic level, since I have been using this approach my students' success on the standardized tests has been excellent in the subjects covered. The students frequently cite and praise this activity in our review at the end of the year as one of the primary reasons they've learned so much.

High-Impact Teaching Strategies Used in This Lesson

- *Involve, Don't Tell.* Students are fully involved in their projects—as well as parents.

- *Keen Visuals.* Taking the pictures, plus the images they add to their journals.

- *Labels.* The word "review" takes on an entirely different dimension when viewed through the perspective of this project.

- *Novelty.* Review without the normal use of paper and pencil.

- *Ownership.* Students can interpret each aspect of the assignment in their own unique way.

- *Socialization.* In this case, the unique aspect is the possibilities for frequent parent–child interactions.

Expansion of the Central Idea

This teacher has taken one of her personal interests and found a way to incorporate it in a meaningful way in her classroom. Learning invariably comes alive for our students whenever we are able to do this. They see the excitement in our eyes and hear the enthusiasm in our voices. Students invariably pick up on our intrinsic passion and feel drawn into it. It might be well worth considering your own passions and deciding how you might include them as a part of your teaching.

In this particular lesson, however, if the actual photographic skill required by the teacher was kept to a minimum, most of us could find a way to adapt the basic idea offered here. The opportunity to review key concepts on a frequent basis—and in a creative way—will very likely lead to significantly better testing results when compared with students who only review at the end of the year.

Educational psychologists refer to this concept as "massed versus distributed practice." Massed practice can best be compared to cramming for two hours on the night before a test, while distributed practice might mean studying for thirty minutes each night for four days before the test. It has been consistently shown that distributed practice is better in the short term—meaning the test result will be higher—but it also is significantly better for retaining information long-term. By using the strategy demonstrated in this lesson, the teacher is giving her students the very real gift of better learning.

Lesson 8: Native American Legends

Students: Third and Fourth Grade

Submitted by: Kris Long

School: Miami Country Day School, Miami, Florida

Ask the Teacher

■ **Why Did You Develop a High-Impact Lesson for This Topic?** To enable my students to create and write a Native American legend of their own, they first need to be exposed to some of these legends. They need to not just hear them, but to also feel the story and atmosphere in which legends were shared. The students also need to digest, discuss, and ask questions about the legends. Through this process they can begin to brainstorm and create ideas from which to create their own legends to share with one another.

■ **How Do You Use High-Impact Strategies to Teach the Topic?** To build excitement, I take my students outside to share a Native American legend. In the background I play music from The Native Flute Ensemble. We sit in a circle and I share a Native American legend. A good one to share is The Girl Who Loved Wild Horses.

After sharing the legend, the students discuss in small groups or pairs why they feel the legend was created in the first place and ask questions about it. I explain that legends are called realistic fiction and usually have a lesson. I share with them the book from which I memorized the story to demonstrate how the legend being spoken again and again turned into a story to share in a more traditional way. Once the students have had an opportunity to ask questions, discuss, and reflect about the legend they heard, they begin brainstorming on their own topics for a legend.

Students first work independently, then gather in small groups and share ideas with each other, which they can add to their own notes. Once brainstorming is finished, each student writes a rough draft of a story. Once the rough drafts are complete, the students share their work in groups of three to four, discussing what they enjoyed about the legend that was created and what could be improved.

Finally, after they have had this peer review, they rewrite and edit their own work. The completed legends are made into a book, and then they each get to share their stories with younger students and peers.

■ **What Is the Result of Teaching the Lesson This Way?** The strategy of telling a story with music playing in the background as a springboard from which to write their own legends is an automatic engager. Stories, and legends in particular, pull in students with the elements of anticipation and interest. Their interest and excitement in writing a legend is enhanced when they realize they will be able to share the stories they develop. As a teacher, this subject has become one of the ones I enjoy the most for one simple reason—once I open the door I stand back and watch in admiration as their natural desire to learn leaps forward.

High-Impact Teaching Strategies Used in This Lesson

- *Entertainment.* Performing in front of the younger students as they share their own legends is a potent influence for full engagement in the activity.

- *Frames.* Explaining where legends come from and how Native Americans used them makes learning about them relevant.

- *Jump Up.* Moving outside to hear the legend.

- *Labels.* The word *legend* will have a new and evocative connotation for these students after the lesson.

- *Music.* The use of the Native American music to set the atmosphere is critical to the success of the lesson.

- *Ownership.* The students create their own stories.

- *Socialization.* The students talk to each other constantly during this process.

- *Yesterday Lives.* The power of stories is self-evident in the students' enthusiasm, excitement, and interest.

Expansion of the Central Idea

It is possible that some readers will view this teacher's decisions to use music—as well as take the students outside—as unnecessary theatrics. And yet, without these elements present, much of the power of the lesson will be lost. The emotions evoked by the music, the setting, and even the teacher's voice will go a long way in making this a memorable lesson.

Hopefully it is obvious that not all content can to be taught with a strong emotional undercurrent. However, that simply makes it even more apparent why we must seize upon those that *can* be offered this way to students and go out of our way to create these experiences for them. If education is in any way preparation for life outside of school, then these are essential experiences for all students to have participated in at some point. Life—*real* life—is chock-full of emotions, and our schools will better serve our children at a fundamental level if in addition helping them learn how to read and write, we also help them grow comfortable with how they *feel*.

Lesson 9: Animals in the Ocean

Students: Third through Fifth Grade

Submitted by: Tina Bernard

School: Hajek Elementary, Burleson, Texas

Ask the Teacher

■ **Why Did You Develop a High-Impact Lesson for This Topic?** I developed this lesson to prepare students for a field trip to the Texas State Aquarium. We were going there as a side trip to our actual overnight trip on the USS Lexington. Although the trip was designed to feature military action during World War II, it was convenient to walk over to the aquarium. This is significant because I knew we didn't have much time to fully experience the aquarium, so I designed a lesson where students took ownership of the material and shared it with each other. Without doing it this way, I could never have taught the students so much in so little time!

■ **How Do You Use High-Impact Strategies to Teach the Topic?** I began by distributing a few brochures from the Texas State Aquarium that highlighted feature exhibits and shows. Students were given one minute to look over the material; then we began to look at the brochures as a class. We decided that there were eight animals that we did not know much about and, because my students know that I like them to ask interesting questions, we knew that we had to know more!

Students were divided into eight learning teams, each responsible for finding as much material about one animal as possible in ten minutes. They then had five minutes to decide how they would teach the material to the rest of the group—using nothing but their bodies and voices to present. Once time was up, I took students to the gym, where I had already made signs for each of the animals and spread them out on the walls, two per wall.

Students were then taken on a mock tour of the aquarium where they traveled to each animal exhibit and the groups presented what they had found as we came to their particular animal. Because the groups had only their voices and bodies to work with, they created songs, poems, dances, and cheers that they taught to each other along the way. At the end of our session, we had learned about our animals of interest and had a great visual, kinesthetic way to connect the information.

■ **What Is the Result of Teaching the Lesson This Way?** Students were completely engaged in the learning process during the entire lesson. We all learned more than we could have in a traditional lecture setting—and had fun the whole time. Students were able to remember almost all the information they had learned about each animal when we were at the actual aquarium, and they even taught some of the aquarium workers their songs, chants, poems, and cheers. When the director of the aquarium stopped me and asked how long we had been studying the animals, I replied, "About an hour!"

High-Impact Teaching Strategies Used in This Lesson

- *Crest of the Wave.* Everything was done in short bursts.

- *Entertainment.* Students were performing for each other.

- *Jump Up.* Students went to another room to perform and moved to a new location for each animal presentation.

- *Keen Visuals.* Pictures of the animals were posted so everyone could see them.

- *Ownership.* Students looked up their own information.

- *Socialization.* Students worked together in teams.

Expansion of the Central Idea

This lesson contains a hidden gem in how to work effectively with Gen Y and Gen Z, which needs to be explicitly revealed. One of the key differences in today's classrooms is that the long-held notion of the teacher having all the information no longer applies. In this particular lesson the teacher could have provided each group with what she thought was the most important information for them to tell the other students about each animal. Instead, they were left entirely on their own, not only to discover the information about their chosen animal, but perhaps more importantly *which* pieces of information to share.

The simple truth is that if the teacher had provided each group with a prompt sheet on the important facts about each animal, it would merely have been *her* opinion on which of the many known facts about each animal were important for them to learn. If she had done that the students would simply have been regurgitating something they were told. Regardless of the creativity of the presentation, a significant opportunity for real learning would have been lost.

By letting them choose which facts to share, while the students did not consciously realize what was happening, they were processing, sorting, cataloguing, organizing, and prioritizing information. As teachers we should intentionally seize any opportunity we have to further students' development in these critical thinking areas—just as this teacher has done in this seemingly quick and easy lesson.

Lesson 10: Plotting Points on the Coordinate Grid

Students: Fourth and Fifth Grade

Submitted by: Jenn Currie

School: Commodore Perry School District,
                      Hadley, Pennsylvania

Ask the Teacher

■ **Why Did You Develop a High-Impact Lesson for This Topic?** I created this lesson to get students up and moving, as well as have them actually use their body to find their coordinates and help remember that they must go OVER and UP to plot their point, rather than vice-versa. Fourth and fifth graders very often confuse these directions.

■ **How Do You Use High-Impact Strategies to Teach the Topic?** I begin by arranging the classroom chairs in a 10 × 10 square fashion. Next, I place about half the students in designated seats. They each hold a card that tells their coordinates. They keep this secret. I now ask the class, "How many of you have played or have seen someone play Battleship?" The majority of the hands go up. "Great! We're going to play Battleship to locate the students in the chairs!"

I now ask a student seated in one of the chairs to stand up and then ask the class what coordinates indicated the location of that person. For example, I might say,

LEARNING SHOULD BE
COLLABORATIVE...

NOT COMPETITIVE

"Which set of coordinates, (5,2) or (2,5), would represent Alexis's location?" If a student responds, "I believe she is at (5,2)," I say, "Alexis, is that what your card says?" She shakes her head no. "Hmm, then she must be at . . . Alexis, show us your card. (2,5). OK, let's look at Caitlyn. Please stand up." We continue on like this a student or two. We then examine the correct coordinates and they self-discover, by using the information they have gathered, that to get where they need to be, they must move OVER and UP to point the plot. We exchange positions to allow others to try. Sometimes I have them discuss in groups where they think someone is before answering, so they have the benefit of talking it through with someone else.

Next, each student receives a set of coordinates on an index card and is instructed to plot him- or herself. Sometimes I even have students plot their friends. Once plotted, the remainder of the class decides if they are sitting in the correct location in relation to their points.

Finally, after these demonstrations, we take the idea to paper and plot points on a coordinate grid. I keep asking, "How is this coordinate grid similar to how our chairs were set up?" Eventually they all start answering, "They are both set up in a grid fashion and we must move OVER and UP to plot our points." Students continue plotting points and I continue to check for understanding.

■ **What Is the Result of Teaching the Lesson This Way?** On most all occasions students will remember to plot OVER and UP. If by chance they do forget, all I need to do is remind them of our lesson: "Remember when we had the chairs placed in a square and we had to plot ourselves in the correct chair? How did you decide where to seat yourself?" That usually triggers the memory of OVER and UP!

High-Impact Teaching Strategies Used in This Lesson

- *Directions.* This teacher is giving clear, precise, and short directions.

- *Entertainment.* Students playing Battleship with each other is very entertaining!

- *High-Quality Responses.* By occasionally allowing them to check with each other before answering, they are preparing their responses.

- *Jump Up.* Movement is being used to teach the concept.

- *Novelty.* Playing Battleship with each other is *unusual*, too!

- *Tiers.* The learning is done in clear, distinct layers, building from physical movement to paper and pen.

Expansion of the Central Idea

The key aspect of successfully teaching using the tiers concept is in how each step builds on the next one—clearly different yet only in a subtly more complex way. This lesson is a very clear example of this concept. Sequential change does occur during the course of the lesson, but at an appropriate pace.

Note that after students have been given multiple opportunities to learn OVER and UP by viewing other students and guessing at their coordinates, the next step builds on this—in a gentle but clearly distinct way. As students move from observing other students to proactively either seating themselves or seating another student in the proper place, the difference is clear, but not overwhelming. While some students may not consciously note much has changed, the experienced teacher can easily identify the difference between observing and guessing, and choosing and moving. They are indeed different and distinct learning modalities.

The challenge in using tiered learning is that, to the teacher's perception, the change between tiers may seem small. To the learner, however, it may well be a massive shift. This difference is a result of the teacher's experience level with the content—if they know it well, the next step seems obvious. However, to someone learning something for the first time, it may be quite another matter. The key, then, is to always look at the difference between the steps from the viewpoint of the student. Only from that perspective can we build the most appropriate tiers for our lessons.

Lesson 11: American History Time Lines

Students: Upper Elementary and Middle School

Submitted by: Cindy Rickert

School: Christopher Farms Elementary School,
                Virginia Beach, Virginia

Ask the Teacher

■ **Why Did You Develop a High-Impact Lesson for This Topic?** Teaching history to fifth graders can be a challenge, especially when the textbook is written on a level too high for my students to read. So, I needed to find a way for students to learn important dates in our state history, in a way that would really stick with them.

■ **How Do You Use High-Impact Strategies to Teach the Topic?** To learn important dates in early Virginia history, we create a "living time line." We work in cooperative teams in my class, and I let each team choose a year to re-enact something important which happened that year in Virginia. The one rule is they must help the rest of us remember that year with ONE sentence—preferably one that rhymes. For example, to demonstrate that in 1620, the Bride Ship came to Virginia, one team dressed up like ladies and acted like they were stepping off a ship, then they shouted: "In 1620, in came the HONEYS!"

■ **What Is the Result of Teaching the Lesson This Way?** We do a living time line at the end of every unit, and my students can't wait to live the history! It gets them excited about a subject that they used to think was boring. As the year goes by, they get better and better at creating vivid reminders of important dates. And, as a result, my students rarely miss time line questions.

High-Impact Teaching Strategies Used in this Lesson

- *Entertainment.* Students acting out key events.

- *Getting Responses.* The response that students are giving in this lesson is practiced repeatedly in small groups first, allowing them to clarify the key idea.

- *Involve, Don't Tell.* Students are truly involved in this activity!

- *Jump Up.* Students are moving during their presentations.

- *Labels.* When taught this way, the word *history* takes on a whole new meaning, and hopefully creates a positive association for these students.

- *Ownership.* Students have a wide range of choices in what they will present, how they will present it, and the key line.

- *Socialization.* Students are working in groups.

- *Uniquely Memorable.* Using a single sentence, acting out the scene, and incorporating rhymes all directly assist students' memories.

- *Yesterday Lives.* History is full of stories. This method of teaching helps these stories truly come alive for the students.

Expansion of the Central Idea

While this teaching strategy is helping students learn their current lesson, it is actually helping them on a much broader scale. By summarizing the lesson in this way, they are discovering on their own the power of using specific memory strategies. As they experience success in the short term, and subsequently perform well on tests, they will certainly be delighted.

However, imagine these same students the following year, or even a few years ahead. Picture them studying a subject in a more traditional classroom setting, perhaps struggling to remember some key pieces of information. It's easy to see how they might reflect back on how they were taught history and say, "Wait a minute, what we did back then made history so easy! Maybe I can do something similar for this subject, for myself, and be able to learn it better."

If students are able to transfer the learning strategy to another content area, then this teacher is truly achieving the highest aims of education. We want students to leave our classrooms self-sufficient, reflective, and armed with good strategies. By taking students through a lesson in this way, this teacher is helping them learn the information in the current lesson, but is also teaching them broader skills that will serve them well for a long time to come.

Lesson 12: Can You Dig It?

Students: Seventh and Eighth Grade

Submitted by: Laurie Gallant

School: McMichael Middle School, Nacogdoches, Texas

Ask the Teacher

■ **Why Did You Develop a High-Impact Lesson for This Topic?** History seems dull to many students. Many feel that all they do is memorize facts and dates about dead people. Most teachers present the subject of archeology by looking at a picture of a dig site, and then there may be a worksheet to find things in a grid. Artifacts are discussed. Test at the end of the unit. Boring.

■ **How Do You Use High-Impact Strategies to Teach the Topic?** To introduce the unit of Texas Indians I also tie in archeology. I buy each student a 2-inch-high clay pot. I then use various websites and show students actual pottery found at numerous archeology sites around Texas. In groups of three or four, students then create an artifact—a painted pot—that represents a Native Texan lifestyle such as hunter, gatherer, farmer, and so on.

After school, without students knowing, I take their pots and break them into pieces! I mix all the pieces of the various pots together and bury these pieces in tubs of dirt. When students arrive the next day, I give each group one of the tubs filled with dirt and buried pottery pieces, and some spoons and brushes, and tell them that their pots are broken and buried somewhere in the dirt. They are all astounded, and begin to dig—or excavate—the pottery pieces, and must also "classify" the pieces for the correct pot. Finally they are given the time to reconstruct the pottery using Elmer's glue!

■ **What Is the Result of Teaching the Lesson This Way?** Since creating this introductory activity, my students are engaged and excited about archeology. When I have a guest archeologist come and speak to my students, they have a better understanding of archeology and are able to ask very insightful questions. It now makes more sense to them when I share with the students that the majority of what we know about ancient cultures comes from the archeological sites. I also say that what we throw away today in our landfills will become the future dig sites—but that's another lesson!

High-Impact Teaching Strategies Used in This Lesson

- *Frames.* The relevance of the activity is woven throughout the lesson and helps clarify what archeology really means.

- *Involve, Don't Tell.* Students are fully involved in this activity, instead of simply being told the information and asked to remember it.

- *Jump Up.* There is plenty of movement in all aspects of the lesson.

- *Keen Visuals.* The creation of the pots, and then uncovering the pieces of pottery in the tubs of dirt, makes this a highly visual lesson.

- *Labels.* After this experience, the word *archeology* will have a much deeper and more powerful meaning to students.

- *Novelty.* Digging up your own broken pot is certainly novel!

- *Ownership.* They created the pots, and they are the ones uncovering them.

- *Socialization.* Students are working together at several different points throughout the lesson.

Expansion of the Central Idea

The level of engagement in both parts of this lesson would be extraordinarily high. Since high levels of engagement lead to High-Impact Lessons, it is worth highlighting the various strategies being used. From group discussions, to groups making the pots, to digging in dirt—all these strategies capture students' attention and engage them in the learning.

One engagement strategy being used here, however, deserves particular attention. When students return to class the next day, can you imagine how surprised they would be to discover that the pots they had so carefully created the previous day had been shattered by their teacher and buried in dirt. This shocking development would no doubt astonish many of the students.

Yet this emotional reaction now becomes the driving force behind the excavation portion of the lesson. Did she *really* do this? Where are the pieces to the pot they created? *Why* did she do this? When a student's curiosity has been aroused, they tend to dive deeply into the activity to which it is connected.

The suggestion here, of course, is not to smash everything your students create! Rather, the idea is to consider what we can as teachers occasionally do to surprise, startle, and shock our students—in a good way, for a good educational purpose. Their emotional response will keep them highly engaged and fully focused on the lesson at hand.

Lesson 13: Review Baseball

Students: Seventh and Eighth Grade

Submitted by: Maureen Stolte

School: Brandon Middle School, Virginia Beach, Virginia

Ask the Teacher

■ **Why Did You Develop a High-Impact Lesson for This Topic?** I developed a baseball review game as a way to acknowledge my class when they have completed a unit of study. Students always look forward to doing this as their reward for working hard. We don't always use it at the end of every unit; however, it's one of their favorite ways of celebrating that we've reached the end of a section.

■ **How Do You Use High-Impact Strategies to Teach the Topic?** To prepare to play review baseball I come up with a series of questions ranging from easy (first base) to difficult (home run). The day of the game, I divide the class into two groups and allow them to devise names for their teams. Next I have the students set up plastic bases and flip a coin to determine which team will be up first. The first team up will line up in batting order and the opposing team will select a pitcher and then man the bases and field.

The student who is up at bat will select a first base, second base, third base, or home run question. If the student answers the question correctly, the pitcher tosses a plastic ball to the student, who tries to hit the ball with plastic bat. Even if the student does not hit the ball, he or she will run to the base that correlates to the type of question that they answered. A student is never out unless they answer a question incorrectly. Therefore, athletic ability is not necessary to experience this form of acknowledgment.

Each team is given three outs, but if the teams are really slamming base hits sometimes I limit them to just one out. While my students really enjoy going outside to do this activity, on rainy days we play the game indoors,

and the only difference is that the students are instructed to hit the ball
gently and walk to the bases.

■ **What Is the Result of Teaching the Lesson This Way?** I always hit
a home run with my students whenever I tell them we'll be playing the
baseball review game. Throughout the school year, they eagerly anticipate
the end of each unit of study, because they know they may get to play the
game once again.

High-Impact Teaching Strategies Used in This Lesson

- *Acknowledgment.* The physical act of walking to the different bases is
  the acknowledgment that they have answered the question correctly.

- *Being Open.* The teacher is deliberately using *closed* questions for a
  specific purpose: For this activity to work, each question must have a
  "right" answer.

- *Involve, Don't Tell.* Students are certainly involved in this activity!

- *Jump Up.* Students are physically active during the lesson, even if it is
  played indoors.

- *Novelty.* Reviewing material by playing a version of baseball is unusual!

- *Revolutions.* The students know the chance to play the game is going to
  come around again, at the ends of most units of study. It's something
  for them to look forward to each time a new unit begins.

Expansion of the Central Idea

The fact that the students know they may be given a chance to do this
activity at the end of each unit is something that draws them forward.
All teachers should have at least two or three activities they know their
students enjoy that reappear on a regular basis. These activities become
something students anticipate, ask for, and sometimes even work hard to
earn—all of which mean they are engaging in the classroom.

Enjoyable—and *recognizable*—activities that occasionally pop up in the
classroom serve an important function. While much has been made in this
book of the use of novelty to engage today's students, the opposite can be
just as effective in certain cases. A ritual that students enjoy, anticipate, and
appreciate can also help to keep them focused and engaged throughout
the year. In this case it's easy to imagine students eagerly reviewing the
material they've learned during a unit in preparation for the next round of
review baseball.

Lesson 14: Docent of Your Own Museum—Understanding the Visual Arts in Relation to History and Culture

Students: High School

Submitted by: Christy Sheffield

Organization: Great Expectations, Ames, Oklahoma

Ask the Teacher

■ **Why Did You Develop a High-Impact Lesson for This Topic?**
"Understanding the Visual Arts in Relation to History and Culture" is one of the national standards that teachers are to meet in Fine Arts, but the dusty title of that concept mostly inspires yawns and questions from students of "What's in it for me?" There certainly is enrichment and enlightenment for students that comes from recognizing how the culture of a society shapes its art and sometimes the art shapes the culture, but the aspect of the "Docent of Your Own Museum" most pertinent to students' lives is the manner they use to explore the lesson topic. I developed this High-Impact Lesson, which delves deep into exploring the art/culture relationship, because students become passionate about the topic since they "own" their museums. Additionally, a snappy class discussion drives home the point that being a competent docent—a tourist guide working in a museum or cathedral—provides skills that fit the requirements for countless careers.

■ **How Do You Use High-Impact Strategies to Teach the Topic?** In a fine arts class, students create scale-model museums featuring visual art from four different cultures and give guided tours to explain the relationships between their museums' works of art and the societies in which the art was produced. The students enjoy being museum curators who make decisions about art acquisitions; they are practicing architects who design impressive exhibit spaces; and they are diligent researchers because they need the information for providing guided tours. The active, hands-on aspects of this project make the work matter to the students immediately and implant insights and skills that have lifelong relevance.

To begin, students search for pictures of visual art from four different cultures. They need three or four works for each culture. The teacher supplies books, magazines, and art catalogs from which students may cut pictures. Excellent sources of such pictures are the catalogs that museum gift shops provide free of charge. Students choose paintings, of course, but they may also feature sculptures, vases, functional native pieces, stained glass, and so on. Their accompanying task is to research the art's relation to history and culture. Next students manufacture four-room museums. Students choose one piece of art from their collection to set the scale of their model museum, although not all pictures will fit this same scale. (Note: Some students need help in calculating scale, but their efforts on this project certainly give relevance to the need to understand ratios from math class!) The teacher supplies materials and tools and a sample scale-model museum put together from cardboard. When students finish their model construction, they install their art at eye level for a scale-model person. The museums are open-sided so that the art inside can be easily seen.

When the museums are completed and students have prepared brochures for their exhibit halls listing the artworks with artist, date of production, real-life size of the piece, and the medium used for each, then the teacher arranges for small groups to listen and look as each student docent provides informative tours of his or her exhibits. The tour day is preceded by discussions and guidelines on how to be interesting and engaging docents. On the day of the tours, students dress in appropriate business casual attire and wear name badges as they welcome "visitors," who are impressed with their exhibits and their knowledge of art, history, and culture.

■ **What Is the Result of Teaching the Lesson This Way?** This has become a thoroughly engaging way for students to study how visual art is related to history and culture because its many facets are relevant to students' interests and needs for the future. Students are given much discretion in the choices they make, and this matches exactly with "problem-solving and decision-making skills," which is one of the Eight Keys to Employability defined by the Occupational Outlook Committee. The assignment integrates research, writing, and the use of technology, and it provides open-ended opportunities for creativity. Students get a boost in self-esteem as they display their unique museums and in their sense of significance when they are the expert-for-the-moment on the art and culture they describe in their tours. Students learn not only about the artwork they exhibit themselves, but they also learn from the "tours" they take of classmates' museums. This project truly connects students to art's relation to history and culture, and in their lives beyond the classroom, students will visit national art galleries and major museums with greater appreciation because they've been museum directors themselves!

High-Impact Teaching Strategies Used in This Lesson

■ *Acknowledgment.* The acknowledgment aspect of this lesson emerges as students share what they have created with others and receive praise in return for the knowledge and ideas in their museum.

- *Frames.* The relevance to a possible future job is very high and can be a motivating force in driving the students to create a high-quality product.

- *Getting Responses.* All students involved in this project not only have plenty of time to prepare their responses but also multiple opportunities to respond as various people ask about their museum.

- *Involve, Don't Tell.* These students are thoroughly involved at every level in this lesson.

- *Ownership.* Students have a high level of ownership with their projects, making numerous decisions along the way from conception to presentation.

Expansion of the Central Idea

Students often struggle to see the relevance of the information they are learning in school. While it is often stated that the primary function of our schools is to create positive, contributing members of our society, that connection is often sadly lacking—especially at the high school level. By choosing this approach to cover a topic that might not be immediately or intrinsically interesting to some students, this teacher is making an extremely powerful link between the lesson and life. It is the kind of connection we need to make more of for our students in every aspect of their educational journey.

At the same time, this project-based lesson also allows students to make numerous decisions—and the opportunity to explain, validate, and justify their choices. Understanding the effects of our decisions, weighing pros and cons, is a critical higher-order thinking skill that this approach allows each student to continue to develop at their own pace. This is equally as important as making the link to life beyond the school doors. Project-based lessons where students are given both the room to make choices, and the opportunity to articulate the reasons behind them, are truly desirable learning opportunities.

Lesson 15: Carrying Capacity of a Landscape

Students:	High School
Submitted by:	Nigel Scozzi
School:	Shore School for Boys, Sydney, Australia

Ask the Teacher

■ **Why Did You Develop a High-Impact Lesson for This Topic?** I've taught this topic before, many times, and students consistently failed to understand what is meant by the use of the word *carrying* in this concept. They normally use this word in a very different way, in a totally different context, and were simply unable to transfer the concept to the idea of landscapes.

■ **How Did You Use High-Impact Strategies to Teach the Topic?** I start with the following supplies:

- Large bucket of tennis balls
- 3 students
- 3 signs (to be stuck on each student's chest)
- A box (or bucket)

First, I briefly explain that the idea of "carrying capacity" used in this context is a geographical term referring to the ability of a landscape to support a certain number of people. The limit, of course, is the resource base of that region, although the students are not told this at first. Three students are selected, and they come to the front of the classroom. I then stick charts to each of their chests with the following restrictions:

- "D Man" can only use one hand to catch and carry the balls.
- "S Man" can use both hands to catch and carry the balls.
- "T Man" can use both hands and the box to store the balls.

I then explain that I'm going to start throwing an equal number of tennis balls to each of them. As soon as they drop one their turn is over. What happens is fairly predictable:

- "D Man" can only catch and carry at the very most four balls.
- "S Man" is likely to catch and carry more balls.
- "T Man" could seemingly go on forever.

I then offer the punch line. I explain that the balls are symbolic of people and the students symbolic of the three primary types of major landscapes.

They quickly identify "D Man" as "desert," and give reasons for its inability to carry many balls/people. A "what if?" scenario is proposed—

for example, suppose he can now use two hands? Students quickly grasp the idea of more hands equaling irrigation or piped-in water, such as in the desert areas of the western USA.

"S Man" is understood—with prompting—to be "savanna" (G could be used here for grasslands).

"T Man" is usually first guessed as "tropical" but with Q & A they work out that is this unlikely due to the degradation of soils very quickly after deforestation. Eventually they arrive at the correct idea—that the T stands for "temperate" areas. A world "biome" map is a good stimulus for the lesson at this point.

I then follow up this initial demonstration by revisiting each of the three areas and elaborating on what it would mean to live there. The word *carrying* is used throughout our discussions, to ensure they understand what it means in this context. Additionally, the meaning of "capacity" is investigated further with more questions and discussion, so they can truly understand the key content based on the original tennis ball demonstration.

■ **What Is the Result of Teaching the Lesson This Way?** This lesson absolutely rocks! I have done variations of it with many grade levels, and the result is consistent. There is laughter and playfulness during the tennis ball demonstration, and yet all students learn the basic concepts much faster than if I taught it using traditional methods. Simply put, what has really surprised and delighted me is that even though it took less time to learn when I use this approach, they usually remember the idea much longer—seemingly forever!

High-Impact Teaching Strategies Used in This Lesson

- *Entertainment.* Students attempting to catch the tennis balls is essentially a skit! There is also lots of laughter as the three students try to catch tennis balls—and of course drop many of them! Very entertaining indeed to high school students.

- *Getting Responses.* The students are being asked to discuss questions and respond to them, with the intention of clarifying and furthering their understanding.

- *Involve, Don't Tell.* Rather than simply stating the key facts and information, students are involved in the learning—whether through being a part of the demonstration or through observing it when it happens.

- *Jump Up.* Movement is used as students are trying to catch the tennis balls.

■ *Uniquely Memorable.* The humorous and dramatic method of teaching the core concept will make the entire lesson memorable.

Expansion of the Central Idea

This lesson offers a dramatically—almost shockingly—clear demonstration of the High-Impact Strategy "Involve, Don't Tell." It is so easy, as teachers, to fall for the trap of simply *telling* students the information they need to know. But here, the teacher has taken the core of the lesson and devised a simple, vivid, physical illustration of the core concept. All subsequent discussion about this topic will benefit significantly from students' clear understanding of the central idea.

Almost any lesson has a critical, central core. Once students are comfortable with their understanding of this essential aspect of the lesson, related information they later learn will adhere firmly to this fundamental tenet. Once they have a strong grip on the heart of the issue, much like a powerful magnet draws in any metal within its reach, their understanding of the concept will draw in related ideas and serve to solidify their understanding.

By the way, while this idea may seem obvious to you right now, many teacher support materials are rarely presented this way. Often the key idea, fact, issue, or statistic lies buried several paragraphs—perhaps several pages—deep in a chapter. In these cases our primary job as teachers is to seek out this key focal point students need to know and find a way to teach it in a memorable way, as this teacher has so clearly and admirably demonstrated.

A Final Thought

For those teachers feeling daunted about trying out High-Impact Strategies for the first time, here's a final thought for you:

The geometry of learning is a circle. Revolving in one direction, success leads to confidence, and confidence leads to hope. Revolving in the opposite direction, failure leads to helplessness, and helplessness leads to despair.

We should *not* leave the direction in which the circle revolves to chance. Using High-Impact Strategies creates a virtuous circle that spins our students up to the highest levels of achievement. Once you start using the strategies, and your students begin to find learning easy and fun, you'll find the increasing momentum of engagement and participation leads to greater and greater success.

Appendix

Stories

This section contains nine stories for you to use in the classroom as analogies, metaphors, or examples. They come from a variety of sources. Feel free to use them in your lessons as appropriate.

The Strawberry ■ 250

The Traveler ■ 252

The Animal School ■ 254

The White Horse ■ 255

The Castle Wall ■ 258

The Two Seeds ■ 260

The 1958 World Series ■ 261

The Caterpillars ■ 262

The Bicycle ■ 263

The Strawberry

There was a monk who lived in a small village in the jungle with a group of other monks. Each morning this monk would go out into the jungle and gather fruit for the other monks to eat for breakfast. One morning this monk went into the jungle and was beginning to gather fruit when he heard a sound behind him. He turned around and saw a tiger. Not wanting to be breakfast for the tiger, the monk slowly began to creep away. But the tiger saw the movement, looked up, and began to walk toward the monk. The monk began to walk faster, and the tiger began to walk faster. The monk began to run as fast as he could, but the tiger began to run also, easily gaining on the monk. Suddenly the monk burst out of the jungle and found himself standing on the edge of . . . a cliff.

He turned around and saw the tiger behind him, reaching through the bamboo with his claws. In this moment the monk decided it was time to take a risk. He saw a vine lying on the edge of the cliff, and he grabbed tightly to it with both hands and jumped off the cliff. The vine held! And the monk began to climb down the cliff. He was halfway down the cliff when he heard a sound below. Looking down, he saw . . . a tiger at the bottom of the cliff! The monk said, "Wait a minute. Either that's the world's fastest tiger, or . . ." He looked up and saw that the tiger at the top of the cliff was still there! Now there was a tiger at both the top of the cliff and the bottom of the cliff! He clung to the vine, trying to decide what to do. As he was thinking, out of a small hole in the cliff, right above where the monk was holding onto the vine, poked the nose of a very tiny mouse. It smelled the vine the monk was clinging to, leaned out, and began to nibble at the vine right above where the monk was holding onto it.

In this moment of crisis, the monk saw something. Growing out of a crevice in the cliff right near him was a strawberry plant, and inside of it was the biggest, most luscious strawberry he had ever seen! And this is what the monk did—he reached out, grabbed the strawberry, plucked it, ate it, and . . . here's the key . . . he ENJOYED it!

Now it happened that just as the mouse finished nibbling through the vine and it fell away, the monk found a tiny ledge to cling to. He held onto it for so long that the tiger at the bottom of the cliff got bored and went away, and the tiger at the top of the cliff got bored and went away. Very slowly the monk made his way back on up the cliff, through the jungle, and back into his village in time for supper.

While they were eating, the monk told the other monks what had happened to him that day. They all smiled and said they were glad that he was safe. The monk thanked them and then said, "Yes, I too am glad that I am safe. However, you know how we all try to learn something each day?" They all agreed with him.

"Well, I learned something today," said the monk.

"What did you learn?" they all asked.

"Life is precious, and time is short. Too often I spend my time worrying about everything that has happened to me in the past (the tiger at the top of the cliff). Too often I spend time unnecessarily worrying about what might happen to me in the future (the tiger at the bottom of the cliff). Or, perhaps worst of all, I spend too much time worrying about the nibbling, nagging worries of each and every day (the mouse). Then, when a true strawberry in my life comes along, sometimes I forget to pluck it, eat it, and most of all . . . ENJOY it!

"So not only should we wish for many strawberries in our lives, but also the wisdom to know they are there—to pluck them, taste them, and fully enjoy each and every precious moment."

The Traveler

A traveler was on a long journey. Each morning he got up and traveled along his path. One morning he woke up and set out again on his journey. However, he soon noticed that on this particular morning the path appeared to be getting more and more narrow. He began to grow concerned that he had taken a wrong turn and decided that he would ask the next person he saw that morning if he was indeed on the correct path. But no one else was on the path that morning. He walked and walked, and it wasn't until noon that he encountered the first person he had seen all day. When he entered a clearing, there at the far side of the clearing sat a very old man. This old man had long, flowing white hair and a white beard, and he had his eyes closed.

The traveler was quite excited to see the old man. He hurried up to him and asked, "Excuse me, but I was traveling along the path this morning, and it began to get very narrow, and I started to wonder if I was on the right path. Can you tell me? Am I going the right way?"

The old man just sat there in silence, his eyes still closed.

The traveler tried again, but could get no response. Finally, in frustration, he started to leave. He was at the far side of the clearing when he heard a sound, and he turned around. The old man had opened his eyes, and was staring straight out in front of him. And when he spoke he said, very softly:

"You're on the right path. Keep going."

But the traveler was at the far side of the clearing and wasn't sure if he had heard correctly, so he asked the old man to repeat himself. The old man did say something, but this time it was something quite different. This time he said:

"Gather what you find before you cross the river." And then he closed his eyes once again.

Now, the traveler had heard this last part quite clearly, but he was confused—what did it mean? But he could get nothing more from the old man, and finally the traveler did leave, continuing on the path as before.

It was hot on the path that day, and the traveler grew sweaty, tired, and thirsty. And the path, while growing ever more narrow, was still visible enough to follow. Finally, late in the afternoon, the traveler turned a corner and found in front of himself a river. He was so excited! He ran down to the river, drank some of the water, and used more water to wash himself. When he was fully refreshed he started to wade to the other side, but as he took his first step the words of the old man came back to him, and he paused.

"What did he say?" the traveler asked himself.

And then he remembered the words: "Gather what you find before you cross the river."

"Did he mean this river?" wondered the traveler. "Ah, he was crazy!" He began to move again. But the words of the old man echoed so strongly in his mind that he found himself backing up to the bank of the river. He looked around.

"If I were going to gather something," he asked himself, "what would I take here?"

He looked around, and saw trees, shrubs, and pebbles by the river's edge, but nothing of any value. But the words of the old man were so strong in his mind that he said:

"This may be the strangest thing I have ever done, but . . ." and he bent down and picked up some of the pebbles and put them in his pocket. Then he waded across the river and continued traveling. However, at the far side of the river he soon lost his way and traveled aimlessly until he found another path to follow several hours later. He knew he could now never retrace his steps back the way he had come.

Late that night the traveler slept by the side of the road. He woke up in the middle of the night, but did not know what had awakened him. Then he realized that he had rolled over on the pebbles in his pocket, and he shook his head.

"That old man was crazy," he said aloud. "I don't know why I picked these up!"

He reached into his pocket and took out the pebbles. He was in the act of throwing them away when suddenly the moonlight shone down on what he held in his hand, and he paused.

"No," he said. "It can't be!"

Because what he was holding in his hand were no longer mere pebbles. Now they were diamonds, rubies, sapphires, and emeralds—precious gems of all kinds. And he realized what had happened—they had been precious gems all along, but when he had first picked them up they had been covered in dirt, and in his pocket they had rubbed against each other so that the dirt had come off and he could see them for what they were.

And then the traveler said the most important thing of all. He said, "Oh. OH! I wish I had gathered more pebbles before I crossed that river!"

The Animal School

Once upon a time, the animals decided they must do something decisive to meet the increasing complexity of their society. They held a meeting and finally decided to organize a school. The curriculum consisted of running, climbing, swimming, and flying. Since these were the basic behaviors of most animals they decided that all the students should take all the subjects.

The duck proved to be excellent at swimming—better, in fact, than his teacher. He also did well in flying. But he proved to be very poor in running. Since he was poor in this subject he was made to stay after school to practice it, and even had to drop swimming to get more time to practice running. He was kept at his poorest subject until his webbed feet were so badly damaged he became only average at swimming. But average was acceptable in the school and nobody worried about that . . . except the duck.

The rabbit started at the top of his class in running, but finally had a nervous breakdown because of so much make-up time in swimming . . . a subject he hated.

The squirrel was excellent in climbing until he developed a psychological block in flying class, when the teacher insisted he start flying from the ground instead of the tops of trees. He was kept at attempting to fly until he became muscle-bound and received a "C" in climbing and a "D" in running.

The eagle was the school's worst discipline problem. In climbing class he beat all of the others to the top of the tree, but he insisted on using his own method of getting there. He received an "F."

The gophers stayed out of school and fought the tax levies for education because digging was not included in the curriculum. They apprenticed their children to the badger and later joined the groundhogs to start a private school offering alternative education.

So the animals held another meeting and criticized the failure of the educational system to produce successful members of society.

Source: Based on a story written by George Reavis when he was the Assistant Superintendent of the Cincinnati Public Schools back in the 1940s. This content is in the public domain and free to copy, duplicate, and distribute.

The White Horse

In a small village there was a poor farmer who owned a beautiful white horse. One day a rich man from the city came through the village and saw the farmer's white horse. He was very impressed, and he went to the farmer to ask him if he could buy this lovely horse. The rich man said, "I will give you a huge pile of gold for your horse!" But the farmer loved the horse and was not sure he should sell it.

"Well," he said, "This horse has been in our family since it was born. I'm not sure we could part with it, although it would certainly be nice to have all that money. In my whole life I've never had much money. Still, we love this horse."

The rich man nodded his head and said that he understood the farmer's problem. "Tonight," he said, "I'm staying here in your village. I'll come back tomorrow and you can tell me what you've decided." So off he went into town.

Now, the farmer had a neighbor. He was a very nosy sort of person, always telling other people what to do and how to solve their problems. When he heard about the rich man's offer, he hurried over to the farmer's home.

"You MUST sell the horse!" he exclaimed. "When will you ever again have the chance to have so much money?"

"Yes, it is a lot of money," said the farmer. "But I'm not sure what to do. This horse is almost like a member of our family. We certainly need him when we plow the fields."

"Forget the fields!" said the neighbor. "With all that money you might never have to work again! You must sell the horse, or this will be very bad for you."

Then the farmer said something that he had believed in since he was very young. He said, "Well, who can ever really tell what will be good or bad?" With that, he went back into his house.

The next day the rich man came to the farmer and asked him if he had made up his mind yet. The farmer said he was very sorry, but after thinking about it all night he had decided that he could not sell the horse. The rich man said that he was very sorry, but he understood, and off he went.

When the neighbor heard about this he was quite upset. He went directly to the farmer and said "Why didn't you sell the horse? That was crazy! You were very foolish! I have a bad feeling about this."

The farmer smiled and again said, "Who can tell what will be good or bad? All I know is that I've decided not to sell the horse." Having spoken these words, he went off to his fields and began working. But that very morning, as he and his son were plowing the fields, the white horse suddenly broke free of his harness and raced away into the woods!

When the neighbor heard this, he came over and said, "See! I tried to tell you! Now look what's happened. You don't have the white horse, and you don't have the gold. This is a disaster for you!"

But the farmer shook his head and simply said, "Who can tell what will be good or bad? All I know is that my horse has run away." And he went back to working in the fields with his son.

The next morning, as they were again out working in the fields, the ground began to shake, almost as if there were an earthquake! The farmer and his son looked up, and saw a sight that amazed them. Out of the woods came their white horse, being followed by one hundred wild horses! Being a smart man, the farmer hurried over to the corral and opened the gate. The white horse entered the corral, and the one hundred wild horses all followed it. When they were all inside, the farmer closed the gate.

The neighbor, of course, had heard all the noise, and saw what happened. Instantly he came over and said, "This was a great plan! Look, now you have your white horse back, plus all these other horses. Now you can sell them and become very wealthy! This is such a wonderful thing that has happened to you. You are so lucky."

But the farmer was not as excited. He simply looked at the horses in his corral and said, "We'll see. After all, who can tell what will be good or bad? All I know is that I now have one hundred wild horses in my corral." And with that he went back to work.

The next morning the farmer's son was out teaching the wild horses how to let a rider get on their backs. He was on one of the bigger horses when suddenly it bucked, throwing him high into the air. When he hit the ground, he broke both his legs!

When the neighbor heard what had happened he came over and shook his head sadly. "See," he said. "I knew you should have sold that horse in the first place. I just knew something like this was going to happen. I could just feel it! Now look, your son has broken both his legs! How will you work in the fields to bring in your crops this year? This is so terrible."

The farmer thought for a moment before speaking. Finally he said, "Yes, having my son break his legs is a terrible thing. But I won't worry about it too much. After all, who can tell what will be good or bad? All I know right now is that my son has broken his legs."

The neighbor threw up his hands in disgust and walked away, because he could not imagine how any good could come of having your son break his legs. But . . .

The very next day the Army from the big city came sweeping through the villages in the countryside. They were taking all the young men and making them go off with them to fight in the wars in a faraway land. The families did not want their young men to go, because it was very dangerous, and there was a chance they could be hurt, or even killed.

When the Army came to the house of the farmer, they saw that his son had two broken legs, and they said, "We can't take him! He's no use to us at all; in fact, he'll just be a burden." They left the farmer's house in search of other men to take.

The neighbor heard about this and he laughed out loud. He told the farmer, "How clever. You must have planned this all along! What a great idea! Your son has two broken legs, and now he doesn't have to go off and fight in the war! How very fortunate for you."

As always, the farmer smiled and said, "One must never get too excited. After all, who can tell what will be good or bad? All I know is that my son doesn't have to go off and fight in the war."

The neighbor chuckled again and walked away. But he shouldn't have laughed, for as he arrived back at his own home, he found the Army waiting for him there. And because the Army needed more men, they took the neighbor away with them, and he was never heard from again!

The Castle Wall

The king had a beautiful daughter. It was time to find her a husband. But the king wanted to find someone who was very clever, someone with deep wisdom, because he knew that one day this man would become the king. How to find such a man? The king pondered at great length and finally came up with a plan. He would devise a test. Whoever could pass the test would be able to marry his daughter.

The castle in which the king lived had huge walls surrounding it. One morning when he was out riding, he saw these walls and knew instantly what the test must be. That afternoon he made a proclamation throughout the land. Whoever could jump over the castle wall could ask for his daughter's hand in marriage.

When they heard about the test, many men came from all across the land to try and win the hand of the king's daughter by jumping over the castle wall. They all practiced very hard. They would build up their leg muscles as much as they could. They would take very long running starts. But despite everything they tried, a whole year went by and no one could jump over the castle wall. The king began to despair that anyone would be able to come forward and meet the challenge he had created.

One morning, however, a young man entered the castle. He was not as large as some other the other men who had come before, but he appeared very confident. He told the king he would like to marry his daughter. The king looked down at this young man and shook his sadly.

"As you must have heard," he said, "I have issued a challenge to all the young men of my kingdom. Before you can marry my daughter, you must show your skill by jumping over the castle wall."

The young man looked at the walls of the castle for a long moment. Finally he said, "Very well, I shall jump over the wall."

Although the king very much liked this young man, he doubted he would be able to succeed where so many others had failed. "You may certainly try," he said, "but I don't know how you could possibly do it when so many others have failed."

"We shall see," replied the young man. And with that he set off through the castle gathering as many wooden boxes as he could find. The king watched him and asked him what he was doing.

"Just watch," replied the young man. With that he stepped very far back from the castle wall and set down the first box. In front of it he placed a stack of two boxes. In front of that he placed a stack of three boxes, then four, then five, and so on until the final stack of boxes was so high that it came to just below the edge of the castle wall. On the other side of the wall he did the same thing. Then he turned and faced the king.

"You did say," he said, "that I must *jump* over the castle wall to marry your daughter. Isn't that right?'

Puzzled, the king nodded and said that was indeed the challenge.

"Very good, then," said the young man. "Here I go."

With that he went very far back to where the first box had been placed. He jumped up onto it. From that box he jumped up onto the stack of two boxes. He jumped from that stack to the one with three boxes on it. He continued jumping from one stack to the next tallest one until finally he arrived at the castle wall. With one last, small jump, he hopped over it, and began jumping down the boxes on the other side until he reached the ground. He ran back to the king.

"As you can see," he said, "I have jumped over the castle wall."

"Yes," said the smiling king. "You have indeed earned the right to marry my daughter. I believe that with the cleverness you have shown today you will not only make a good husband for my daughter, but you will also make a very wise king."

The Two Seeds

It was springtime, and a lovely young woman planted her garden. Two seeds ended up lying in the ground next to each other. The first seed said to the second one, "Think of how fun this will be! We will let our roots grow deep down into the soil, and when they are strong we will burst from the ground and become beautiful flowers for all the world to see and admire!"

The second seed heard this, but was worried. "That sounds nice," he said, "but isn't the ground too cold? I'm frightened to try to put my roots into it. And what if something goes wrong and I don't turn out very pretty? And what if the lovely lady doesn't like me? I'm scared of not succeeding!"

The first seed, however, was not about to be stopped. He pushed his roots down into the ground and immediately began to grow. When they were strong enough he burst from the ground and soon became a beautiful flower. The lovely young woman tended carefully to him and proudly showed him to all her friends. He was very happy. "Come on," he said to his friend every day, "it's wonderful and warm up here in the sunshine!"

The second seed was quite impressed with what the first seed had become. However, even though he could see what was possible, he was still very scared. He tentatively pushed one of his roots into the ground. "Ouch," he said. "This ground is still much too cold for me! I don't like it. I think I'll just stay inside my shell where I'm comfortable. Besides, I'm quite safe inside my own shell. I'll become a flower later. There's plenty of time." Nothing the first seed could say would change his mind.

One day, when the young woman was away, a very hungry bird flew in the garden. It scratched at the ground looking for seeds to eat. The second seed, still lying inside its shell, was terrified of what would happen if he was found. But this was his lucky day, and the bird did not find him. Finally it flew away.

When the bird was gone, the second seed breathed a sigh of relief. But he also had come to a decision. While hiding inside his shell he had realized that perhaps he had been wrong in thinking that there was always plenty of time to become a flower. Perhaps, he thought, no one should take for granted that there will be plenty of time to explore their hopes and dreams. Perhaps, sometimes, everyone needs to simply take a chance and reach for a goal. So that's exactly what he did. Without another word, he pushed his roots out into the ground and quickly grew into a beautiful flower.

The 1958 World Series

In the 1958 World Series, the New York Yankees and the Milwaukee Braves were tied three games each going into the seventh and deciding game. Warren Spahn, who was the 1957 Cy Young winner, was pitching for Milwaukee late in the deciding game. His team was up by one run when the Yankees star catcher Elston Howard came up to bat.

Milwaukee manager Fred Haney came to the pitching mound and told Warren Spahn, "If you throw it high and outside he'll hit it out of the park." That statement did it! Spahn's mind was programmed and the next pitch was high and outside and Elston Howard blasted it for a home run. The Yankees went on to win that game, and the World Series four games to three.

As Elston Howard triumphantly rounded the bases after his home run, Warren Spahn threw his mitt down in disgust and shouted something. Reporters later asked what he had said. He replied, "Who would ever tell somebody what to do by telling them what *not* to do?"

The Caterpillars

Processionary caterpillars feed on pine needles. They move through the trees in a long procession, one leading and the others following, each with his eyes half-closed and his head snugly fitted against the rear extremity of his predecessor.

Jean-Henri Fabre, the great French naturalist, after patiently experimenting with a group of these caterpillars, finally enticed them to the rim of a large flowerpot where he succeeded in getting the first one connected up with the last one, thus forming a complete circle, which started moving around in a procession that had neither beginning nor end.

The naturalist expected that after a while they would catch on to the joke, get tired of their useless march, and start off in some new direction. But not so . . . through sheer force of habit, the living, creeping circle kept moving around the rim of the pot. Around and around it went, keeping the same relentless pace for seven days and seven nights, and would doubtless have continued longer had it not been for sheer exhaustion and ultimate starvation. An ample supply of food was close at hand, and plainly visible, but it was outside the range of the circle, so they continued along the beaten path. When Jean-Henri realized that if they were left alone they would follow this circle until they perished, he gently broke the chain and led the entire procession to the food and water

The problem is that they were stuck firmly in a habit (instinct, custom, tradition, precedent, paradigm, past experience, standard practice—whatever you may choose to call it), but they were following it blindly. They kept expending their energy in a quest that was ultimately taking them nowhere. They failed to see the larger picture. In the end, they simply mistook *activity for accomplishment.*

The Bicycle

Imagine that you were digging through your garage one day and came across an old bicycle. Perhaps it looks to be as much as 25 years old. But you're pleased with your discovery, so you move aside everything else and pull out this classic contraption. It's so old that it only has three speeds! And there are even some worn playing cards still stuck to the spokes so that they make noise when you pedal! You apply some much-needed grease to the chain, and off you go. It works! While you're pedaling around you notice that there's a race being held shortly down at the local school. Eager for some exercise, you head there and enroll in the race. When the race begins, you give it all you've got, pedaling as hard as you can. Will you win this race, even giving it 100% of your effort and energy? Well, probably not, given that the *technology* you are using is lagging significantly behind the other competitors. Your bike is just too old.

Now imagine another scene. One day you go to the sports equipment store and buy the latest bicycle available, one with all the bells, whistles, and gadgets. It has thirty gears, an aerodynamic shape, and weighs so little that you can lift it with just your pinkie finger! You happen to notice a sign indicating that there's that same race at the local school, so you head there at once. You are confident, given that you have the latest in technological wonder at your beck and call. The race begins, and you are so confident you will win that you don't even to make much effort, relying on the technology to take you across the finish line first. Will you win this race? Again, probably not, because technology in and of itself is simply not enough. It takes the effective *application* of the technology to make the real difference.

To be a contender in the race described here would take, at the least, a combination of technology and effort. Just putting in a tremendous amount of energy would not be enough, nor is it sufficient to simply possess the appropriate technology. It is the combination of both, applied in the correct manner, which helps one maximize the effort for the best result.

To succeed in life requires that we have two things and that we use them together. The first is the drive, the willingness, the energy, and the enthusiasm for the task. The second is the technology. One must have the proper tools for success. These tools can take many forms. They could be physical tools, such as a technologically advanced bike, or they might be interpersonal skills, such as knowing how to communicate effectively with another person. Putting these two things together makes for people who are the most successful in many aspects of life.

References

Alna, O. (1999). Importance of oral storytelling in literacy development. *Ohio Reading Teacher, 33*(1), 15–18.

Anderson, J. R. (1990). *Cognitive psychology and its implications* (3rd ed.). New York: W. H. Freeman and Company.

Bayor, G. W. (1972). A treatise on the mind's eye: An empirical investigation of visual mental imagery (Doctoral Dissertation, Carnegie-Mellon University). Ann Arbor, Michigan: University Microfilms, 1972. No. 72-12, 699.

Berliner, D., & Biddle, B. (1995). *The manufactured crisis.* Reading, MA: Addison-Wesley Publishing Company.

Berlyne, D. E. (1965). Curiosity and education. In J. D. Krumboltz (Ed.), *Learning and educational process* (pp. 67–89). Chicago: Rand McNally.

Berstein, D. (1994). Tell and show: The merits of classroom demonstrations. *American Psychology Society Observer, 24*, 25–37.

Brand, S. T. (2006). Facilitating emergent literacy skills: A literature-based, multiple intelligence approach. *Journal of Research in Childhood Education, 21*(2), 133–148.

Brigham, F. S., Scruggs, T. E., & Mastropieri, M. A. (1992). Teacher enthusiasm in learning disabilities classrooms: Effects on learning and behavior. In N. L. Gage & D. Berliner (Eds.), *Educational psychology.* Boston: Houghton Mifflin.

Brophy, J. E. (1979). Teacher praise: A functional analysis. *Review of Educational Research, 51*, 5–32.

Budd, J. W. (2004). Mind maps as classroom exercises. *Journal of Economic Education, 35*(1), 35–46.

Burko, H., & Elliot, R. (1997). Hands-on pedagogy vs hands-off accountability. *Phi Delta Kappa, 80*(5), 394–400.

Calvin, W., & Ojemann, G. (1994). *Conversations with Neil's brain.* Reading, MA: Addison-Wesley Publishing Company.

Campell, J. (1983). *Man and time.* Boston: Princeton Publishing.

Canfield, J., & Hanser, M. V. (1993). *Chicken soup for the soul.* Deerfield Beach, FL: Health Communications, Inc.

Chapman, M. (2007). Theory and practice of teaching discourse intonation. *ELT Journal, 61*(1), 3–11.

Cialdini, R. (1984). *Influence: The new psychology of modern persuasion.* New York: Quill Publishing.

Covington, M. V. (1992). *Making the grade: A self-worth perspective on motivation and school reform.* New York: Holt, Rinehart & Winston.

Covington, M. V., & Omelich, C. (1987). I knew it cold before the exam: A test of anxiety-blockage hypothesis. *Journal of Educational Psychology, 79*, 393–400.

Cropley, A. (2006). Dimensions of creativity: A social approach. *Roeper Review, 28*(3), 125–130.

Cruz, B. C., & Murthy, S. A. (2006). Breathing life into history: Using role-playing to engage students. *Social Studies and the Young Learner, 19*(1), 4–8.

Cusco, J. B. (1994). Critical thinking and cooperative learning: A natural marriage. *Cooperative Learning and College Teaching, 4*(2), 2–5.

D'Arcangelo, M. (1998). The brains behind the brains. *Educational Leadership, 56*(3), 20–25.

Dastoor, B., & Reed, J. (1993). Training 101: The psychology of learning. *Training and Development, 47*(60), 17–22.

Deporter, B., Reardon, M., & Singer-Noire, S. (1999). *Quantum teaching: Orchestrating student success.* Boston: Allyn & Bacon.

Diamond, M. (1988). *Enriching heredity.* New York: The Free Press.

Driscoll, M. P. (1994). *Psychology of learning for instruction.* Boston: Allyn & Bacon.

Emmons, R. (2007). *Thanks.* Boston: Houghton Mifflin.

Fernandez-Berrocaal, P., & Santamaria, C. (2006). Mental models in social interaction. *The Journal of Experimental Education, 74*(3), 229–248.

Gage, N. L., & Berliner, D. (1998). *Educational psychology.* Boston: Houghton Mifflin.

Gagne, R. M., & Glaser, R. (1978). Foundations in learning research. In R. M. Gagne, (Ed.), *Instructional technology: Foundations.* Hillsdale, NJ: Erlbaum.

Glaser, R. (1984). Education and thinking: The role of knowledge. *American Psychologist, 39*, 93–104.

Goldberg, C. (2004). Brain friendly techniques: Mind mapping. *School Library Media Activities Monthly, 21*(3), 22–24.

Goleman, D. (1995). *Emotional intelligence.* New York: Bantam.

Green, J. (2005). *The Green book of songs by subject: The thematic guide to popular music* (5th ed.). Nashville, TN: Professional Desk References. www.greenbookofsongs.com

Greenco, J. G., Collins, A. M., & Resnick, L. B. (1996). Cognition and learning. In D. Berliner & R. Calfee (Eds.), *Handbook of educational psychology* (15–46). New York: Macmillan.

Grinder, M. (1988). *Righting the educational conveyer belt.* Portland, OR: Metamorphous Press.

Hannaford, C. (2005). *Smart moves.* Salt Lake City, UT: Great River Books.

Hansen, E. J. (1998). Creating teachable moments . . . and making them last. *Innovative Higher Education, 23*(1), 7–26.

Heath, S. B., & Wolf, S. (2005). Focus in creative learning: Drawing on art for language development. *Literacy, 39*(1), 38–45.

Hughes, C. A., Hendrickson, J. M., & Hudson, P. J. (1986). The pause procedure: Improving factual recall from lectures by low and high achieving middle school students. *International Journal of Instructional Media, 13*(3), 217–226.

Jensen, E. (1988). *Superteaching.* Del Mar, CA: Turning Point Publishing.

Jensen, E. (1996). *Brain-based learning.* Del Mar, CA: Turning Point Publishing.

Jensen, E. (2000). *Music with the brain in mind.* San Diego, CA: The Brain Store, Inc.

Jensen, E. (2005). *Teaching with the brain in mind* (2nd ed.). Alexandria, VA: ASCD.

Johnson-Laird, P. N. (1988). How is meaning mentally represented? In U. Eco, M. Santambrogio, & P. Violi (Eds.), *Meaning and mental representations.* Bloomington: Indiana University Press.

Kagan, S., Kagan, M., & Kagan, L. (1997). *Cooperative structures for team building.* San Clemente, CA: Kagan Publishing.

Keller, J. M. (1987). Motivational design of instruction. In C. M. Reigeluth (Ed.), *Instructional design theories and models: An overview of their current status.* Hillsdale, NJ: Erlbaum.

Kincheloe, J., Slattery, P., & Steinberg, R. (2000). *Contextualizing teaching.* New York: Addison-Wesley Longman.

LaBerge, D. L. (1990). Attention. *Psychological Science, 1*(3), 156–162.

Larkins, A. G., McKinney, C. W., Oldham-Buss, S., & Gilmore, A. C. (1985). Teacher enthusiasm: A critical review. In N. L. Gage & D. Berliner (Eds.), *Educational Psychology*. Boston: Houghton Mifflin.

Lazar, A. M. (1995). Who is studying in groups and why? Peer collaboration outside the classroom. *College Teaching, 43*(2), 61–65.

Levenson, R. W., Ekman, P., & Friesen, W. V. (1990). Voluntary facial action generates emotion specific autonomous nervous system activity. *Psychophysiology, 27*, 213–215.

Lin, H., Chen, T., & Dwyer, F. (2006). Effects of static visuals and computer-generated animations in facilitating immediate and delayed achievement in the EFL classroom. *Foreign Language Annals, 39*(2), 203–219.

Litecky, L. P. (1992). Great teaching, great learning: Classroom climate, innovative methods, and critical thinking. *New Directions for Community Colleges, 77*, 83–90.

Loftus, E. (1992). When a lie becomes memory's truth: Memory distortion after exposure to misinformation. *Psychological Science, 1*, 345–349.

Loftus, E. (1993). The reality of repressed memories. *American Psychologist, 48*(5), 518–537.

Lozanov, G. (1979). *Suggestology and outlines of suggestopedia.* New York: Gordon and Breach Publishing.

Margulies, N., & Valenza, C. (2005). *Visual thinking: Tools for mapping your ideas.* Carmarthen, UK: Crown House Publishing.

Marzano, R. (2004). *Classrooms that work: Research-based strategies for increasing student achievement.* Upper Saddle River, NJ: Prentice Hall.

Maslow, A. H. (1968). *Toward a psychology of being* (2nd ed.). New York: Van Nostrand.

Maslow, A. H. (1970). *Motivation and personality* (2nd ed.). New York: Harper and Row.

Mehrabian, A. (1981). *Silent messages—A primer of non-verbal communication.* Belmont, CA: Wadsworth.

Mercer, N., & Sams, C. (2006). Teaching children how to use language to solve math problems. *Language and Education, 20*(6), 507–528.

Moore, J. R. (2007). Popular music helps students focus on important social issues. *Middle School Journal, 38*(4), 21–29.

Moreno, R., & Mayer, R. E. (2000). Engaging students in active learning: The case for personalized multimedia messages. *Journal of Educational Psychology, 92*(4), 724–733.

Moura, H. (2006). Analyzing multimodal interaction within a classroom setting. *Visible Language, 40*(3), 270–291.

Myhill, D., Jones, S., & Hopper, R. (2005). *Talking, listening, and learning.* Maidenhead, UK: Open University Press.

Ormrod, J. E. (2000). *Educational psychology* (3rd ed.). Upper Saddle River, NJ: Prentice-Hall.

Paulin, M. G. (2005). Evolutionary origins and principles of distributed neural computation for state estimation and movement control in vertebrates. *Complexity, 10*(3), 56–65.

Pierce, J., & Terry, K. (2000). Breathe life into history through story in the elementary classroom. *Southern Social Studies Journal, 25*(2), 77–90.

Pineda De Romero, L., & Dwyer, F. (2005). The effect of varied rehearsal strategies used to complement visualized instruction in facilitating achievement of different learning objectives. *International Journal of Instructional Media, 32*(3), 259.

Pontefract, C., & Hardman, F. (2005). The discourse of classroom interaction in Kenyan primary schools. *Comparative Education, 41*(1), 87–106.

Prensky, M. (2001, October). On the horizon. *NCB University Press, 9*(5).

Prensky, M. (2005). Engage me or enrage me: What today's learners demand. *Educause Review, 40*(5), 60–64.

Qais, F. (2007). *Enlightening advantages of cooperative learning.* ERIC online submission.

Ratey, J. (2008). *Spark: The revolutionary new science of exercise and the brain.* New York: Little, Brown and Company.

Ready, M. (1978). The conduit metaphor: A case of frame conflict in our language about language. In A. Otny (Ed.), *Metaphor and thought* (2nd ed.), pp. 164–201. Cambridge, UK: Cambridge University Press.

Reid, L. (2000). Professional links: Active and interactive approaches to poetry, drama and classics. *English Journal,* May, 151–155.

Robinson, K. (2001). *Out of our minds: Learning to be creative.* Oxford, UK: Capstone Publishing Limited.

Ruhl, K., Hughes, C., & Schloss, P. (1987). Using the pause procedure to enhance lecture recall. *Teacher Education and Special Education, 10*(1), 14–18.

Sapolsky, R. M. (1999). *Why zebras don't get ulcers* (4th ed.). New York: W. H. Freeman and Company.

Schacter, D. L. (1990). Impulse activity and the patterning of connections during CNS development. *Neuron, 5*(6), 745–756.

Schmier, L. (1995). *Random thoughts: The humanity of teaching.* Madison, WI: Magna Publications.

Sutton, J. (1998). Setting the stage: Creative drama in the writing classroom. *Stage of the Art, 9*(7), 11–15.

Sviniki, M. D. (1990). *The changing face of college teaching: New directions for teaching and learning.* San Francisco: Jossey-Bass.

Tomlinson, C. A., & Kalbgleisch, M. L. (1998). Teach me, teach my brain: A call for differentiated classrooms. *Educational Leadership, 56*(3), 52–55.

Vergneer, G. W. (1995). Therapeutic applications of humor. *Directions in Mental Health Counseling, 5*(3), 1–11.

Vygotsky, L. S. (1987). *The collected work of L. S. Vygotsky, vol. 3.* In R. W. Rieser & A. S. Carlton (Eds.), *Problems of theory and history of psychology.* New York: Plenum Press.

Weinberger, N. M. (1998, November). The music in our minds. *Educational Leadership, 56*(3), 36–40.

Wells, G., & Arauz, R. M. (2006). Dialogue in the classroom. *Journal of the Learning Sciences, 15*(3), 379–428.

Williams, R. B. (2007). *Cooperative learning: A standard for high achievement.* Thousand Oaks, CA: Corwin Press.

Woolfolk, A. (2000). *Educational psychology* (7th ed.). Boston: Allyn & Bacon.

Yerks, R. M., & Dodson, J. D. (1908). The relation of strength stimulus to rapidity of habit formation. *Journal of Comparative Neurology, 18,* 459–482.

Index

Acknowledgment strategy, 15–22
  application of, 18–21, 175, 177, 223, 225, 227, 242, 244
  classroom management and, 17–18
  concepts underlying, 15–17
  forms of acknowledgment, 19–21
  learning environment and, 21
  overview of, 10
  teachers' views of students and, 16–17
Acronyms, 184
Acrostics, 184–185
American history, lesson about, 237–239
Anchoring, 210
Animals in ocean, lesson about, 233–235
Archeology, lesson about, 239–241
Assessment
  drama use in, 63
  framing and, 72
  preparation for, 228–230
Associations, as memorization technique, 185
Attention span. *See also* Crest of the Wave strategy
  groups/grouping and, 33–34
  influences on, 30–31
  lectures/lecturing and, 30, 31–32, 35–36, 38–39, 165
  learning environment and, 30–31, 32, 34–35
  learning style and, 29–30
  pausing and, 142, 167
  refocusing of, 128, 129
  shortness of, 29–30, 101, 190, 191–192
Attitudes, framing of, 71–74. *See also* Framing

Being Open strategy, 22–29. *See also* Questions/Questioning
  application of, 26, 219, 242
  classroom management and, 24–26

concepts underlying, 22–24
overview of, 10
types of questions for, 23–27
Biological process, lesson about, 176
Body location, as memorization technique, 185–186

Canfield, Jack, 207
Carrying capacity, lesson about, 245–248
Chalkboards/Whiteboards, 106, 143
Chicken Soup for the Soul (Canfield), 207
Choice, and responsibility, 133–135, 138–139. *See also* Ownership strategy
Chlorophyll, lesson about, 216–218
Classroom management
  acknowledgment/feedback and, 17–18
  attention span and, 33–35
  dramatic activities and, 59–60
  framing and, 68, 112
  giving directions and, 43–45
  humor and, 148, 149–150
  identifying key ideas and, 95
  instruction zones and, 210–211
  labels/labeling and, 112
  movement and, 101, 102
  memory/memorization and, 183–184
  music and, 117
  novelty and, 129
  open loops and, 156–157
  ownership and, 135–136
  pausing and, 142
  positive attention/focus and, 201
  questions/questioning and, 24–26, 79, 147–148
  responding to questions and, 79, 88
  social interaction and, 165–166
  Tiers strategy and, 173–176
  visual images and, 107
  vocal emphasis and, 192
  volume of speaking and, 196–197

Closed vs. open questions, 23–27. *See also* Questions/Questioning

Completing the action, and students' responses, 81, 82–83

Compliments, 20

Congruence, in giving instructions, 53

Constructivist approach, 7

Content
coverage of, 35, 36
framing of, 69–70. *See also* Framing

Contextualizing Teaching (Kincheloe, Slattery, and Steinberg), 5

Conversations. *See* Social interaction

Coordinate grid, lesson about, 235–237

Coupland, Douglas, 1

Crest of the Wave strategy, 29–42
application of, 35–40, 223, 234
attention span and, 29–33. *See also* Attention span
classroom management and, 33–35
concepts underlying, 29–33
learning environment and, 30–31, 32, 34–35
learning style and, 29–30
overview of, 10–11
state changes and, 36–40

Diamond, Marian, 5–6

Digital divide, 2

Digital immigrants vs. digital natives, 2, 3. *See also* Generational differences

Direction zones, 211, 212. *See also* Zones of Instruction strategy

Directionalizing, of instructions, 54

Directions strategy, 42–58. *See also* Giving directions
application of, 45–56, 236
classroom management and, 43–45
concepts underlying, 42–43
language use and, 46, 48–49, 53–54
learning environment and, 50–51
learning style and, 42–43
overview of, 11

Distributed vs. massed practice, 230

Drama
activities for, 60–63
assessment and, 63
classroom management and, 59–60
music and, 61–62
need for, 58–59

Ebbinghaus's Curve, 31–32

Engagement activities/strategies, 174–175, 240

Enriching Heredity (Diamond), 5–6

Entertainment strategy, 58–66
application of, 60–63, 217–218, 225, 232, 234, 236, 238, 247
assessment and, 63
classroom management and, 59–60
concepts underlying, 58–59
overview of, 11
strategies for, 60–63

Feedback. *See also* Acknowledgment strategy
forms of, 19–21
students' expectations of, 16, 20–21
for young students, 20–21

Fine arts, lesson about, 243–245

Flipcharts, 143

Frames strategy, 66–76. *See also* Framing
application of, 69–74, 219, 221, 232, 240, 245
assessment and, 72
classroom management and, 68
concepts underlying, 66–68
overview of, 11
purposes of framing, 67–68

Framing. *See also* Frames strategy
assessment and, 72
of attitudes, 71–74
classroom management and, 68, 112
of content, 69–70
purposes of, 67–68

Games, 174–175, 241–242

Generation X: Tales for an Accelerated Culture (Coupland), 1

Generational differences, 1–2, 3, 6, 29–30

Geography, lessons about, 222–224, 245–248

Getting Responses strategy, 76–85. *See also* Questions/Questioning; Responding
application of, 80–83, 238, 245, 247
classroom management and, 79
concepts underlying, 76–79
language use in, 80–81
overview of, 11

Giving directions. *See also* Directions strategy
  classroom management and, 43–45
  framework for, 54–56
  guidelines for, 45
  language use and, 46, 48–49, 53–54
  learning environment and, 50–51
  learning style and, 42–43
  zone for, 211
Groups/Grouping
  apprehension in, 88
  attention span and, 33–34
  music with, 120–121
  preparation for, 88, 89
  purposes of, 88, 89
  questions/questioning for, 149
  speaking voice for, 195–197
  strategies for, 167, 168, 172–176, 196–197

High-Impact Teaching Strategies. *See also specific strategies*
  adaptation of, 166–167, 216
  application of, 7, 9, 10, 248
  concepts underlying, 7
  creation of, 215–216
  effectiveness of, 248
High-Quality Responses strategy, 85–93. *See also* Responding
  application of, 89–90, 221, 236
  classroom management and, 88
  concepts underlying, 85–88
  groups/grouping for, 88, 89
  overview of, 11
Humor
  classroom management and, 148, 149–150
  memory/memorization and, 207
  questions/questioning and, 148, 149–150

Instruction zones, 211, 212. *See also* Zones of Instruction strategy
Instructions. *See* Giving directions
Interaction zones, 211, 212. *See also* Zones of Instruction strategy
Involve, Don't Tell strategy, 93–100
  application of, 95–98, 217, 221, 229, 238, 240, 242, 245, 247, 248
  classroom management and, 95
  concepts underlying, 93–95

key ideas and, 93, 94–98. *See also* Key ideas
  overview of, 11

Jump Up strategy, 100–105. *See also* Movement
  application of, 102–104, 219, 225, 227, 232, 234, 236, 238, 240, 242, 247
  classroom management and, 101, 102
  concepts underlying, 100–102
  learning environment and, 101–102
  learning style and, 100–101
  overview of, 12

Keen Visuals strategy, 105–110. *See also* Visual images
  application of, 107–108, 217, 221, 223, 229, 234, 240
  classroom management and, 107
  concepts underlying, 105–107
  overview of, 12
Key ideas. *See also* Involve, Don't Tell strategy
  identification of, 93, 94, 95
  memory/memorization of, 94–95, 181, 219
  pausing and, 168
  teaching of, 95–98, 168
Kincheloe, Joe, 5

Labels strategy, 110–115
  application of, 112–114, 230, 232, 238, 240
  classroom management and, 112
  concepts underlying, 110–111
  context and, 113–114
  language use and, 111, 112–114
  negative vs. positive labels, 110–111
  overview of, 12
Language use
  in giving directions, 46, 48–49, 53–54
  labels/labeling and, 111, 112–114
  learning environment and, 111
  mental images created by, 199–203
  in questions/questioning, 80–81
Learning environment
  acknowledgment in, 21
  attention span and, 30–31, 32, 34–35
  changes in, 30–31
  emotion and, 5, 8
  giving directions and, 50–51

Learning environment (*continued*)
  instructional zones and, 209, 211–212
  language use and, 111
  movement and, 4, 101–102
  music and, 5, 115–117, 118, 120–122, 225, 231, 232
  ownership and, 135–136
  social interaction and, 5, 6, 42, 164–165
  state changes in, 36–39
  students' expectations of, 2, 3–4, 5–6, 7, 10, 30–31, 42
Learning style
  attention span and, 29–30
  changes in, 2, 3–4, 5, 20–30
  giving directions and, 42–43
  instruction zones and, 210
  memory/memorization and, 183–184
  movement and, 100–101
  music and, 119
  open loops and, 153–154
  pausing and, 140–141
  social interaction and, 5, 6, 42
Lectures/Lecturing
  attention span and, 30, 31–32, 35–36, 38–39, 165
  effectiveness of, 31–32, 165
  pausing during, 142, 167
  questions/questioning after, 149
  responding to, 149
Lyrics, of music, 120–121, 122. *See also* Music

Magic, use in instruction, 216–217, 218
Mapping devices, 107, 108. *See also* Visual images
Massed vs. distributed practice, 230
Memory/Memorization. *See also* Uniquely Memorable strategy
  classroom management and, 183–184
  humor and, 207
  influences on, 180–181
  of key ideas, 94–95, 181, 219
  learning style and, 183–184
  movement and, 187
  storytelling and, 181–183, 185, 206, 207
  techniques for, 175–176, 179, 180–183, 184–188, 206, 219–220
  traditional focus on, 179–180

Mental images, 199–203. *See also* X-Ray Vision strategy
Mismatching, 167
Movement, 100–105. *See also* Jump Up strategy
  academic content and, 226
  activities for, 103
  apprehension about, 103–104
  classroom management and, 101, 102
  concepts underlying, 100–102
  learning environment and, 4, 101–102
  learning style and, 100–101
  memory/memorization and, 187
  music and, 119, 227
Multimedia productions, 62–63
Muscle memory, 187. *See also* Memory/ Memorization
Museums, lesson about, 243–245
Music. *See also* Music strategy
  classroom management and, 117
  dramatization of, 61–62
  learning environment and, 5, 115–117, 118, 120–122, 225, 231, 232
  learning style and, 119
  lyrics of, 120–121, 122
  movement and, 119, 227
  points to use, 117, 121
  types of, 122–123
  volume of, 121–122
Music strategy, 115–127. *See also* Music
  application of, 117–123, 217, 223, 225, 227, 232
  classroom management and, 117
  concepts underlying, 115–117
  learning environment and, 115–117, 118, 120–122
  learning style and, 119
  overview of, 12
Musical padding, 120–121

Native American legends, lesson about, 230–232
Natural resources, lesson about, 218–220
Notetaking, pausing during, 143–144
Novelty strategy, 127–133
  activities for, 129–130
  application of, 129–131, 217, 219, 221, 227, 230, 236, 240, 242
  classroom management and, 129

concepts underlying, 127–129
memory/memorization and, 186
overview of, 12

Ocean animals, lesson about, 233–235
On the Horizon (Prensky), 2
One-act plays, 63. *See also* Drama
Open vs. closed questions, 23–27. *See also* Questions/Questioning
Open loops, 153–163. *See also* Revolutions strategy
classroom management and, 156–157
definition of, 153
examples of, 157–161
framework for, 157
learning style and, 153–154
Out of Our Minds (Robinson), 3
Ownership strategy, 133–140
activities for, 136–137
application of, 136–139, 221, 225, 230, 232, 234, 238, 240, 245
classroom management and, 135–136
concepts underlying, 133–135
definition, 133
learning environment and, 135–136
overview of, 12
responsibility and, 133–135, 138–139

Pause procedure, 32. *See also* Pause strategy
Pause strategy, 140–146. *See also* Pausing
application of, 142–144
classroom management and, 142
concepts underlying, 140–142
learning style and, 140–141. *See also* Visual images
overview of, 12–13
Pausing. *See also* Pause strategy
attention span and, 142, 167
classroom management and, 142
for key ideas, 168
learning style and, 140–141
during lectures/lecturing, 142, 167
during notetaking, 143–144
timing of, 168–169
with visual images, 140–141
for vocal emphasis, 192–193
Peer acknowledgment, 19
Peer coaching, 165
Peer review, 231

Peg system, as memorization technique, 186, 218, 219
Photo journals, lesson about, 228–230
Physical acknowledgment, 20, 175
Plays, 63. *See also* Drama
Plotting points, lesson about, 235–237
PowerPoint presentations, 141, 142–143
Prensky, Marc, 2
Press and release, 30, 34–35
Priming, of students' responses, 81–82, 225
Procedural memory, 187. *See also* Memory/Memorization

Question-clarify-question format, 146, 147, 148–150. *See also* Questions strategy
Question marks, lesson about, 220–222
Questions/Questioning. *See also* Being Open strategy; Getting Responses strategy; Questions strategy
apprehension about, 24
assumptions underlying, 24
classroom management and, 24–26, 79, 147–148
framework for, 146, 147, 148–150
for groups/grouping, 149
humor and, 148, 149–150
language use in, 80–81
after lectures/lecturing, 149
open vs. closed questions, 23–27
responding to. *See* Responding
specificity of, 78–79, 80–81
time allowed following, 85–86, 87–88, 89
Questions strategy, 146–153. *See also* Questions/Questioning
application of, 149–150
classroom management and, 147–148
concepts underlying, 146–147
overview of, 13

Rap music, 123
RAS. *See* Reticular activating system
Redundant retrieval routes, 32
Relevance, of content/instruction, 68, 69–70
Repetition
as memorization technique, 187
for vocal emphasis, 193

Responding, 76–85, 85–93. *See also* Getting Responses strategy; High-Quality Responses strategy
  apprehension about, 76–77
  classroom management and, 79, 88
  completing the action and, 81, 82–83
  concepts underlying, 76–79, 85–88
  groups/grouping for, 88, 89
  to lectures/lecturing, 149
  opportunities for, 165
  priming students for, 81–82, 225
  skills needed for, 87, 88
  specificity of questions/questioning and, 78–79, 80–81
  time allowed for, 85–86, 87–88, 89
Responsibility, and choice, 133–135, 138–139. *See also* Ownership strategy
Reticular activating system (RAS), 154–156
Review, lesson about, 241–242
Revolutions strategy, 153–163
  application of, 157–161, 242
  classroom management and, 156–157
  concepts underlying, 153–156
  learning style and, 153–154
  overview of, 13
Rhyming, 186–187
Rituals, in classroom, 130–131, 242
Robinson, Ken, 3
Role play/playing. *See also* Drama
  assessment using, 63
  of conversation, 167
  in talk show format, 62
  of teaching, 167, 168, 225, 226

Schema theory, 220
Self acknowledgment, 19
Sentences, lesson about, 224–226
Signaling mechanism, music as, 118–119. *See also* Music
Skits, by students, 60–61. *See also* Drama
Slattery, Patrick, 5
Social interaction. *See also* Socialization strategy
  activities for, 174–175
  classroom management and, 165–166
  learning and, 163–164
  learning environment and, 5, 6, 42, 164–165

  learning style and, 5, 6, 42
  lectures/lecturing and, 165
  volume of, 198
Socialization strategy, 163–171. *See also* Social interaction
  application of, 166–169, 221, 223, 227, 230, 232, 234, 238, 240
  classroom management and, 165–166
  concepts underlying, 163–165
  overview of, 13
Social studies, lesson about, 176
Songs, dramatization of, 61–62. *See also* Drama
Spelling, lesson about, 226–228
State changes, 36–40. *See also* Crest of the Wave strategy
State geography, lesson about, 222–224
Steinberg, Shirley, 5
Step checking, 51–52
Step down technique, 196–197. *See also* Walk Away strategy
Storytelling
  instruction using, 206–207. *See also* Yesterday Lives! strategy
  as memory/memorization technique, 181–183, 185, 206, 207
Students
  attention span of. *See* Attention span
  as Generation Y and Z members, 2
  learning environment of, 2, 3–4, 5–6, 7, 10, 30–31, 42. *See also* Learning environment
  learning style of, 2, 3–4, 5, 42. *See also* Learning style
  out-of-school lives of, 6, 58–59, 116, 127–128
  planning by, 7–8
  school history of, 135–136
  volume of speaking by, 195–199
  work future of, 3–4

Talk shows, role playing in, 62
Teachers
  background/education of, 2, 3–4, 6
  content coverage by, 35, 36
  as Generation X members, 2
  planning by, 8
  strategy adaptation by, 166–167, 216
  teaching styles of, 8
  views of students of, 16–17
  volume of speaking by, 196–197

Themes, and music, 119–120

Tiers strategy, 171–179
  application of, 173–176, 227, 236, 237
  classroom management and, 173–176
  concepts underlying, 171–173
  framework for, 172–173
  overview of, 13

Time lines, lesson about, 237–239

Uniquely Memorable strategy, 179–190.
    See also Memory/Memorization
  application of, 184–188, 219, 238, 247
  classroom management and, 183–184
  concepts underlying, 179–183
  learning style and, 183–184
  overview of, 13

Visual–conceptual skill, 223–224

Visual images. *See also* Keen Visuals
    strategy
  classroom management and, 107
  learning with, 105–107
  lesson about, 221–222
  time for processing of, 140–144. *See*
    also Pause strategy
  traditional uses of, 106
  types of, 107–108. *See also* Mental
    images

Vocabulary
  content learning and, 190, 191–192
  learning of new words, 176, 190,
    191–192
  lesson about, 176

Vocal emphasis. *See* Vocal Italics
    strategy

Vocal inflection
  as state change, 37
  for vocal emphasis, 193

Vocal Italics strategy, 190–195
  application of, 192–193
  classroom management and, 192
  concepts underlying, 190–192
  overview of, 13–14

Volume
  of music, 121–122
  of students' speaking, 195–199
  of teachers' speaking, 196–197

Walk Away strategy, 195–199
  application of, 197–198
  classroom management and, 196–197
  concepts underlying, 195–196
  overview of, 14

Whiteboards/Chalkboards, 106, 143

Wordtoons (website), 108

X-Ray Vision strategy, 199–205
  application of, 202–203
  classroom management and, 201
  concepts underlying, 199–201
  language use and, 199–203
  overview of, 14
  positive vs. negative mental images,
    199–203

Yesterday Lives! strategy, 205–209. *See*
    also Storytelling
  application of, 206–207, 232, 238
  classroom management and, 206
  concepts underlying, 205–206
  overview of, 14

Young students
  feedback for, 20–21
  memorization techniques for, 183

Zones of Instruction strategy, 209–212
  application of, 211–212
  classroom management and, 210–211
  concepts underlying, 209–210
  learning environment and, 209,
    211–212
  learning style and, 210
  overview of, 14